OLD GLEADLESS

Just a little country village

PAULINE SHEARSTONE

Artist and writer, Pauline Shearstone, was born in Sheffield and is keenly interested in Local History. This is her fourth Local History book and the second relating to Old Gleadless. After the publication of her first Gleadless book, *Gleadless from Village to Suburb*, Gleadless was well and truly put on the 'Local History' map!

She is well known for her paintings of 'Old Sheffield' with her most recent commission being a series of watercolour paintings of the City for the new 'HMS Sheffield' ship.

Married with a son Timothy, she enjoys recording Sheffield's historical past, in particular the Gleadless and Norton areas.

Other books by the Author:

Sheffield Sketches including Norton and the Chantrey Story (1980)
Portraits of the Cutlers' Hall (A guide book) (1983)
Gleadless from Village to Suburb (1985)

Cover and book design by Pauline Shearstone.

Front Cover: Gleadless around 1900. The 'Heeley & Sheffield House' survives but the rest, Webster's Butchers shop and 'The Ball Inn' (later Guymer's shop) have not.

Back Cover: Simpson's shop at the end of 'Honeymoon Row' around 1900. Mrs Simpson (left) and Clara Birtles (middle) are pictured. The girl is unknown.

ISBN 0 9510362 1 1

Publisher Pauline Shearstone (0742) 390197
First published 1989.

Typeset & printed by Sheffield Women's Printing Co-op (TU) Ltd. Tel. 0742 753180

This book is dedicated to
all Gleadless people
past and present

"Where shall I begin please your Majesty?" he asked.
"Begin at the beginning,"
the King said gravely,
"and go on till you come to the end;
then stop."
('Alice in Wonderland.')

Old Gleadless Village 1929 (H. Clayton)

The photo shows Norton Avenue being cut. On the far right is the Gleadless Methodist Church, then the Chapel Yard cottages and 'Piggy' Ward's cottages (now 'Tea Time at Angela's'). On the far left is Teddie Hoyland's farm. At the time this photo was taken, Gleadless was an idyllic country village.

ACKNOWLEDGEMENTS

I would like to express my grateful thanks to the following who have very kindly helped me with this book:

The staff at the Local Studies and Archives Dept., Sheffield City Library.
The staff at the Local Studies, Derbyshire Library Service.
My husband Walter and son Timothy for their constant encouragement.

Irene & Brian Thompson
Winifred & Cecil Higgins
Douglas Higgins
Ethel Pass
Annie Benton
Frank Cantrill (Australia)
Hetty & Herbert Hobson
Sam Gill
The late Walter Gill
Stanley Crofts
Walter Cook
Ruth Gould
Rose Mottershaw
Stan & Maggie Taylor
Jessie Oldfield
Gordon Bradley
Elizabeth & Colin Rhodes
Zena Fidler
John & Margaret Hinchcliffe
Jim Bird
Madge Waller
Mabel Liversidge
May Hartley
Kathleen Cupit
Albert & David Jackson
The late Reg. Cartledge
Mr & Mrs Stan Robertson
Nora Richardson
Mr & Mrs Dennis Webster
Miss Shipston
Mrs Layden
Mr L. Siddall
The late Mrs West
Clifford Wakelin
Vera Torr
Ronald Ward F.R.P.S.L.
Brian Cregand
Mrs Dunham
Rita Berney
Vera Baker
Mrs Hullah
Dolly Worrall
Rose Martin
Mrs Smith
Vincent Bradley, O.B.E.
Mrs Bradley
Mrs Thorpe
The late Jack Marriott
Henry Hobson
Ted Higgins (Canada)
Noreen Walker (Canada)
Fred Stubbs
Mr & Mrs Wild
Mrs Twigg
The late Mr Gabbatiss
Ellis Walker
Mrs Willey
Horace Clayton
Mrs Cottey
Mr & Mrs John Naylor
Mrs Timmins
Dorothy Needham
Winifred Robins
Mrs MacDonald
Audrey Brooks
Mrs Wragg
Mrs Johns
The late Hannah Gubbins
Mr & Mrs Henry Birtles
Mrs. Moxon

Also others too numerous to mention here.

CONTENTS

LIST OF ILLUSTRATIONS

Drawings

Maps

AUTHOR'S INTRODUCTION

Within the last fifty or sixty years, Gleadless has changed beyond all recognition. The old cottages and farms have been demolished and roads widened to allow an enormous amount of traffic to swallow up the once tiny village. No longer do we have the villager's pig at the bottom of the garden or hear the chug and clank of the mighty traction engine as it moved from farm to farm at threshing time. The sound of corncrakes in the fields and the procession of miners marching to work, are only echoes of the past.

All this has vanished as if it had never existed and yet it still remains in the minds of the men and women who have shared their memories with us in this book. Most of them were born in the first few decades of this century and were brought up in a rural environment. They have lived through great changes from a time when life was lived at the more gentle pace of the horse and cart to the hustle and bustle of our hectic, modern age.

Gleadless people have been more than generous. I have spoken to a large number of the older residents and everywhere I was received with kindness, patience and generosity (not to mention tea and biscuits!). Often I left, not only with treasured photographs and useful information, but also with gifts of flowers and eggs! Indeed I regard the people in the book as friends and I'd like to believe that they see me in the same way. My grateful thanks to everyone who has helped me compile this book, without your help it could never have been written.

After listening to so many stories, one cannot help but be touched by the hardships that these people endured. Yet through it all they survived with a sense of humour and an ability to get on with their lives regardless of what life held in store.

"I'm glad I lived in those days," I was constantly told.

Was life so much better? Can we forget that many children died through illnesses that could have been cured to-day, or that the miner's life was such a fragile one with an accident at the pit meaning hardship for the entire family. Conditions in the home were, compared to our luxurious living standards of today, quite unthinkable. No proper lighting and a tin bath filled with water and used by all the family on a Friday night and that dreaded ritual of black-leading the stove! Middens and pig-sties at the bottom of the garden, children without shoes and real poverty and hunger.

Yet through all this, everyone I spoke to agreed that, "Life was much better then," when Gleadless was, "just a little country village."

For these people their fond memories are something we can only marvel at and they, treasure.

As the reader may be aware, this is my second book concerning Old Gleadless. My first one, *Gleadless from Village to Suburb*, created such an unbelievable stir in the village (I mean Gleadless!). Old friendships were re-kindled and I received numerous letters from 'home and abroad' from many ex-Gleadlessites who wrote me heart-warming letters and sent me copies of old photos. (I'm always interested to hear from anyone with further information or old photos, relating to the Gleadless area.)

Although I should have liked to have included many more stories, one must stop (or rather call a temporary halt) somewhere. So if I have not included some item of interest in the following pages that you think I should have done, then I must ask you to accept this book merely as a sampler of the rich and varied reminiscences that survive in the minds of the older residents of Gleadless.

To-day, in schools, Local History is becoming part of the curriculum and hopefully, what I have written in this book will become a source of interest for future generations. For a time will come (if it has not already arrived) when people living in the area will wish to know what the old village was once like.

This book is dedicated to all Gleadless people (and Hollinsenders). May they (and anyone else who loves a trip down 'Memory Lane') derive as much pleasure in reading it as I have had in putting it all together!

Pauline Shearstone

43 Seagrave Crescent,
Gleadless Town End,
Sheffield
S12 2JL.

1. THE VILLAGE

Within living memory Gleadless, once described in the early 20th century, as a "village on the confines of Yorkshire, 3½ miles South East of Sheffield" and "inhabited mainly by colliers", has altered dramatically. Rural Gleadless remained unspoilt until the 1950's. This once quiet, small community of farmers, colliers and craftsmen lived apart from the hustle and bustle of neighbouring Sheffield until it became a part of it under the Sheffield Extension Order 1921, then as a Sheffield Suburb, Gleadless formed part of the Handsworth Ward.

Later in April, 1924, the opening of Ridgeway Road, brought an influx of traffic pouring through the village destroying the tranquillity of the area. Housing estates were built and roads were widened and constructed engulfing in their wake the old cottages.

Before this invasion of Gleadless took place, the village consisted of three main 'pockets' of living areas, Town End, Lane End and the Common or Common Side. People living in these parts formed their own little individual community and were more likely to know people in their immediate vicinity and less likely to be acquainted with other villagers living only a short walking distance away.

Apart from the ordinary cottages there were several farms dotted about — Charnock Hall, Base Green and White Late Farms along White Lane while Park House Farm perched on land at the top of the Common. In the Newfield Green vicinity were Paddock and Hurlfield Hill farms and in what is now Hollinsend Park, was Cartledge's Farm.

These farms employed some of the villagers while others were colliers, working at the local drift mines or the main Birley Pits, often trudging several miles to the pit head before they descended the mine to walk yet again before they reached the coal face. Some worked at Seagrave Nurseries, others in rural trades, blacksmithing or table blade or edge tool forging. Alternative work meant a walk to Intake to board the tram to Sheffield where the steel works offered further employment. Girls stayed at home to look after their younger brothers or sisters or went away into 'Service' or served in shops.

Most of the cottages were built of stone and the long gardens at the backs were filled with cabbages, potatoes, pigsties and the middens. The heart of the small community was the church and chapel where not only the religious needs of the villagers were met but their social ones too.

There were pubs as well, 'The Old Harrow,' 'The Red Lion,' 'The Heeley

& Sheffield House' and the 'New Inn' satisfied the 'thirst' of the villagers, while 'The Yew Tree,' 'The Hollin Bush' and 'The Noah's Ark,' in Hollinsend were never short of customers!

Then there were the small 'corner' shops often the front rooms of cottages, with their tiny windows bursting with an assortment of groceries. A haven for a child with a penny to spend on sherbet dabs, liquorice pipes and aniseed balls. There were ladies who baked bread to sell and the milkman who came round with his horse and cart, clanking along the dusty road to dole out the milk.

Gleadless had travelling men who came puffing up the hills. People like 'Pot' Jack who came every week with a clothes basket full of wares and children would shout to their Mothers, "Pot" Jack's coming! Do you want anything?"

August saw the show people arrive for the annual Feast Days when swings and roundabouts were carefully pieced together like some giant jigsaw puzzle. This was a time of celebration when the villagers watched as the exotically painted caravans came rattling into the area. Youngsters like the children of Hamelin followed the parade of fairground people in the hope that they could help and later cadge a ride on those beautiful, galloping horses with gaping mouths and flaming nostrils!

From the Fair to the Harvest Festival from Christmas to other social activities and so on throughout the year. There was little or no money to spend, yet the fun of those simple, unforgettable days always remains in the hearts of those people to-day.

Friday night was 'Bath Night' when the 'set pot' or 'copper' would be stoked up and filled with water. Turns would be taken to sit in the zinc washing tub with just a drop more hot water added as each child or adult stepped in!

Some women always seemed to be having babies and since a visit from the Doctor was rare, the village women acted as mid-wives with the most notable one being Elizabeth Sharpe.

Villagers didn't greet each other with a simple 'Good mornin' but would usually follow it up with "How are tha' this mornin' then?"

Nick-names were given to many of the locals 'Pop,' 'Mush' and 'Piggy' were just a few of the names that some individuals were 'christened'.

Superstitions, bad and good luck omens were evident in the collier's daily life whose survival down the pit was all to often left to Providence.

Village funerals were very simple affairs with the coffin being carried to the church and the mourners all wearing deep black.

Gleadless was a poor village but if anyone had anything to lend anybody worse off than themselves, then they would do so without any second bidding. Not every family could afford a clock but that didn't really matter for there were several ways by which the time of day could be reckoned. The daily journey to the pit each morning could be heard for miles with the stillness and quietness being broken by the sound of the miners' clogs on stone. The army of miners, on their way to the Birley Pits, marched along together and passed the little cottages, the men being joined along the way by more reinforcements.

Another way that the villagers knew the time, at least if the wind was in the wrong direction, was when the middens were being emptied. This was a daily ritual with the deposits sometimes being left in the nearby fields. Sanitary conditions and the water supplies were extremely primitive, creating perfect conditions for disease and yet this harshness of life helped to create and strengthen bonds of close friendships.

Now we begin the journey back in time, to days when Gleadless was 'Just a little country village' and the people were, as the old saying informs us, "the salt of the earth!"

The Village (Gleadless) — The Facts

Gleadless is located on the south side of Sheffield and close to Norton and nearby Frecheville and Ridgeway. It is a very ancient village dating back to its earliest recording of 1307 when being one of the several hamlets of the Parish of Handsworth, it was mentioned in a deed dating from the latter end of Edward I's reign. In the document Gleadless is spelt Gladeleys.

Gleadless — its meaning and spelling

Some of the earlier spellings:
le Gladeleys
Gledles (1610)
Gladelesse (1637)
Gleedles (1771)
Gleadleys (1790, 1832)

Its meaning:
There are various explanations for the meaning of the word Gleadless:
(Old English, gleoda) 'Forest clearings haunted by a kite'
(Old English, glaed) 'Clearings in glade'
(Old English, glaed) 'Bright clearings'
The Anglo-Saxon place names which indicate the early English settlements *(glida -leah)* 'kite grove'

Being on a boundary it is acceptable that the word 'less' formerly spelt 'leys' referred to clearings on a boundary, e.g. Eckington Lees, but it is believed that Gleadless received its name from the Old English word 'glida-leah' meaning 'kite grove.'

Other local names

Hollins End — from the word 'Hollin,' a name given to the Common Holly.

Intake derives its name from the time of the Enclosures when the common land was enclosed and became an 'Intake.'

Hagg Lane (now Hurlfield Road) meaning 'fence.'

Handsworth — 'the soil' or 'the enclosure belonging to Hand.'

The 'Shirebrook' stream

The Boundary

The little stream called the 'Shirebrook' marked the boundary line between the West Riding of Yorkshire and the County of Derbyshire. (Before Gleadless was taken into Sheffield). The Meersbrook was also a boundary brook, rising a hundred yards or so from the source of the Shirebrook which "is a tributary of that more ancient boundary stream, the Rother."

The County Boundary line cut right through the 'Red Lion' at Gleadless Town End so the majority of the village lay in the West Riding of Yorkshire while areas along White Lane (on the other side of the 'Shirebrook') such as Smithfield Road, Charnock Hall and Base Green farms, were in the Parish of Eckington in Derbyshire. While the Gleadless Toll House at Herdings was in Norton Parish.

An Ecclesiastical Boundary

The Shirebrook also marks an ecclesiastical boundary between the Archbishopric of Canterbury and York. All churches south of the stream are under Canterbury and those north are under York.

The Ancient Boundary of Mercia and Northumbria

About 410 A.D. the Romans evacuated Britain and subsequently we were invaded by the Angles and Saxons, who divided the country into kingdoms. Among these kingdoms were Mercia and Northumbria, and the boundary between them was the tiny stream called the 'Shirebrook.' So what we now call Frecheville was in Mercia and what is Hollinsend was in Northumbria.

2. MINING IN THE GLEADLESS AREA

"If there is one thing that has dramatically changed both the landscape of England and the life of many of its inhabitants then this is coal . . ."

Mining was the main occupation in Gleadless, Hollinsend and Intake and although there was not a Pit head dominating the scenery, the area was a mining community. There were local drift mines at the 'Nabb' on Fox Lane, Vardy's near the 'Phoenix,' Bradley's on Base Green and Mr Wakelin's at the top of Hurlfield Hill and others but the major Pits such as the Nunnery, Birley East and Birley West, and Orgreave were where most of the local miners worked.

The Gleadless area has always been rich in coal. From as early as the 16th century one finds documentary evidence to the fact. In 1515 reference is made to a "collier" — William Fox of Gleadless, and also to a John Hyll who made nails. While another document, dated 1579, shows that permission was granted to "digg and get coles" on "customary land near Gleydleis."

Historically speaking, from the 9th century, England had discovered coal as an energy source but it did not become a commercial viability until the late 18th and early 19th century. Therefore, early coal digging in Gleadless, which was in small quantities, was for local convenience and use.

The problem of transport made everything else, until the early 1900's, more or less out of the question. Even after certain roads had been turnpiked, the roads continued to be in a shocking condition. If we consider that the turnpikes had been fit for the passage of heavy traffic (and they certainly were not) then the price of a load of coal would have been prohibitive. The only alternative was to use the other roads or tracks into Sheffield.

A common route from Gleadless was through the Duke of Norfolk's "Park." Conflict arose in 1692 between the Duke and his neighbouring inhabitants (*i.e.* Gleadless, Handsworth and Intake) when he closed the road, declaring that the road in question was a private one, and by doing so he prevented his "competitors" getting their "Coals to town."

However, with the demand for coal (arising from the industrial growth of the City of Sheffield) more mine shafts were sunk. In 1868, the number of collieries in the Sheffield district were thirty five and of these Base Green (Gleadless), Beighton, Birley, Handsworth, Manor, Orgreave, Woodhouse (Handsworth) and Woodthorpe, were in the immediate vicinity of the Gleadless area.

Conditions in the mines were appalling and when the first Commissioners' Report into Mines was published in 1842, it revealed how cramped, dark, wet and rat infested they were.

Young children suffered the ordeal of working down the mines too. Boys of eight years of age were "trappers" sitting in the dark all day while other child workers suffered injuries from which they never fully recovered.

In Gleadless, the drift away from the mines began when the hardships endured by the colliers during the 1926 Strike made them look for alternative work in industrial Sheffield. Also, the closure of the Birley West (1908) and Birley East (1943) pits, made the miner move further afield to Orgreave, Beighton, Treeton or Brookhouse to work in the pits there, and so the exodus of the collier from Gleadless and Hollinsend began. To-day, a visitor to the area would be totally unaware that it was once a mining community and the sound of the miners' clogs in the early morning is only a memory of the past.

Coal Mines where Gleadless/Hollinsend miners would have worked

1. Orgreave	N.C.B. since 1947	1851 - Closed Nov. '81
2. Treeton	N.C.B.	1877. Still working
3. Beighton	N.C.B.	1902. Closed
4. Brookhouse	N.C.B.	1929. Closed Oct. '85
5. Handsworth	N.C.B. (ex Nunnery Colliery Co.)	1903. Closed
6. Birley East	Sheffield Coal Co.	1888 - 1943
7. Birley West	Sheffield Coal Co.	1855/60 - 1908

The 'Deep Pits' was sunk in 1800. The Nunnery

Living in a Mining Community

Although as we have stated, Gleadless was predominantly a mining community, it was a rural environment and consequently many colliers' houses were scattered amongst those of their neighbours who were country dwellers: farm labourers, carters, blacksmiths, file-cutters and smallholders and so on. For the Gleadless miner he walked a fair distance to his place of work and his home was not close to the pit head, unlike other colliery villages. For example the mining village of Shirebrook is a place where almost everyone was (at one time) dependent on the pit for a living, either directly or indirectly.

Hollins End was however, principally a mining community with the rows of terraced houses being built to accommodate the influx of colliers into the area. The earliest pit houses were built either in long rows, often back to back, or in single rows constructed in squares and they often bore such names as High, Low or Middle Row or The Square.

People living in a mining community sometimes feel themselves to be in some ways perhaps different from others. They belong to a fraternity of mining people where villagers see themselves as separate from neighbouring villagers. The pit was the common identity in the Gleadless and Hollins End communities.

Before the pithead baths were introduced between about 1925 and 1945, the collier walked home in his pit dirt and had his wash in a tin bath on the hearth in front of the black-leaded stove with a boiler on one side of the fire and an oven on the other.

Most colliers had allotments and many kept poultry and had a pig sty. Their sports included pigeon flying, fishing and whippet racing. One lived in one's own village and it was sufficient for a shared adversity undoubtedly draws people together. The short terraces seemed to generate a warmth of community feeling and sharing. There was a sense of insularity with people being very attached to one's village and there was very little marrying out with husbands and wives usually coming from the same village.

This sense of dependence on one another was a common identity in the community and lasted well after the coal workings ceased.

The Coal Strikes

The Background

Unrest in the pits was no new thing. From a radius of up to 10 miles, people journeyed (usually walked) into Woodhouse, to work. Between 1855 and 1860, Birley West shaft was sunk by Messrs. Jeffcock and Dunn.

Up to 1875 children could start working underground at the age of 10 often looking after the trap-doors as well as helping the men. They worked long hours and often only saw the sun for short periods during the week. Sundays was the only day they saw sunlight during the winter time. In 1875 the age for children to work down the pit had risen to 13 while in 1922 it was 14 and in later years it was limited to 15 and 16 year olds.

The miners began to feel a sense of wrong and they gathered together to try and ease the conditions in which they were forced to work. They realised tht the only way to improve their working life was to withdraw their labour and this took the form of a strike.

In 1876 the colliers were out on strike to resist a reduction in their wage demand, while in 1888, the year that the Birley East Pit was opened, there was another strike for a 10% rise, which most of the "bosses" granted. In 1889 a further increase in wages resulted in a miner earning 30/- per week (on average). However, the miner, in an attempt to improve his and his family's living standards, continued to have struggles with his 'masters' who were (by Victorian standards) several 'layers' higher than himself on the social level. So when in 1893 the Pit Managers tried to impose a 25% wage reduction on the miners, there were strikes, demonstrations and mass meetings.

On September 1st, 1893, "1,000 miners from Hollinsend, led by 'Domino Joe', marched and sang through the village (Woodhouse) in what was really quite a peaceful demonstration — and others joined them as they progressed." (*Woodhouse* by J. Roberts.) The days that followed resulted in the Heavy Dragoons being posted to Woodhouse to quell 'the lawless mob' (see Le Tall's *Woodhouse* for a fuller account).

Many works in Sheffield were closed for lack of fuel and it was only by the intervention of Lord Rosebury that the lock-out ended on October 19th, with the old rates being kept till a board of conciliation was formed.

There continued a smouldering discontent in the collieries resulting in further Pit Strikes in 1912, 1919, 1921 and 1926, during which great hardships were suffered.

The 1912 Coal Strike

From 1900 to 1914, wages remained stationary, although the cost of living continued to increase. Many workers still outside the unions were often very badly paid and a large proportion of the working class suffered from shocking housing and inadequate social services together with fluctuating employment.

These conditions, together with the new freedom to strike secured by the Trade Disputes Act, led to the most acute industrial strife Britain had yet known. In 1911 a Railway Strike paralysed a large part of the country while the following year saw 850,000 miners being idle for several weeks.

'Sympathetic strikes' were another feature of the period, when men of one union came out to help another. These strikes were aimed not at the employers but at the Government which ended the coal strike, by introducing a Minimum Wage Act.

The 1912 Coal Strike lasted from February till early April, and outcropping went on at Darnall, Tinsley, Millhouses, Arbourthorne and other areas of the city. Gleadless, being a mining area, was inevitably affected by the strike. *Frank Cantrill*, now living in Australia, recalls his memories of it:

"In my boyhood days the coalminers only saw the sun on Sundays in winter, as they worked a twelve hour day but after a strike they got an 8 hour day. They had quite a few strikes and I remember soup kitchens and being given breakfast at school, tea and a thick slice of bread and jam.

During the 1912 Strike, the Wesleyan Chapel gave a tea every night for weeks to those around Town End. Mrs Sharpe, the local midwife, used to bear the cost of one and once we got ham sandwiches and cake!"

It must be noted here that during the coal strikes that hit Gleadless, all the local community gave as much help and assistance as they could, which not only included the Chapels and Church but individuals as well.

(For further information regarding the Coal Strikes refer to *Gleadless from Village to Suburb*, p. 116 - 122).

The distribution of food was organised and soup kitchens were opened. Many children were fed by the local education authority as the Gleadless School Log Book reveals:

8.3.12. In consequence of the great Coal Strike many children are away from school as they are getting coal from the surface in various parts of the Parish.

27.3.12. Called a meeting to consider the distress in the district — particularly as affecting the children.

29.3.12. Commenced to provide free breakfasts for the children. The teachers make all the necessary arrangements and distribute the food to the children in one of the class rooms. The breakfasts are to consist of cocoa with bread and butter alternatively with bread and jam.

The Soup Kitchens

Annie Benton: "We lived at Ivy House on Gleadless Road and my father, James Smith, was a very generous man. In the 1926 Strike he gave milk free for the wives and children down at Hollinsend School. There was a soup kitchen down at the school and every day he gave so many gallons of milk. They gave out soup, bread and milk at the soup kitchens. They needed them because nearly all Gleadless people were colliers."

Hetty and Herbert Hobson: "At one time there used to be an old shed at the side of the 'Royal Oak' (Hollinsend) which they used as a slaughterhouse. Anyway, during the Pit Strike (it was before the 1926 one), they used the copper (where they used to boil the water) for a soup kitchen. This was inside the slaughterhouse.

You used to go down there with your jug and they'd fill it up for you. It didn't matter how big your jug was, the bigger the better. People round about used to take their jugs.

Sid Flowers, the Coal Merchants, used to provide coal for it and potatoes, because they had some fields across here (Hollinsend). Then Walshams and Willeys used to provide meat for it. 'Jud' Flowers and two others used to be boiling it up all morning and then we'd all take our jugs. I was only a kid at the time but I remember it well."

Charity Main — The 1921 Strike

The strikes of '21 and '26 caused a great deal of hardship within the village. Ways and means were devised to help feed the needy and to make life more bearable during the length of the strikes.

In an endeavour to finance the Distress Fund during the 1921 Coal Strike, a pit was sunk on the land opposite the Gleadless Congregational Chapel and was known by the locals as *'Charity Main'.*

On April 14th 1921, Councillor Raynes, Secretary of the Gleadless Congregational Chapel, formed a Committee which included Mr W. Gubbins and Mr J.T. Siddall, to devise ways and means to combat the distress caused by the Strike. The committee of eight were added to by another eight who went out for subscriptions and distributed food parcels to those desperately in need.

By the 16th April, the feeding of the children came into operation with fifty children being fed in the Sunday School and by the 18th, breakfasts were being served in the Council School. That week 550 meals were served, these being paid for out of the Distress Fund. Soon after 800 children had been provided with meals and a number of families had been supplied with provisions, the fund was exhausted.

The Committee were desperate for finance when Mr Fidler, the village builder and property repairer, was approached by his son-in-law and another young man who asked permission to try for coal on his land. Permission was granted and after digging for only a short time more experienced help was called for and two pit deputies, Mr Fred Cartledge and Mr Albert Wilson, took charge on the understanding that it was not to be a money making concern, but must only be for those in distress in the neighbourhood. Also it was agreed that no-one should be paid for working.

Permission was given by Mr I. Harrison, owner of Seagrave Nurseries, to mine under his land. The money left, after paying Mr Fidler for ropes, bags, buckets, planks, scaffold poles etc., was to be donated to the Distress Fund and the War Memorial Fund.

The men worked three hour shifts and received 1 cwt. of coal per shift. Some worked two shifts and mention is made of three men who worked several twelve hour shifts but still only received one cwt. of coal. That was how it became known as 'Charity Main'.

The amount of coal obtained was 230 tons and the money handed over amounted to £140. £55 of which was used for the Distress Fund, £45 was deposited in the bank for the War Memorial Fund and £40 was given to Mr Fidler for the cost of the materials.

To enable the reader to imagine the scale of distress that a strike would cause a village, with no unemployment or social security pay, I have included here the number of meals provided from the sale of coal derived from 'Charity Main':

1175 dinners for the miners
500 teas for adults, 2000 teas for children
1500 breakfasts for children (Bread, margarine and jam, or bread and dripping)
36 food tickets, value 2s 6d each

The community spirit shone through with Bob Beverley opening his field for recreation and the Rev. T.C. Crossland, the Vicar of Gleadless Church, opening his grounds for bowling and providing prizes for competitions.

The Chapels provided help too with a similar scheme being operated in Intake, while 4,000 meals were provided under the Handsworth District Council Education Act. Throughout the strike the premises of the Gleadless Independent Congregational Chapel was opened from early morning until late at night.

Many of the women who helped with the meals would be up at 6.30 am to be down at the Council School by 7.30 am to service breakfasts, back at the Sunday School by 11 am to prepare dinner, then off home for 2.00 pm to bake a stone of bread for the following day. Such was the Community spirit! (For a more detailed account of 'Charity Main' see p.117-9 'Gleadless from Village to Suburb')

The 1926 Coal Strike

On May 3rd, 1926, there began what became known as the General Strike, with the overwhelming majority of workers in many vital industries going on strike in support of the miners' demands. However, the strike was only to last nine days but the miners stayed out for another six months, until poverty and hunger compelled them to accept longer hours and lower wages.

Walter Gill talks of memories during the '26 Strike and of the Mangle Main Pit which came to be worked during that time.

"What created the 1926 Strike was they wanted to put us on eight hours and reduce our wages. In those days we were on a wage structure plus a percentage. For example they might have paid you 9/- plus 35% but what they wanted to do was to drop that % and put another half an hour on. So we all went on strike.

I was on strike from 1st May until November 14th, about six months and when strike ended we went back for same, nothing had been gained.

During the strike I did some odd jobbing for local farmers, potato picking and some gardening at Mr Pagett's house at the top of Gleadless Common, me and my cousin got 5/- doing gardening for him.

Then they opened these local pits like Mangle Main which was in a field just off Kirkby Road. There were others like Charity Main which was worked at the top of Fidler's field (opposite the "New Inn"). Bill Gubbins, Fred Cartledge and others worked on that. Gilbert Gould's pit were at top o' Common, but I worked at Mangle Main.

The Mangle Main Pit

When the strike came in 1926, my Father, Sam Gill and four or five of his mates sank a pit, called Mangle Main, which was in a little field on the left off Kirkby Road. The field belonged to the Taylor family and Walter Taylor owned the field. They got permission to sink two shafts there. The shafts were about nine or ten yards down and they met coal about a 4' 6" seam.

You've never seen anything like it down there. In the bottom there were roadways that had been dug years and years before. They were so straight too. They were marvellous. Every so often the old miners, who had worked there before, had left a little piece of coal — so high — like a stool and we assumed that's what they used to sit on in the olden days. These roadways went towards Kirkby Road.

Its name

The pit was called Mangle Main because they used to wind the coal up by an old fashioned wooden mangle, an old roller. A rope with a hook attached to it was fastened onto the roller and they'd hang a bucket on to this hook. They'd send the bucket down the shaft and when it was full of coal then it would be wound up by turning the mangle.

Working the Pit

I used to go down the pit and we'd climb down on steep ladders.

My Dad and his brothers, Ike and Walt. Gill and Tommy Critchlow, Len Crofts, Andrew Barber and another worked the Main between them. They worked two and three on a shift and then there were five or six of us lads who used to work the Pit top. We used to sell the coal.

People used to queue for coal at the top of field. They'd come through the gate and I'd take their money from them. I was the money man. I wore two pouches for the money and a book. Everything that was sold I had to book. We sold coal at 6d, 1/- and 2/- worth. People used to come from as far as Heeley for it.

With the strike being on, the other miners threatened us once and we notified the police about it. I'll never forget it. Superintendent Hughes and his colleagues came to see if we were alright and they said that if there was any trouble, to let them know and they'd sort it out for us. But nobody bothered us because we didn't sell the coal to firms and industry but only to householders.

We used railway sleepers for supports in pit. Mr Hinchliffe had a piggery and lived up Smithfield Road and he had a lot of them and he'd swop them for coal.

The closing of the Main

The Pit began to fill with water (Gleadless has a series of underground streams) and we were having a lot of trouble getting this water away. A chap from Hollinsend, called Fred Dodd came and said "I'll get rid of water for you." Anyway he didn't! He couldn't get rid of it. The water came half way up the shaft which was nearly ten yards deep. Then overnight it went. Nobody knew where but it went. Every drop of water had gone. So we started working again, moving towards the bungalow. Suddenly, the workings collapsed and caved in so that finished Mangle Main. We daren't go any further.

After that me Dad went to work at some outcrops at Ringinglow and they called it the "Other Main" and I just did odd jobs until the Strike finished in November, 1926."

Stanley Crofts first worked at Orgreave Colliery before moving to Birley New Pit and hadn't been working long when the General Strike in 1926 occurred.

"I was about 14 years old and hadn't been down the pit long when I was called on strike. All the villagers were out except for a few people who worked in Sheffield in steel or on the land.

During the first few weeks of the strike, Colliers received £1 (100p). Fillers 10/- (50p) and Boys 5/- (25p) per week strike pay. These amounts gradually dwindled down to nothing but we were given loaves of bread and we had to walk to Handsworth to collect these loaves in pillowcases.

Mangle Main

A few of the senior colliers got together and knowing where coal was in existence under the land in the area, decided to open up a pit which had workings under Gleadless Nurseries. Tommy Critchlow, Sam and Walt, Gill, my brothers Harry and Arthur (who was the Check Weighman-Book Keeper) and others whose names I can't recall, worked it.

I remember the pit vividly because the men worked in water and the coal was always wet. My brother Harry used to get quite a ribbing because of the way he used to shout, to our Arthur, "Watter coming up!"

The people used to queue for long hours every day for coal.

Life during the strike

Thus some money was obtained to help with the provision of teas for all the village children at the Congregational Chapel. I have never seen the closeness of people in a better light than those days. The Churches and the Pubs worked together. In fact the Congregational Chapel (the United Reform) was open all the day through so that men could be occupied in games. It was also the information centre of all activities. All the pubs had soup kitchens, mainly at lunch times.

As to the women, during the strike they went on a 'Roster' for duty at the Chapel, preparing and serving the children's teas. They were good marriages and the women stuck to their men through thick and thin.

After the strike, the Under-Manager at Orgreave Colliery came round Gleadless to all his old workforce, offering Colliers £1 and Fillers and Others 10/- to go back to work because they were good men and hard workers."

View from the top of Gleadless Road. (A. & D. Jackson)
Seagrave Nurseries are on the left. To the right of the bungalow can be seen 'Mangle Main' (where the truck is in the picture).

The Gleadless Common Drift Mine

Another mine which was working during the 1926 Coal Strike was Gilbert Gould's on Gleadless Common. Gilbert, described as a little man, energetic, with a cheery manner, was a deputy at Woodthorpe Colliery for twenty five years before he left the coal face and went into business himself.

"He would have been about 48 when he bought a hardware shop in Meadow Street and put me in it," says *Ruth Gould,* and I revelled in it!"

Born in 1899, Ruth remembers her father, Gilbert, working the pit, and the day when she was put in a wagon to be taken down the mine.

"I rode down only once, just to have a look and the coal glittered! It was lovely but I was glad to get out! The men found a woman's slipper and a fossil of a fish. We just looked at them but didn't take them to the Museum. In my day women didn't work down the pit."

Gilbert Gould's Drift Mine on Gleadless Common in the 1920's. (Miss R. Gould)
L to r: Gilbert Gould, Willis Gould, Ellis Mellor, Joseph Gould & David Gould.
Ellis Mellor was the engine winder for the Common Pit. His father's shop was at the top of Grassthorpe Road.

The Mine's beginning and ending

"I believe my father started working in the mine in 1920 or 22 and because it wasn't profitable it had to close in 1928. To make a mine safe they have to leave so much coal to keep the roof intact and Father found a lot of this coal, not solid seams, and so it closed."

Although he had his hardware business, Gilbert was always "hankering" to get back into mining so he and his sons made exhaustive inquiries and searched through old records before they decided to open their own pit on the Common.

After leasing the land from the Duke of Norfolk, they sank their first shaft amidst laughing remarks from some local miners who believed there was no coal there but after many months of hard work they did find coal (the old workings were believed to have been 130 years old). It was good, hard Silkstone coal, six feet thick, similar to that at Nunnery Colliery. From then on the pit prospered and produced about 2,000 tons.

By modern standards the pit was a tiny one, although it was fully equipped and fitted with a splendid ventilation system of Gilbert's own invention!

A newspaper cutting dated 1926 describes the pit as follows:

'It has no shafts, but two "drifts" one 150 yards long and dropping into the earth at the rate of one yard in three, and the other 100 yards long with a fall of one in two. The workers walk to and fro, and the coal is wound up in three small tubs by means of a steam engine.'

The pit during the 1926 Strike

Being a non-Union concern the pit was worked during the 1926 Strike. As one reporter of that time stated:

'Up on Gleadless Common, overlooking the city, where so many miners are sitting idle, wondering how much longer the strike will last, there is a pit, sunk, owned and worked solely by the members of one family, that has gone cheerily on with its work.'

However, the pit did not continue working without a fight. When the strike began Mr Gould stated that he intended to carry on working. A deputation was sent to see what could be done. The men "instructed" Gilbert not to sell a heap of slack, (which stood in the yard) for industrial purposes.

"Alright", said Gilbert, "you can have that, and give it away amongst the poor people in the district."

But the gift was refused and after further discussions with the Union it was decided that the coal could be sold. This decision was not a popular one with the strikers who gathered in large numbers when the coal was being moved. They attempted to hinder the whole process so the police were sent for and when they arrived they came in motorcars! The sight of police in motorcars, must have caused quite a stir in the quiet country village of Gleadless.

Consequently, the police held back the crowd while the coal was taken away and they remained there to guarantee that no more disturbances were likely to arise during the Strike.

The pit continued to be worked until it was uneconomical which led to its closure in 1928. A staunch Churchgoer and Trustee at the Gleadless Independent Church, Gilbert was, in his daughter's own words, "a worker and a strong family man."

The Drift Mine near the Toll Bar

Annie Benton: "There was a drift mine at the top of Hurlfield Hill. Mr Wakelin and another man worked it together. It was near the Toll Bar at the right hand side of the chain. Well, they went underground there and they got outcrop and sold it in the '26 Strike and they even kept it on afterwards. The coal wasn't too bad and we had some because we'd fires in every room. In the dining room we had a deep grate in the hearth and we had to empty it each week and there was dust all over when you shovelled it out into a bucket!"

Mining Customs

One would suspect that the matter-of-fact, down-to-earth miner would not be superstitious but yet he was. In the early part of the century, few safety precautions were available in the mines and so luck tended to play its part in the miner's survival. Bad luck omens were taken seriously.

If a miner met a woman on his way to work, he would return home and he would be reluctant to go to work if he happened to forget anything and had to re-enter his house.

The sight of a crow perched on a wheel would result in the miner refusing to go down the shaft and regarded as very bad luck was the crowing cockerel.

Miners were concerned about their strength and if a miner washed his back he believed it would weaken him. *Mrs. Mottershaw* relates:

"The miners were a very tightly knit community and they were very rough and ready but very kind to people. They were also very superstitious. One of the superstitions was that if they met a woman on their way to the mine in the morning they turned back because it was a sign of disaster and so if by any chance one woman was foolish enough to be out and be seen, the other women used to set on her because they'd lost a day's money.

Another superstition was that a collier must never wash his back. That's true and my Father's said when he was a little boy he's seen the miners come home, the wife would have plenty of hot water ready and the old tin bath would go in front of the fire and Father said it didn't matter whether Mrs. So and So from next door was in or not, the miner would just get into the bath and wash but he would not wash his back only once a week on a Friday night because they believed that their strength was in their back and they mustn't wash it.

Also when somebody died it was the custom to go in and see the person who'd died. I suppose it was paying your last respects. I spoke a little while ago about Father's Uncle William who lived in the cottage that was the Toll Bar (Norton Ave.) Now actually he was killed down Birley Pit. There was a roof fall and the story is that he tried to get away by going to some old workings where you had to climb up a rope to get out and he got as far as the rope but when he got there he couldn't get any further and that his hands, or rather the ends of his fingers were rubbed raw by him trying to climb but failing to do so.

Well after the disaster at the colliery, the other miners, as a mark of respect, would not have his body brought back in a horse and dray but he was put on the dray and the colliers themselves pulled the dray back from Birley Pit to the cottage to bring him home and that was their way of showing respect."

Accidents

Mining was a family affair with Father and sons working together down the same pit. If an accident occurred, families lost many members of their family. *Stan Taylor*, whose family and relations all worked down the pit comments:

"In the early twenties there must have been something like thirty to forty members of the Taylor family in the village, most of the males were miners. They all worked down Birley Pit and were all members of the Gleadless Independent Chapel. It was said that it was possible to field both a soccer and a cricket team capable of giving a good account against any club but the mine took its toll.

Thomas, Fred and a near relative John were killed in the pit. Sam and Herbert and two more brothers both suffered accidents which hindered their work in the pit and Freddie, that was the son of Thomas, although suffering many accidents including loss of several fingers, was the only one remaining to carry on in the mines until retirement.

To be quite honest, there wasn't a family in the village that suffered in the mine like our family did; there's no doubt about that and both my

Father and Uncle Fred were killed instantly and my Uncle Sam had a broken back and never worked again. My other brother Fred, carried on and finished up in charge of demonstrating machinery. That was after he'd had quite a few accidents. His ribs were crushed and I think he broke a leg and then all his finger ends were ripped off when he got 'em fast in one o' belts.

There was a ruling that if your father got killed in pit or happened an accident then their sons were found a job. Anyway I was 13 when me father got killed and of course the letter came, when I was 14 and leaving school, for me to go and see the Pit Manager to find me a job. So I went and took one look down the pit and said, "Not for me thank you!"

Sam Gill had the same reaction to working down the pit and his decision to stay out of the mine was reinforced by his Father.

"My Dad had good reason to hate the pit. There were many accidents there. My Dad had his collar bones broken and his ankles. My Uncle David and Uncle Tom both only had one eye which were all due to working in Pit. My Uncle Mick went blind in pit and so that's why me Dad said to keep out of it or he'd throw me down shaft!"

Reckoning Day

Another of the Miner's customs was the weekly ritual of paying out wages. Where a father and his sons worked together, they would have a Friday get-together called a 'Reckoning' when the money would be distributed.

Mrs J. Oldfield: "My Father-in-law worked in the pit (I believe it was Orgreave) with his father. The family had their own "hole" and the men and the family worked that "hole". There were three brothers and two brothers-in-law and the father.

The Father made them walk to the pit in the morning and he wouldn't let them catch the paddy home. He used to say that they got more cold standing than walking, so they had to walk from Orgreave to Intake.

At the end of the week his Father received a certain amount for the coal they'd fetched out of that pit. They had a "Reckoning Do" at his Father's house on a Friday night. Everything was meticulously reckoned and if anybody had been ill his share was put on one side. The Father was the head of the "hole" and he collected the money for the coal they'd fetched out. Nothing else. If anything was stone or rubble they wouldn't get paid for it. They only got paid for the acutal coal. They all went down to the Father's house for the "Reckoning" and that's how they worked then.

My Father-in-law came out of the pit in 1926 during the Strike and he never went back again."

Walter Gill *(ex-miner):*

"At Orgreave my Dad's family used to have what was called a "Benk" of their own. There used to be two work up, two work down and one who worked in the "eddings". They used to take the coal off in layers and my Dad and his family used to work in one "Benk" you see. That's how we used to work in them days. A family used to work and reckon together.

They had what they called a "Ready Reckoner". They used to say, "I'm going to reckon." On Friday, pay day, they used to all gather round and kneel down and get their share of money. We didn't queue at the office window to get paid in them days, that came later. At Orgreave we were on contract and we received so much a yard.

If you worked with somebody who you didn't know, you used to ask them where they reckoned so you could go and draw your money off them on Friday. They wouldn't tell you and would just joke and say, "At top o' chimney!"

Ethel Pass:

"Families all worked together in the pit. In our family there were eight family and two sons-in-law who worked together. My father sub-contracted — he pitched the price. They got so much for the coal they got out. They had to lay down and cut, the coal with a pick. I've heard my Father say that when a seam was running out it was only 6 inches high so they had to lay down and get the coal out like that.

Reckoning Day: The pit paid my Father for what the family had dug out during the week and he used to share the money out and work out how much each one of his brothers and sons-in-law should get. They called this the 'reckoning'. When my Dad finished working at the pit his wage was only 8/- a day then."

A Miner's Ways

The early riser

Ethel Pass: "One Boxing Day, I was invited to a party. I was seventeen and I was enjoying myself when a knock came on door and me Mother was there and she said, "Your Dad's locking up so I've got to come and fetch you."

These people whose party it was were better off than us and they told me Mother that they'd bring me home because it was only 7 pm. But no, me Mother daren't go home without me. So home I went. Oh, I did feel embarrassed!

When I got home my Father said, "I've got to be up early in the morning so I'm going to lock up."

You see, only my Father locked up at night. No one else ever did and he was working 'on days' that week so he had to get up at 4 am. But I did feel daft having to leave at 7 o'clock when I was seventeen!

The Miner's Silk

In those days all miners wore what they called a "silk". They didn't wear a collar and tie but they had like a sort of scarf around their necks which they called a silk. It was square and they used to fold it in two, then roll it. That's how they got the silk narrow. It used to go round their necks and over and then they used to wind it round their braces.

Well, my Father used to like to go to the Theatre called the 'Old Alec' ('Royal Alexandra Theatre' in Blonk Street) and they used to get Dan Leano but this particular night he went to the old 'Empire' in Union Street (both of these theatres are now demolished) because there was somebody he wanted to see. Well, when he came to pay they said, "We don't allow you in here without a collar and tie. You're not properly dressed."

So he said, "This silk of mine has cost more than anybody's collar and tie that's gone in here!" But they wouldn't let him in.

Eventually, my Dad did get around to wearing a collar and tie. He always went to this particular shop called 'Paceys' at the bottom of King Street. They used to have lovely ties and they were always crocheted.

What's a Daycala?

My father lost his eye in the pit. A spark came off his pick and it burnt the back of his eye and he lost it. So his job as a miner at the coal face was finished and so he became a 'Daycala'.

This was at Orgreave Colliery. During the Strike they started to sack miners. They wanted my Father to take compensation and the lump sum they offered him was £75.00. Well, he wouldn't take it and he said to the chap who came to offer him the money, "Would you sell one of your eyes for £75.00?"

This chap would come (we used to love him to come when we were kids because we knew him and me Father were in for a battle of words) and he'd open his brief case and out would come all his papers and he'd say, "Now then Mr Gill, can we make a settlement?"

My Dad used to reply, "It's no good thee coming because I'm not taking lump sum. I'm going in for part compensation."

Anyway, this business of part compensation went through and me Father was allowed 10/- a week for life. Well, when he came out of work, he had to go to Orgreave Colliery on the Friday for this 10/- (50p) but the dole knocked it off, so instead of fetching 26/- for him and me mother, he fetched 16/- and 10/- from Pit.

Before me Dad got stopped, this chap with the brief case came one particular day when me dad was working as a Daycala, which meant he ran about doing odd jobs.

Well, when this chap came (I shall never forget it because as kids we thought it was hilarious!) he said to me Father, "What do you do Mr Gill, in the Pit?"

So me Dad said, "I'm a Daycala."

"And what's a Daycala?" chap asked.

"Shall I tell thee?" me Father said.

"I'd like to know for my report," chap replied.

"Well, I shift muck when it falls," answered me Dad.

So this fella, says to me Father, "And what do you do when none falls?"

"Oh, I don't shift that!" me Dad answered — so dry!

Well, chap just shut his book and went! We thought it was hilarious! Me Father was so witty and had such a dry sense of humour.

Birley Pit Trip

Every year Birley Pit had a day trip to Cleethorpes and all the miners and their wives used to go on the train. The train used to come out of the sidings where the coal waggons came from. This was where the Paddy left each day, near the bottom of Birley Moor Road (opposite where the Birley Bingo centre is today).

Kids used to go on this trip as well and most of them had no shoes. They even went to school without shoes. Oh, there was some poverty, it was terrible. Thank God, we were never as bad as that! We were only a small family. Some got Parish Pay but it was only about 5/- and they had to be destitute to get that. This was paid by the Parish."

St. Monday

Herbert Hobson: "Colliers never worked on a Monday. They used to have it off. Saint Monday they called it. Once on St. Monday, four or five went fishing on their bikes. Well, they finished up with punctures and to get them home they stuck tyres with grass.

The sound of the Miner's Clogs

Hetty Hobson: "When we lived up Smithfield Road we could hear the Colliers coming right down Gleadless Road to Town End and you could tell when to put kettle on by the time they got to Town End."

It must certainly have been quiet in Gleadless during the 20's and 30's. *Mrs Liversidge* also comments on being able to hear the miners coming home from a distance far away.

"My husband, Fred Liversidge was a miner and he came from Hollinsend. When he was on afternoons, I could tell, (when I lived on Irish

Channel) when he was coming home because I could hear his clogs when he was passing Independent Chapel on bottom of Common. It was so quiet (oh, it was lovely!) I could hear him coming home so I used to put kettle on."

Hetty continues, "When you first got a house in them days, you just fitted out a bedroom and where you were living. Then you went into it and you built it up afterwards.

When we came to live on Hollinsend Road that's what we did. Well, we soon hurried up and got the back bedroom decorated because of hearing miners walking past our house in the morning. At first you could just hear the sound of their clogs, just faintly at the top of Gleadless Road and Hollinsend Road and then it got louder and louder as more and more miners kept joining them and by the time they got down here, at the bottom of Hollinsend Road, it was like a regiment. We didn't need an alarm clock in the morning!

At 6 am when last cage had gone down at Birley Pit, they used to blow a siren.

Harley Street Specialist

The Cook family used to live up Wood Lane and they had a son called Rhodes. Rhodes worked down the pit and broke his neck in an accident. He was in hospital such a long time that he began to get interested in helping Doctors. He became so involved in helping patients that he studied it and never went back to pit. Instead he became a Harley Street specialist in London."

(I believe he became what we know today as an osteopath.)

Life down the Pit

Life in any pit village was difficult but the community had a common identity in the pit. To a miner the pit dictated his and his family's life. Due to the harshness of life and each miner depending on his workmates for his safety in dangerous working conditions, close friendships between neighbours were formed. These links were carried on into social life too with the miner playing at football and cricket with other miners who were his workmates.

For the majority of Gleadless and especially Hollinsend boys, the pit was their only destination on leaving school. Although fathers were unwilling to send their sons down the pit, there was little alternative work.

Walter Gill was a miner from the age of 14 until his retirement. Having worked at four pits in the neighbouring area, he witnessed many changes, from the old days when coal was hewn by hand by the collier to a more modern approach of machine coal cutting equipment. Born in 1910, Mr Gill recalls life down the pit:

"I started work in 1924 and I was 14 years old. I left school on the Friday and started at Orgreave Pit on the Monday. I was up at 4 am and I'd walk to pit and it was an hours walk there and when I'd got there I'd another 1½ miles to walk to where I was going to work so I walked about 4 to 4½ miles each morning. Then when I'd finished my work I had to walk home again.

My first job in the pit was as a haulage lad working in pit bottoms. From there I went onto 'workings' then I moved onto what they called a 'Clipping' job which meant I fastened clips onto tubs. At 18 years old I went on what they called 'Filling' on 'Pan Hole'.

Conditions in the pit

Conditions in Birley Pit were shocking. In some places you were up to your knees in water. We all used to wear Wellingtons. We worked at one place where we used to make coats out of rattice cloth. We called them 'westcotes' (waistcoats) but we made them long so that water would run off your back and this lattice cloth used to divert the water.

The water would run down 'jinny' (from the pit bottom to the top of the run way) and flow down constantly. There were no baths so you had to work in it and then come home like that and from Birley it was nearly 1 hour's walk home.

We worked in places where it wasn't fit for dogs to work in. When I say that I mean there were no oxygen or air. Your head used to thump and your heart used to pound like a hammer. They couldn't get ventilation to us because we were working in 'eddings'. Eventually, they did bring fans in and they'd blow air to you. When you got home all you wanted to do was to lie down and go to sleep.

Waistcoats

These 'westcotes' we wore had two pockets. One to put our 'snap' in and another for our drinking bottle. When we got to work we'd take it off and hang it up.

This particular time I had a 'filler' with me and when it came to our 'snap' (a break for 20 minutes) I went to my westcote and put my hand in my pocket and it felt all fluffy and I thought, "What the devil's that?"

I discovered it was a great, big rat in my pocket, eating my 'snap'! Well! Rat jumped one way and I jumped other!

But Birley Pit was full of rats. They'd smell your food so we'd try and throw stones at them but we had to be quick because they were like lightening. At Orgreave there were a lot of mice. Once when I was just a lad of 16 I put my 'westcote' on and I could feel something running up and down my back and found it was a mouse! Brookhouse didn't have as many rats as Birley though.

Meals

We had our dinner underground. It was bread and jam or bread and lard or dripping. We took water (some took cold tea) to drink. I'd take 5 pints of water in a 'dudley' which was a tin container with a spout at top and you arranged it so you could carry it on your shoulder.

At Orgreave with it being so hot and no air, I would have drunk up by 'snap' time. All we used to wear down pit were little pants and clogs. Clogs were the cheapest form of shoes you see.

Accidents

Birley Pit closed in October, 1943 and I remember that on the very last shift a miner was killed. When there was a fatal accident we used to 'knock off' and the pit stood for 24 hours.

They only used wood in those days. Wooden bars and wooden props. With the heavy weight on the props the timber used to crack and bang and we'd call it 'shouting Jack' when timber was cracking.

There were many accidents in the pit but the worst one I remember was when a junction caved in. I knew the men killed. Some men were bringing a machine out of the area and they must have caught a 'prop' or something and all the lot caved in. One bloke was dead standing up but they wouldn't let us bring him out while we got the two others out who were buried underneath. We could hear them shouting. We worked for three hours at the side of the dead chap before we brought the two out. The men were alive but they both died during the night.

Wages

I used to get 4/6d (22½p) a shift when I first started work. They'd wind men down pit between 6.00 am and then we'd come up again at 2.00 pm so that was like a 7½ hours shift.

Pits worked

I worked at four pits altogether. Orgreave, Birley, Treeton (twice) and then Brookhouse (twice). I was made redundant from Orgreave Pit but without any redundancy pay. In late 1929 and early 30 they shut down the Silkstone Seam and I'd been there about six years.

From there I went to work at Treeton Pit where my Father worked but we went from bad to worst there. I was only working on two days, Tuesday and Friday. But my pal, Henry Corker was working at Birley Pit and he got me a job there working on a machine and it was more money. I'd only been getting 18/- a week at Treeton but I got £2 (7/11d a shift) at Birley.

When I worked at Birley I got my wage in a packet for we were on what they called a 'day' wage but at Orgreave we were on a 'contract' which meant that we got paid so much a yard (see also 'Reckoning Day').

I left Birley Pit (which was Woodhouse) in 1943 when they closed it down and turned it into a Bevan camp where lads who didn't want to go into the Army could be trained to go down pit. They were called 'Bevan Boys'.

From Birley, I was transferred to Brookhouse. During my time in the pit, I became a Deputy which meant I was in charge of thirty or forty men at coal face and handled explosives."

Both Stanley Crofts (one of the Mush Crofts), born 1912 and Walter Cook, born 1911, worked down the Pit. Between them they possess a remarkable technical knowledge of the actual workings of a mine. Unfortunately, limited space here does not allow me to go into too much detailed technicalities of a mine worker's job.

Stanley Crofts: "Everybody's first job as a boy down a mine would be coupling tubs or empties as we used to call them. Some were steel and some were wooden and they used to hold about 15 cwt."

Walter Cook: "I started as a Pony Driver at Birley Pit and I went out into workings on my first day with a pony. I had to take a spare pony out and another lad was learning me and I just had that one day learning. Next day I was left on my own.

Pillar and Post system

This tub-way ran for about a mile. They called it a 'level'. Then from the main runway, they (the tubs) were brought up by an endless rope then lowered back into this pass-by. They used to drop 14 empty tubs into this pass-by and I had to take 14 tubs from there with pony. It were a bit down hill and then it started to go up an incline.

Well this pony couldn't take 14 tubs all the way, so what you did, you left them in what we called a 'Swilly' where they'd stand on their own these tubs.

You uncoupled 7 and took 7 up and I'd meet another lad about 3 or 400 yards higher up and we had a pass-by. It was like shunting two trams on two separate roadways. Well, we'd take empty tubs on there, then 'Far End lad' would take them to coal face to miners.

The miners were getting coal to the left hand and to the right hand and we called them a 'Board'. We used to take 7 tubs up either side. There might be three sets of miners working in two's on right hand and there were only 7 tubs so that was three sets of two's equalled six with one tub left. They used to fall out as to who was going to have the odd one. This system was called the 'Pillar and Post system."

Stanley Crofts: At Orgreave in the Silkstone Seam, there was no 'Pillar and Post System' there. There was what we called 'Long Wall'. You had a long wall and you had stints of ten yards each. But everybody had to start at the Pit bottom."

Walter Cook: "When I started work as a boy (1925) I got 2/9d a shift when I was a Collier at 21, we had to buy our own tools and we were getting less than 10/- a shift.

The Pit Ponies stables were underground and they could only see in the dark but not in the light. They only came out of the mine at holiday time and then they'd put them in a field. They used to go mad when they had to go back down again.

The Paddy Train ran from Birley Vale and it cost 6d. a week to go on it. When it first started it had two very good railway carriages but within six months it was like a ghost train!

There were a lot of lads from Park and district and nearly all the miners smoked in those days but you weren't allowed cigarettes and matches down a Pit so if you wanted a cigarette when you came out of work, you hid a cigarette and a match in seating. Seating got ripped and Paddy was soon in a bad state.

Westcote

We used to wear an old 'westcote' (waistcoat) and your Mother used to put a big pocket in it so it could hold your big bottle or 'dudley' as we called it. Then we had another pocket at other side for your 'snap'. When I was a lad, I took a quart of tea and when I set off in the morning it used to be hot but during the day it were cold. You never put milk in because it'd go sour so we drank cold tea. But they were good days."

Stanley Crofts: "Mining communities were great. People were happy, hard-working and they had community spirit. The company of the people were good to each other.

It was a marvellous time to live in because you had like a code. You knew what you were doing and everybody knew where they stood with everybody else."

3. LIFE ON THE LAND

Gleadless, until the housing programme of the 50's, was a rural area, which was self-suffiicent and relied on the farms in the immediate surroundings not only for produce but also for casual labour. Pea and potato picking times brought an influx of women (especially from Hollins End) offering to work in the fields to earn much needed money.

The fields at Harvest time would have been busy with activity as men, women and children helped to gather in the harvest. While on threshing days one could hear the chuff and rattle of the engine and threshing-machine on the road with children racing to meet it. The smell of hot steam and oil would fill the air while the iron monster with more chuffing and much complicated shunting would be steered into position ready for its work to be done.

Today, mechanisation and new scientific methods have replaced the labour of dozens of farmworkers and horses on every farm.

Cartledge's Farm (The late Reg. Cartledge)
The miners in the photo are using the pathway which led through the fields to Intake.

There were numerous farms scattered around Gleadless: Newfield Green, The Paddocks, Hurlfield Hill, Hoylands, Cartledges and Foxs, to name but a few. While in the White Lane area were the very big farms of Base Green, Charnock Hall and White Lane. Secluded down Carter Lane was Carter Lodge and Carter Hall farms.

One can only be saddened when one realises that we have lost two ancient, early 17th century buildings, namely Base Green farmhouse and Charnock Hall. Buildings such as these would never have suffered a similar fate today we contend to believe. In an effort to house Sheffield people in surrounding villages such as Gleadless, the agricultural land disappeared and ultimately the farms.

Fox's farm buildings on Gleadless Common, Carter Hall farm and White Lane farm are the sole survivors from the building aftermath in Gleadless.

Charnock Hall consisted of a vast estate covering 105 acres of land while Base Green, which had earlier been a name given to the Commons and waste lands near Charnock Hall, was also a vast farm. My most grateful thanks to Mr. Gordon Bradley, the Rhodes family and John and Margaret Hinchliffe for their kindness and help with this chapter.

The Gleadless countryside has changed beyond recognition. The villager's pig has gone, protesting to the factory farm and the cheese-press to the museum. The 'farm chaps' no longer sit down to a breakfast of fat pork and skimmed milk while the mighty traction engine chugs and clanks no more from farm to farm at threshing time. However, in the following pages these times live on in the minds of people who enjoyed life on the land in the once rural Gleadless.

Base Green Farm

Mr. Gordon Bradley was born at Base Green Farm in 1913 and lived there until he was married in 1940. The Bradleys were well known in the Gleadless area and were the last family to live at the farm before its lands were taken for the building of the Base Green Housing Estate in the 1950's. Mr. Bradley remembers vividly what life and times were like on the farm.

Market Days

"Base Green was a very mixed farm. We used to grow corn, potatoes, cabbages, cauliflower, peas and rhubarb. We used to do a lot of market work in the old Rag Market (This was the old Rag and Tag at the bottom of Dixon Lane). We'd stand with the horse and dray in there. In those days we used to sell direct from the carts. They allowed us to go in and there were perhaps eight or ten horses and drays, all in a line. You paid a toll every time you went in and you sold direct to the customers from there.

We had to be out by 9.45 am so all the other pot and retail stalls could be put up when we'd gone.

I worked down there until they built the new Parkway Market in 1955 or 6. I'd go with my lorry and stand in there (The old Rag Market) after my Father (Brewster Nelson Bradley) had died in 1948. I sold direct from the waggon but after the new Parkway Market was built we weren't allowed to sell direct from the waggon anymore and we were stopped and had to go through a wholesaler.

Sometimes my Father used to walk from Base Green to Rag Market. He'd go across the fields from Jaunty Lane to old Intake and if he missed a horse tram he'd walk it.

In those days, they drove all the cattle along the roads to the abbatoir. There were no waggons for the cattle. Cattle to be slaughtered were taken to the Shambles (Sheffield) and cattle were brought from markets all over; Retford, Worksop, Chesterfield and Doncaster. They were all driven along the road to the Shambles.

We only took our goods to Sheffield Market but others came from further afield. One chap called Leadham came from Rotherham, another called Pontiss came from Wickersley and two uncles, one named Ellis came from Richmond and the other called Helliwell came from Woodhouse. Another chap name Croft came from Intake and they all lined up with us in the Market place with their horses and drays.

Shire Horses

In my Father's day we had ten Shire horses. Goods were loaded onto the cart and they would travel along Gleadless road to the "Heeley and Sheffield" House, then turn right down the steep hill (the top of Hollinsend Road, now a cul de sac) then turn left up Gleadless Common to the top, then down Windy House Road to City Road.

We never travelled down Hurlfield Hill because it was far too steep but when they opened Ridgeway Road we used that then. All this road work would wear the horses out in three or four years. We had two horsemen. The first man set off at 3.15 am with his first load and had to be in Sheffield for 4.30 am - 4.45 am. Then he brought the manure back under Breweries (Breweries at this time used horses for delivering beer). Before he went again, he fed his horses and himself. In the meantime the second horseman would have gone one hour after him.

It used to be all bed and work in those days. The horses had to do all the ploughing and getting the "greens" out of the fields which were sometimes steep in sludge.

-Base Green
Farmhouse-
-Pauline Shearstone-
-1985-

Where there's Muck . . .

We had a lot of cattle on the farm too; bullocks and pigs. We had to make manure for fertiliser (Most of the night soil was put on the fields at the bottom of Base Green.) A big "crew" yard was full of bullocks and pigs during winter time. It was about eight foot deep in manure and we'd cut it out in squares with a hay knife. It was so solid. You can imagine bullocks, ten and twelve cwts. running about in it all day through. Everyday, we had to put down fresh straw and when it reached the mangers where they were feeding, the manure was about six to eight foot deep! Any silver coins in your pocket turned green caused by the ammonia in the manure!

Farm hands

Farm people didn't live in the farmhouse except the horseman and his wife and family who lived in the end of the house (the cottage). One of our horsemen was called Sid Williams and he came from the old Town End at Gleadless but others came from different places like Hollinsend. A chap called Jack Porter who lived at the bottom of Ridgeway Road, once worked for us. So did Violet Crouch, who lived in the Barracks at Hollinsend. She was a pea-picker.

Working on the farm was my Father, his three sons (when they'd all left school) four or five men and then casual workers like pea-pickers etc.

Wages

Money went a long way in those days. When I was going to school (1920's) the working men on the farm got about 36/- to 38/- a week for working 12 hours a day and they got overtime when they went to market. Mind you, you could buy a lot with just £1 then. In 1940 a packet of Woodbines and matches cost 5d while a glass of beer cost just 2½d. You can't do that now!

Early days

Mother sent me to Ridgeway School when I was four but they sent me back again until I was five! We used to walk there and back and think nothing about it. Mind you there wasn't much traffic on the roads then. My mother had a pony and trap and on Sundays she used to take us a ride in it, jogging around here.

One of my first jobs was to help on threshing day. We had the Earnshaws threshing machine. There were three brothers, John, Tom and Ben. They had two sets and lived up Smithfield Road before they went to live up Gleadless Common. When I was only 14 years old, I had to keep water for steam engine and had to carry two 3 gallon buckets. I'd walk 200 yards down a field to a pump, pump the tank full, then carry these buckets to the steam engine to keep it going. I had to do that all day and I daren't stop or the water supply would go down. It was hard work!

One particular haymaking time there was the worst thunderstorm in living memory. It was in 1924 and when my Mother put us three kids to bed the sky was green, orange, red and every colour you could imagine. The thunder and lightning was terrific. All the hay had been cocked up in "cocks" in the fields but the next morning it had all gone! It was all down at the bottom of Jaunty Lane. There were dykes, six feet deep, carved out of the ground and there were tons of soil like that all over the farm. These great big ravines were caused by the huge bulk of water. I've never seen anything like it. I'll never forget it.

Inside Base Green Farmhouse

I'll try and describe what it was like inside the farmhouse.

Most people usually went round to the back door. Well, you went up the drive (the drive was about 30 yards long up to the house for St. Peter's Church was built nearer to the road than the house was.) Then you'd walk past the gable end of the house to the back door. This door came into a lobby where you put all your dirty clothes and wellies.

Next door was a large kitchen which had an old type Yorkshire Range. There was a big "set pot" with a fire underneath which was used for cooking and washing the clothes in. Hanging from the ceiling was a big rack with 6 to 7 foot long rails on a pulley which we used to pull up and down. This was for drying the clothes on. My Mother used to have herbs in the kitchen and she used to grind them and put them into bottles.

From the kitchen you'd turn left into a passage way and there was a toilet on your right and on your left was a long passage which went down to a very large pantry. This pantry was bigger than an ordinary room and it had stone benches in it. From the pantry we went down some steps into a big cellar where they used to cure the pigs in winter time. We made our own bacon and it was beautiful to eat.

To the right of the pantry was a place we called "the shop" which was a great big room with everything in it belonging to the farm, like bits and pieces of machines and whatever you wanted. Medicines and all sorts were kept there.

Coming back down the passage way you went straight forward into the lounge — the dining room cum lounge which was a very large room. There were oak beams in there and the floor was wooden like the living room. The other rooms had mostly stone floors.

From this great big living room you went across into another doorway and there was another little lounge there. That's where we had the pianola in those days. You had to put a roll in then pedal away like mad! This lounge was only used perhaps once a month or once every four months when special guests came. We children weren't allowed in.

In the living room were the stairs which went upstairs to the bedrooms. At the top of these stairs on your first right was the bathroom and toilet (there was an outside toilet for the workmen). Then there was Father and Mother's big bedroom.

Along a passage again we came to our bedroom (the chidlren's) and we had two double beds in there. Further along was another bedroom which looked towards the back of the house. Upstairs were attics but we never used those. Between all the bedroom floors and ceilings were oat husks. These husks (just the skin from the black oats) acted as a form of insulation. We had a few mice but we soon killed them.

It was a beautiful farmhouse and it was built in the 1660's. It's a pity it had to be demolished.

The beginning of the Base Green Housing Estate

The land belonging to Base Green farm was built on before the war by private builders. My father sold some land at Town End and a man called Jack Jones built some houses there. During the war the building stopped but after the war the Sheffield City Council came along and compulsory

Base Green Farmhouse (Mr Charlesworth)

purchased it. This would be around 1946/7 or 8. My Father died in 1948 and after that my brother had it for a few years before he lost it. So it would be in the early 50's when they started building.

The farm building was very similar to Kent Memorial House at Ridgeway. They tried to save it. St. Peter's Church is on the site of the farm's outer buildings. You can still see one of the stone pillars belonging to the farm now. The Church is built nearer to the road than the farm was."

It is perhaps worth mentioning here that attempts (although unsuccessful) were made to save the farmhouse.

A report in *The Star* dated 1952 headlines "300 year old farmhouse to become Church". Architects prepared plans to convert the interior of the farmhouse into a church. The reasons for this were three-fold. Firstly, it would provide a permanent place of worship for the residents of the growing Base Green Estate, secondly it would be less costly than building a new church and lastly it would preserve the rural aspects of the village.

At this time Base Green only had the facility of a mission church held in a Nissen hut.

However, plans for the conversion were not carried out. The farmhouse had been empty for some time and the interior was badly damaged. A *Star* reporter states, "Eventually, the farmhouse which a few years ago stood in an area described by townspeople as "the country" will be entirely surrounded by private and Corporation houses."

Inevitably, the farm building, which had been built during Charles II's reign, was eventually demolished.

Coal at Base Green

The Gleadless area was rich in coal and although this was mainly "surface" coal it led to various "drift" mines being opened in the neighbourhood.

From very early days, coal had been 'dug' at Base Green so it was hardly surprising that during the 1926 Coal Strike, Brewster Bradley decided to open a drift mine in the fields behind the farm house.

Mr Gordon Bradley continues, "My father, Brewster Bradley, knew there was coal underneath Base Green. He had a deputy and about seven people working for him. A Fordson tractor/winch was used to pull up the tubs while a horse and cart took the coal to a screen behind the farm-house The breweries had steam waggons in those days and they fetched all the small stuff for their boilers. They had a lot of horses and we used to fetch all their manure.

The mine was closed a year after the Strike. The "props" were pulled out and it dropped in in places. We took the tubs and rails out and then filled it up with rubbish. The last hole dropped in when they were building the houses on the estate. They put a concrete raft across it.

There's still some coal under Base Green! It was good Silkstone coal."

Early Coal workings on Base Green

In bygone days, the increasing surge in steam power brought an urgent demand for coal and coke. The ridge which gives Ridgeway (one mile from Gleadless) its name, is the Basset Edge of the vast Silkstone Seam. With coal being so close at hand, it is hardly surprising that during the 19th century, there were seven or eight mines or drifts along this ridge of less than two miles.

The largest one was at Base Green and had 36 coke ovens. This belonged to Jonathan Rhodes and ceased working in February, 1836. In 1832, the mine at White Lane, owned by Wilkinson Jeffcock & Co., stopped working. One at High Lane, owned by Philip Sayles and Pringle, ceased working in 1827. Opposite the Phoenix Works, the drift, owned and operated by Andrew Vardy, was worked for many years.

Later in 1869 a "colliery" at Base Green was owned by Joseph Rhodes, while John Rhodes owned Woodthorpe Colliery and Jeffcock and Dunn owned Birley Colliery.*

Brewster Bradley had a pit at Marsh Lane, Ford Road with Harry Cowley (grocers), Walter Seaton of Ford Farm and Harry Crowcock, haulage from Sheffield. This was during the 1940's and best Silkstone coal then fetched just £1 a ton! When water flooded in the pit it had to close.

During the building of the Base Green Estate, an interesting incident occurred. On April 5th, 1951, *The Sheffield Telegraph* reported, "Tractor finds 18th century mine on Estate."

Apparently, while excavating on the estate, a tractor fell into a hole and revealed the presence of an 18th century coal mine. In excavating five or six feet down in one place they had thinned the surface crust so much that the tractor had fallen in.

It was reported that the working which were found on agricultural land near White Lane, "included about five headings and several shafts going down to a depth of 10 ft to 15 ft. Further under the hillside towards Norton, where houses were not to be built, the depth was possibly much more.

The headings had been made when there had been no machinery. "All had been hand cut, and the job of cutting out the rock 'bind' had been remarkably well done. This is the Silkstone Seam. Pillars of coal had been left in to serve the purpose of timber", said Ald. Curtis.

* *Yorkshire Past & Present Vol 1* Thomas Baines pub. William Mackenzie

There had been no records of a mine being there and the N.C.B. could not tell them for their records only dated from 1820 and this pit was operating before that time.

The pit was believed to have been working at the end of the 18th century. An 86 year old Gleadless man recalled his grandfather telling him of his father having worked there when women had been employed for pulling the "sledge" which preceded the tubs.

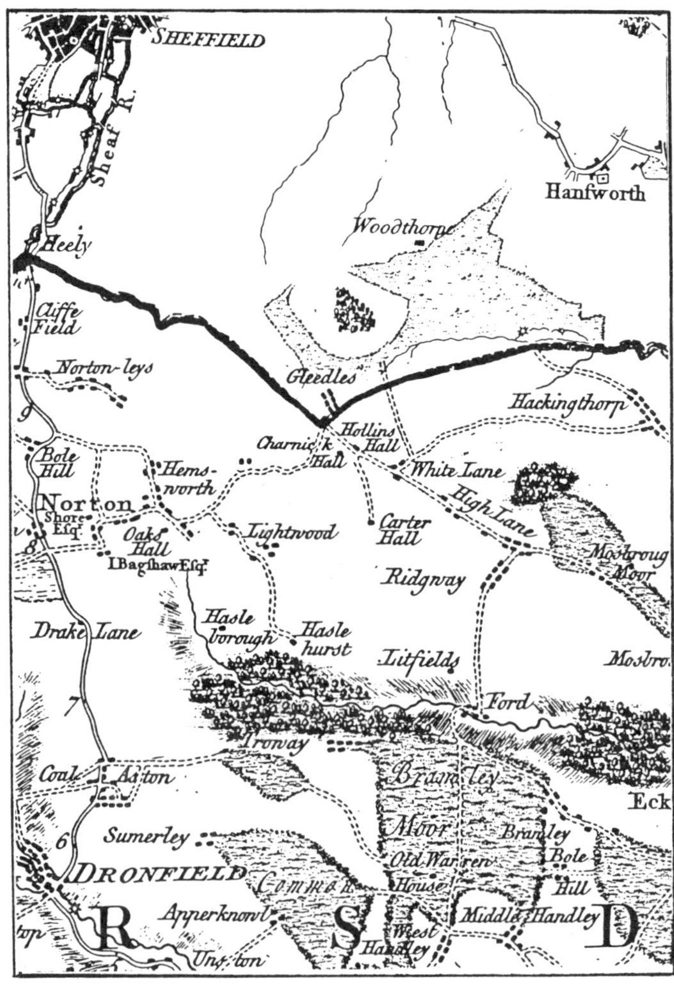

Burdett's Map of Derbyshire, 1791 (Courtesy of Derbyshire Library Service)

Attempts to save the Base Green farmhouse

Efforts, as I mentioned earlier, were made to try and prevent the demolition of the 300 year old farmhouse. Plans were made to convert the interior of the farm into a church. The Rev. A.C. Porteus, Vicar of Ridgeway, is reported as saying that proposals were being made to make a small church on the first floor of the farmhouse without altering the exterior. Partition walls and a loft floor would have to be taken out to do that. One advantage was that the farmhouse was built in the form of a cross. The east wing — a cottage — would be made ready for a caretaker. Alterations would also have to be made for a Sunday school and parochial hall. An appeal for funds was made to cover the cost of these alterations.

A printed booklet was distributed amongst the local parishioners and appeals were made to 'buy a brick for as much as you can'. Meanwhile vandals had played havoc with the structure while it had been empty. Despite determined efforts the farmhouse was demolished and St. Peter's Church was built on the site behind the old farm.

The Church in the Upper Room of the House.

THE OLD
The building shown opposite was scheduled for demolition. Like many such buildings of character which have stood for more than three centuries, it would have been removed in the name of progress.

THE NEW
We are determined to save the shell and make of it a church centre providing for both the religious and social needs of this Community of Gleadless. This will cost about £3,000. The Bishop of Derby's Ten Year Plan has advanced £1,700 of which £1,250 will be required for the purchase of the site and legal costs.

Item from the 'printed booklet'

Base Green

1640 Mention of Bays Green in 'The Parliamentary Survey of 1640'. Basegreen Common was between Charnock Hall and the present Charnock School.

1717 Joseph Banks owns the land at 'Bays Green'. His tenant was Thomas Scholey.

1791 Burdett's Map of Derbyshire shows the area where Base Green Farm was situated being called 'Hollins Hall'.

1795 George Woodhead owns the Farm.

1796 The Eckington Enclosure Act is enforced and the common land in the Base Green area is enclosed.
The Base Green 'copyhold estate' is for sale and is described as having 71 acres of good arable, meadow and pasture land. The estate also had ironstone and coal which could be sold to the local cutlery and scythe and sickle trade.
Anna Marie Hodgson owner in 1796.

1841 *(see Census)* James Rhodes at the farm

1851 Joseph Rhodes

1856 Owned by George Anderson and others, tenant Joseph Rhodes.

1861 Joseph Rhodes

1862 Basegreen Sale. Occupier Joseph Rhodes.

1871 Joseph Rhodes

1881 John Rhodes

1899 The copyhold estate "Base Green" was to be sold by auction. In the occupation of Mr Charles Bradley, the area consisted of 81 acres, and "farm house, with cottage, barn, stables, cowhouses, piggeries, cart sheds, chambers and other buildings."

1922/48 Brewster Nelson Bradley (son of Charles Bradley)

1948 Brewster's son Ron. Bradley at the farm until the building of the Base Green Housing Estate.

1950's The Sheffield Council.

Base Green Farm

1841 Census *(Census for Base Green, believed to be the Farm)*

James Rhodes	25 yrs	Farmer
Harriot Rhodes	25 yrs	
Jonathan " "	3 yrs	
Harriot " "	2 yrs	
William " "	1 yr	
Geo. Barber	15 yrs	Male Servant
Ester Barker	30 yrs	Female Servant
Ann Harrison	12 yrs	Female Servant

1851 Census

Joseph Rhodes	Head	M	37 yrs	Farmer of 102 acres employing one labourer	Yorkshire, Sheffield
Hannah Rhodes	Wife	M	41 yrs	Farmers Wife	Derbs. Whittington
John "	Son		14 yrs	Farmer's Son	Yorks Sheffield
Hannah "	Dau.		12 yrs	Scholar	Yorks Richmond

Joseph "	Son		10 yrs	Scholar	" "
Elizabeth "	Dau.		4 yrs		Derbs. Base Green
Mary "	Dau.		2 yrs		" "
Emily "	Dau.		6 m.		" "
James Steward	Serv.	U	20 yrs	Ag.Lab.	Yorks, Thurgoland
Ann Staton	Serv	U	17 yrs	House Servant	Derbys. Eckington

1861 Census

Joseph Rhodes	Head	M	47	Farmer of 95 acres of land	Sheffield
Hannah Rhodes	Wife	M	51	Farmer's wife	Eckington
John "	Son	U	24	Farmer's son	Sheffield
Hannah "	Dau.	U	22	Farmer's Daughter	Handsworth
Joseph "	Son	U	20	Farmer's Son	Handsworth
Elizabeth "	Dau.		14	Scholar	Eckington
Mary "	Dau.		12	Scholar	" "
Emily "	Dau.		10	Scholar	" "
Thomas "	Son		8		" "
Harriet "	Dau.		5		" "
George Rowbotham	Serv.	U	22	Farm Servant	Beighton

1871 Census

				Occupation	*Place of Birth*
Joseph Rhodes	Head	M	58 yrs	Farmer of 116 acres employing 2 men.	
Hannah " "	Wife	M	61 yrs		
Emily " "	Dau.	U	20 yrs		
Thomas " "	Son	U	18 yrs	Farmer's Son	Base Green, Derbys.
Harriet " "	Dau.	U	15 yrs		Base Green, Derbys.
George Chambers	Servt.	U	24 yrs	Ag. Servant	Unknown

1881 Census

John Rhodes	Head	M	44 yrs	Farmer of 110 acres employing 1 Lab. & 7 Boys	
Sarah Rhodes	Wife	M	45 yrs		Yorks, Handsworth
Annie,Eliz. Rhodes	Dau.	U	16 yrs		Derbys, Eckington
Joseph Rhodes	Son	U	12 yrs	Scholar	" "
John William Rhodes	Son	U	6 yrs	Scholar	" "

Charnock Hall

'Johnty' Rhodes of Charnock Hall

One cannot speak of Charnock Hall without mentioning a character who lived there in the 18th and early 19th century. He was Jonathon Rhodes (known as 'Johnty' Rhodes) and the most important person in the local coal trade. He owned a large colliery consisting of 36 coke ovens at Basegreen and it is more than likely that Jaunty Lane which was once spelt 'Johnty', derives its name from this gentleman.

There are two stories relating to this man which the reader may wish to

As I Remember Charnock Hall Farm. Gleadless.

hear. The first shows what a character he was when he attended the auction at which Charnock Hall was up for sale. He was dressed in a smock, the usual garb at this time for an agricultural labourer. He bid £4,000 for the Hall and at this price it was knocked down to him and when the auctioneer asked for the customary deposit Rhodes refused and one can imagine the auctioneer's feelings. However, 'Johnty' lifted his smock and rolled down his stockings and handed over four notes each of £1,000 as the full purchase price!

On another occasion the men at one of his collieries went on strike and 'Johnty' promised to meet their demands if they would start work again. This they refused to do until their demands had first been met. On hearing this he closed the colliery saying that if the men could manage without work, he was sure that he could manage without the men and the colliery never worked after that.

John Hinchcliffe, together with his wife Margaret and family lived in one of the little cottages that were attached to Charnock Hall. The Hinchcliffes spent many happy years there before the fields were taken for building land and the Hall was subsequently demolished.

Conservation seems to have counted very little at this particular time and all we have left now of a once beautiful 17th century building, are people's fond memories. (I have tried in vain to obtain a photo of Charnock Hall and if any reader has one I would be delighted to see it.) Due to this lack of visual record of Charnock Hall, Mr Cecil Higgins very kindly agreed to draw an artist's impression of how the Hall once looked. This drawing was based on his personal recollections and from an architect's plan of the Hall. My most grateful thanks to Cecil for his splendid drawing!

John Hinchcliffe: "The first family I remember living at Charnock Hall were the Moody family. This would be in the 1920's. They had two daughters and the eldest daughter married a farmer at Herdings Farm. There were two farms at Herdings, the one on the left was Rhodes' farm and the other on the right belonged to a family called Marsh (this building still survives today). Later the Nutt family moved to the farm where the Rhodes lived.

Then in the 1930's the Fidlers took over Charnock and they came from the Mawfa Lane area of Norton. Arnold Fidler wanted to go farming so his parents, Mr & Mrs Fidler senior, bought Charnock Hall Farm and they'd be about 100 acres to it then. Charnock was like one great big park, in fact we used to call it 'Charnock Park' because it stretched from Gleadless Town End to Carter Lane.

There were cottages attached to the Hall. One at the front faced White Lane and there was another at the back. Mr and Mrs Fidler lived in the

Hall in the front part and faced down the Park like we did living in the cottage. Mrs Cadman lived in the other cottage and then Lilian Martin. One man worked on the farm, called Billy Jones and he helped Arnie. When I left school I went farming and helped Arnie Fidler. I used to work from 6.30 am to 6 pm, six full days and when you had your weekend off you still went and milked on Sunday.

Charnock was a mixed farm with cows, geese and pigs. There were two ponds and one was at the front of the Hall and on the far side was the stack yard. I can picture the farm now. There was a big door where you went into the yard at the back and there were cow houses, our cottage, a coal house and where we used to boil up. Then there was the Stack Yard — the Dutch Barn.

At one time they'd been an old fashioned coach house where they must have kept their carriages. Moodies used to keep their 'tub' (similar to a Governor's cart) in there. It was a round 'tub' with a little door in the back and they had a half-Shetland pony called Kitty. Every Sunday Mr Moody used to take Mrs Moody and their daughter in this little tub to the Chapel at Town End. He'd come down the drive at Charnock in his pony and tub.

Later when Arnie got married, Mr and Mrs Fidler (senior) moved into the carriage house part (with alterations of course) and had the back side of the house. The main Hall came out from that forwards about 6 feet, and it was all beautiful stone. There was a big window there with bedrooms above. That was the main part of the Hall.

There was a little wall with iron railings and a walled-in garden and four big windows of the Hall faced out onto this garden. Inside the hall was a beautiful spiral staircase. It was made out of wrought iron and mahogany — it was like a balustrade. There was a half landing with a big grandfather clock standing there and you went up some more stairs to the next landing.

Our cottage at Charnock was just one room, one bedroom above and one attic above that. It was three storeys high. Our downstairs room had a window and a little sink and a fireplace. Behind our back wall was the mill and the cowsheds were at the back of our pantry which went under the stairs. We had electric in our downstairs room and just the bedroom. Stone flags were on the floor but then I put lino down and the walls were all shapes and were damp but I treaded them and bought some slate lats and fixed some boards on top to make the room square. The walls were very high.

We lived with our two little sons in this cottage at Charnock but we managed. It was a beautiful wide area with big sycamore trees and squirrels playing in them. We spent ten very happy years living there before we moved out in 1957. All the farm land had been built up except for the Hall and that piece of land at the front. Arnie and his wife Zena were into competition dancing and they were building the Azena Dance Hall."

The 'Azena' Ballroom was opened in May, 1957. Later in 1963 four young Liverpool lads called John, Paul, George and Ringo, namely 'The Beatles' took the stage there for the princely fee of £85! They played to an audience of 1500 while a further 1,000 ardent fans flocked outside! Today, the 'Azena' is no longer, with the building being used as a supermarket.

The building programme on the Charnock Estate began as early as 1937 but when the war began, the building ceased, only to continue again after the war. Today, street names such as Arnold Avenue and Charnock Hall Road are the only reminders of a once historical and ancient building.

Charnock Hall Farm

1628/29 Richard Wilson is paying £24 for 'the same and the lands thereto belonging' Charnock Hall. Mr Stephen Bright is the receiver of the rents belonging to the Earl of Pembroke.(From the*Bright Papers*, 'Rentals of Totley and tithes of Bradfield', 1625-30, S.C.Lib. Archives.)

1650 Francis Wigfall (Executor of John Wigfall late of Renishaw).
Mr Wigfall to Mr Newham

1792 2nd Jan. Mr John Newham, Mr John Eyre to Henry Tudor Esq. his Trustee. Conveyance of a freehold Estate situate at Charnock Hall in the County of Derby and an Assignment of a Mortgage Term for 1,000 years. (Indenture in four parts.)

1818 21st Nov. George Tudor Esq. to Henry Garrett Key Esq. "Release and conveyance of all the Share and Interest Geo. Tudor Esq. in Charnock Hall and lands in the County of Derby."

1820 Mr Henry Garrett Key and others to Mr James Skelton. "Lease of Charnock Hall farm in the County of Derby."

1829 John Henry Key Esq. and others to Mr Jonathan Rhodes. "Release in fee to bar dower of Charnock Hall and Lands and Hereditaments in the Parish of Eckington in the County of Derby."

1841 Jonathon Rhodes *(census)*

1851 George Rhodes *(census)*

1861 Thomas Rhodes *(census)*

1871 George Rhodes *(census)*

1881 Thos. William Rhodes *(census)*

1893 Sale of Freehold land and homestead known as Charnock Hall Estate. "The day for the completion of the Purchase shall be the 29th Aug. 1893. The title shall commence as to all the lots with a specific devise contained in the Will (proved in 1845) of Jonathan Rhodes, late of Charnock Hall, Coal Master, deceased, which devise shall be presumed to have passed the property for an estate in fee simple."

1895 William Andrews

1922 William Charles Moody

1928, 1932 William Charles Moody

1936/41 Fred Fidler

1937/50's The building of the Charnock Housing Estate

1841 Census *(From Matlock)*

Jonathon Rhodes		65 yrs	Farmer	
Sarah Rhodes		60 yrs		
George Rhodes		20 yrs		
Joseph Elliot		15 yrs	Male Servant	
Mary Broughton		60 yrs	Female Servant	

1851 Census

George Rhodes	Head	U	33 yrs	Farmer of 130 acres employing one labourer	Sheffield
Thomas Rhodes	Bros. in-law	M	48 yrs	Farmer	〃
Hannah Rhodes	Sister	M	41 yrs	Farmer's Wife	〃
Thos. Will. Rhodes	Son		2 yrs		Charnock Hall
Nathaniel Rhodes	Son		1 mth		Derbyshire, Charnock Hall
Benjamin LeTall	Visitor	M	45 yrs	Surgeon & member of Royal College of Surgeons, Edinburgh and of Apothecarie's Hall, London	

(1843 Benjamin LeTall — mentioned in Le Tall's *Woodhouse* p. 82
"My father died at Hallows Houses this year, he was the son of John LeTall, Schoolmaster of Laughton."
Benjamin B. LeTall
Son of Benjamin, went his tour to the east this year, bringing back curios, Galilee shells, etc.
Emma LeTall
The youngest of John LeTall's family, died a short time before my father at Derby.)

Elizabeth Cooper	Visitor	M	46 yrs	Visitor	Yorks., Ecclesfield
Elizabeth Cowlishaw	Visitor	U	39 yrs	Nurse	Sheffield
Henry Ward	Serv.	U	23 yrs	Ag. Lab.	Yorks., Richmond
George Gleadhall	Serv.	U	14 yrs	〃 〃	Nottingham
Charles Wooley	Serv.	U	19 yrs	〃 〃	Yorks., Saint Johns
Ann Goodwin	Serv.	U	39 yrs	House Servant	Derbys., Dunston Chesterfield
William James LeTall			63 yrs	Woodhouse's local Doctor	

1861 Census

Thomas Rhodes	Head	M	58 yrs	Farmer of 103 acres employing one labourer	Sheffield
Hannah Rhodes	Wife	M	51		Sheffield
Thomas W. Rhodes	Son		12 yrs	Scholar	Eckington
George Rhodes	Cous.	U	44 yrs		Sheffield
Charles Woolley	Serv.	U	30 yrs	Farm Servant	York., Saint Johns
William Hayward	Serv.	U	16 yrs	〃 〃	Worksop
Matthew Bowler	Serv.	U	14 yrs	〃 〃	Heage, Derbys.

Harriet Rollet	Serv. U	19 yrs	House Servant	Beighton
John Hibbard	Visitor M	44 yrs	Agr. Lab.	Sheffield
Ellen Hibbard	Visitor M	30 yrs		〃
Benjamin Roberts	Visitor	7 yrs	Scholar	〃

1871 Census

			Occupation	*Place of Birth*
George Rhodes	Head U	53 yrs	Farmer 120 acres employing four men	Yorks., Sheffield
Hannah Rhodes	Sister M	61 yrs	Housekeeper & Manager	Yorks., Sheffield
Thomas, William Rhodes	Neph. U	22 yrs	Corn Miller	Derbys., Charnock Hall
Elizabeth Staniforth	Serv. U	12 yrs	General Servant	Derbys., Mosbro.
Johnny Kenny	Serv. U	21 yrs	Ag. Servant	Ireland, County Galway

1881 Census

Charnock Hall in 1 House. (This would have probably been one of the cottages connected to Charnock Hall).

1 House

James White	Head M	38 yrs	Ag. Lab.	Notts.
Mary White	Wife M	39 yrs		Derbys., Sheffield
Mary White	Dau.	13 yrs	Scholar	Derbys., Eckington
Elizabeth Anne White	Dau.	11 yrs	Scholar	Derbys., Eckington

Charnock Hall

Thos. Will. Rhodes	Head M	32 yrs	Farmer & Corn Miller	Derbys., Eckington
Sarah Ann Rhodes	Wife M	31 yrs		Yorks., Sheffield
Edith M. Rhodes	Dau.	8 yrs		Yorks., Handsworth
Sarah Rhodes	Dau.	7 yrs		〃 〃
George B. Rhodes	Son	5 yrs		〃 〃
Hannah Rhodes	Dau.	3 yrs		Lincs., Saxelby
George Rhodes	Uncle U	63 yrs	Annuitant	Yorks., Sheffield
Hannah Gill	Serv.	19 yrs	Domestic Servant	Yorks., Handsworth
Mary Daniel	Serv.	15/16	〃 〃	〃 〃
Ellis Rippon (male)	Visitor M	49 yrs	Sicklesmith	Derbys., Eckington
Ellen Rippon	〃 M	45 yrs		〃 〃

Farms in Gleadless

John Hinchcliffe: "Gleadless used to have quite a few farms. There used to be a farm at the side of the 'Heeley & Sheffield House' pub where Percy Nutt lived before he moved to Herdings Farm. The Nutt family used to live down Bartle Road and Mr. Nutt married Mrs. Shaw who was a widow and lived at the farm.

There was a little farm at the side of the Post Office where Woodhouse's kept pigs but before them a chap called Maxfield lived there and he had some travel horses – Shires.

Then there was Stubbs nearby and they were the milk people

Across the road was Southclose Farm (still there today) But it was only like a farmhouse with a field at the back. Bill Bird used to live there with his steam wagon and threshing machine. Bill worked the threshing machine and lived there; afterwards Crappers used to have a milk round.

Opposite there was a stack yard that belonged to Corker's Farm which was the next one down. There were two cottages in a field and then Corker's Farm and next to it was Teddie Hoyland's farm and they were both together. They had the land opposite where the old Co-op used to be and the land down to Seagrave Nurseries (before the Kirkby Estate was built). Ridgeway Road wasn't built then and to reach Elm Tree you had to walk along White Lane, round by the Gleadless Methodist Chapel, up to the old Post Office, down Gleadless Hill, up to the 'Punch Bowl' up Gleadless Common and along Hurlfield Road to Mansfield Road (A 'Booth & Fisher' bus used to run from there to Ridgeway).

Cleadless Road with Teddie Hoyland's farm on the right. (Irene & Brian Thompson) The farm is where the Freezer Shop is today. Until recently the Co-op was on the left of the picture. South Close farmhouse can be seen in the distance.

The next group of houses after Hoyland's farm was in the Chapel Yard. Some of the houses are still there where Mrs. Sizer lived (now 'Tea Time at Angela's') and her father 'Piggy' Ward owned all those cottages. Somebody called Wragg used to farm there and his farmland went down the low side (now Seagrave Crescent) and along the wall and where the mile-stone was opposite the 'Red Lion' and the fields dipped down there.

Brewster Bradley's farm land started from where the old Chemist shop used to be (on White Lane) and continued along White Lane right on to the 'Old Harrow'. Bradley's fields went right down to the 'Long Fields' that came down to Jaunty Lane. The Long Fields belonged to the Birley Lane farm.

There were some cottages near the 'Old Harrow' and from me being a child up to 1939, Mr. Taylor was the landlord there.

He had two sons and the eldest one was a shoemaker and repairer. He was called Fred. Maurice Taylor went hawking fish in his horse and cart. The 'Old Harrow' was a little old place not like it is today.

White Lane Farm's land stretched from Carter Lane up to Sunnybank and then after that, it belonged to Birdfield farm. Henry Corker moved from Town End to go and farm at Birdfield he went into the pig business with large pedigree whites and he did well with them. Previous to that Woolleys had had Birdfield before Corkers. But after Woolleys left, it belonged to 'Piggy' Ward. He owned it at that time.

At Eckington Lees (now demolished) there used to be two cottages and there were two farm men there. Alf Croves and a Mr. Wilson. Alf was a horseman for years for Colin Rhodes' father.

There was a pit at the Nabb then and we used to go and fetch coal for the boilers from there. A Mr. Firth owned it and before you got to the 'Phoenix' pub, there was a 'footrill' there. Andrew Vardy owned that but Mr. Cook was in with him. Mr. Cook lived at Wood Lane and he bought Cottam's Pop business. Cottams lived in Gleadless.

Everything has changed now and nearly all the farms have gone since they lost their farmland."

The Pig: The Villager's Friend

'Make (your pig) quite fat by all means. The last bushel, even if he sit as he eat, is the most profitable. If he can walk two hundreds yards at a time he is not well fatted. Lean is the most wasteful thing that any family can use . . . . . The man who cannot live on solid fat bacon, well fed and well cured, wants the sweet sauce of labour, or is fit for the hospital.'

The above quote is from William Cobbett's 'Cottage Economy' (1822) and although it was written in the early 19th century, similar doctrines continued until after the Second World War, when the 'housewife' began to demand 'lean meat' which neither the old methods nor the old breeds could provide. Thus the pig began its move from the country cottate sty to the factory farm. However, until that time began, nearly everybody kept a pig in the country.

Perhaps 'everybody' is an exaggeration but many who could scrape together enough money to buy one – did so, providing that they could find a corner to keep it in. Then the modern bye-laws of prohibiting pig-keeping as a 'nuisance' would have been dismissed as unreasonable by the majority of landlords who allowed their tenants to build their pigsties at the bottom of their gardens.

Indeed the pig, with its unrivalled talent for converting odds and end into meat: was the one bright spot in a diet which might otherwise consist of bread, potatoes, cabbage and weak tea for the poorest villager.

John: "Gleadless was a rural area and you lived off the land. Everybody had gardens and a lot had pigs. We used to kill two pigs a week and sell it locally. My father used to keep many pigs and he used to deal in them. He sold a lot to a man called Gyte and to pork butchers' shops. We used to live down Smithfield Road and we'd drive about fifty to sixty pigs down there and into pinfold opposite 'Red Lion'. There was only a narrow gateway in pinfold and we'd load pigs into a horse drawn 'float'.

At that time of day you had to get the pigs to a certain weight for pork pigs and bacon pigs were a lot bigger. Once Father had sold a lot of pork pigs to Mr. Gyte and he was just loading them up at the pinfold when a policeman came on his bike and said "You'll have to take them back."

The area was closed due to 'Foot and Mouth' and they had to close so many miles. Our pigs hadn't got it or anything like that but we had to bring them all back home again. Well, they had to be fed and the area was closed for four months. They grew too big for pork pigs and my father lost money on that.

When we were at the cottage at Charnock Hall, we killed two pigs a year. We used to kill towards the back end because there was no refrigeration in those days. At the Hall they had big cellars and stone benches. Arnie had a licence for slaughtering so he could use the humane gun. He used to kill pigs for one or two people and I used to go with him.

We'd take with us a stand that had three iron legs. They were all fastened together at the top and you stood it up like a tent. There was a ring in the top where you put your rope through and that was onto a 'cambrel' and you pulled your pig up onto that.

Then we scalded and scrapped the pig. (The pig had to be scalded and shaved as soon as it had been killed to get all the hairs off). Then you'd cut the sinews through its back legs and the cambrels were put through (The cambrel was like a piece of wood with notches on). Then you hauled it up and split your pig. We saved the pig's bladder because they used to blow it up and use it as a football. Only the squeal of the pig was wasted."

So often the villager's pig became 'one of the family'and hearts had to be hardened, for most 'family friends' were both killed and eaten at home and as not all of the pig's meat could be cured (in pre-refrigeration days there was very little means of preserving it) then any momentary sadness surrounding the pig's passing was quickly dispelled by the prospect of plentiful fresh food and the rush to produce an extraordinary variety of dishes that could be concocted from pieces now normally thrown away.

John: "The old lady (Mrs. Fidler senior) was an ace at pork pie making. The first pig we killed when we were at the cottage at Charnock, Mrs. Fidler came to Margaret (Mrs. Hinchcliffe) and said, "Have you ever put a pig away, Margaret?". Margaret says, "No." So the old lady says, "Well, I'll show you." So she went right through it. Right to making pork pies and showed her how to do leaf fat. There's leaf fat inside but you don't mix that with any of the other fats. She used to make apple pies with leaf fat and it was beautiful."

Margaret: "We used to have a coal fire range and for making pork pies we'd make them in ordinary cake tins. We'd put fat in the tins first, then put them in the oven. We'd press it right in and put the chopped up meat in and then put the top on it. Then we'd do it over with an egg and then cook it but you had to make sure that you left a hole in the top. Then we cooked the pig's feet and used the juice out of the feet for the pork pie by pouring the jelly into them."

Black pudding was made from the pig's blood and although still popular in the north, it seems to decline in favour the further down south you travel. White pudding was offal which was all put together and minced. It was boiled first then taken out and put in a big bowl then seasoned with peppers and salt and later fed into skins, like sausage skins nd cooked for three or four minutes. The chines which were a delicacy, was the backbone which had about three big bones on it and in some parts of the country, the chine, stuffed and boiled was virtually the 'national dish'.

John: "The first pig we killed was 17 stone and there was a lot of meat on it! We had to hang our pigs in the attic and in the summer time it got very warm. To keep them we had to get a ration and join a Pig Club. A lady called Mary Marsh at Ridgeway, ran the Club.

The Deep Freeze

Once when I went to Mary's she'd just cooked some bacon and it was beautiful and when she told me it had been killed 18 months ago, I couldn't believe it. I said, "Ours goes 'rearsty' before that."

She said, "Well, it doesn't this way," and she showed me how she'd kept it so long. She'd got a blanket chest and put some hydrated lime in it and laid a flitch in it then covered it with lime. Then put a ham in and covered that with lime and carried on, building it up like that. As soon as she'd cut a piece off for what she wanted for the week, then back in the chest it went and again covered with lime. It was as white as driven snow because it kept the air out and no air could get to it. The lime kept it sweet."

The pig may have been less humbler than the big horses that powered the farm but it was equally as necessary, for it fed its workers. However, certain pig breeds became extinct in the early 1970's for their qualities to produce prodigious amounts of fat pork and 'solid fat bacon' did not appeal to modern producers of factory-farmed 'lean meat'.

Rhodes' Farm on White Lane

Across the road from the 'Old Harrow' stands Rhodes' Farm. The building has seen much quieter days, situated where it is on a very busy road. The old stone wall surrounding the farm helps to shield it from the constant stream of heavy traffic. From the old farm house one looks out across the distant fields, patterned in greens and browns and it is a most welcome sight for anyone who loves the countryside. Here, one can capture the atmosphere of old Gleadless perhaps more than anywhere else, for the surrounding views are beautiful.

For the Rhodes family, who have spent all their lives at the farm, they have seen some considerable changes. Changes one feels not always for the better.

My grateful thanks to Colin & Elizabeth Rhodes for their kindness and help with this section on White Lane Farm.

The Rhodes Family

Miss Rhodes: "My grandfather, John Rhodes lived at Base Green Farm then he bought some land where Charnock School is today. He had this farm built on White Lane and then came to live here, leaving Base Green Farm.

There was an old cottage which belonged to White Lane Farm but my grandparents never lived in it. The cottage was where the pear trees are now in the garden. (The cottage is marked on Burdett's Map 1791). They knocked the cottage down and planted the trees and came to live here.

Grandma Rhodes, died here in 1900 and Grandpa (John) Rhodes died in 1920.

My Father, John, William Rhodes, had a brother called Joe Rhodes and he lived at the Herdings, at Norton. There were two farms at the Herdings. The one on the right hand side was all covered in ivy but they lived in the one on the left. Joe had a sister and she married and went to live at Canklow near Rotherham.

I don't know whether we've any family connection to Charnock Hall Farm. My grandfather had a brother called Thomas Rhodes. The Thomas Rhodes I knew lived in a caravan near the "Heeley and Sheffield" house.

White Lane Farm was a mixed farm both arable and dairy with over one hundred to one hundred and thirty head of cattle at one time. Forty to forty five being milk beasts. Pigs and poultry were reared there too with the pigs being sold to local butchers.

Pig killing

This time on the farm was met with mixed emotions. Hated because it was such an unpleasant job but enjoyed because of the good food afterwards. Indeed it is said that only the 'squeal' of the pig was ever wasted.

Miss Rhodes: "When we were children, the pig killer who came to the farm was Charlie White. The pig was put across a pig form and then killed. We didn't enjoy the killing part but you knew afterwards that you were getting some good stuff to make brawn and pork pies. The pig was killed near Christmas time, never in Summer because it didn't keep in the Summer.

To preserve the pork we used to salt it on the cellar 'benk' (bench). We used salt and so much salt 'peter'. It had to stay there for so many weeks and then we used to brush the salt off and wash it down. Afterwards, it was hung from the ceiling on hooks to dry out. We didn't cover it. The bacon and hams were lovely!

We used about six hooks (two hooks for one side) and one for the pig's face (chap). When the pig's face was cut off to make brawn-chap, that was salted — it didn't taste quite the same as bacon and ham, it was different. We used to boil it in a lump and when it had gone cold we used to have it for a meal like that.

The pig's feet were stewed and jelly was poured off and put into pork pies and it certainly had a bit of taste about it. My mother taught me how to cook and do such things."

Black Puddings

One of the delicacies that came from killing a pig was black pudding and it is perhaps interesting to read the recipe for making the pudding. After the pig's blood was caught in a jug it was then mixed with other ingredients to make this delicacy.

'Take two quarts of Blood, one quart of Groats, strain your Blood thro' a sieve, put your Groats to the Blood, let it stand all night, boil a pint of Cream in the morning, put it to the Blood and Groats, put in three quarters or a pound of crumbs, eight eggs, beat well, sweet Leek, Penny-royal, Parsley, wild Thyme, and Marjoram, a little of each and Beat, a nutmeg, Pepper and salt to your taste, two pounds of Suet shread very small; and a pound and half cut into little dices.'

(From "*Yorkshire Fare*" by Margaret Slack pub Dalesman.) (Wentworth MSS, 18th century, MD 6333. Original in Sheffield City Archives.)

Although this was taken from an 18th century recipe one can imagine that apart from locality variations, the recipe was the basic one for all such puddings.

Earliest recollections

Life at White Lane Farm was always busy and Miss Rhodes remembers as a little girl, doing odd jobs about the farm.

Miss Rhodes: "When I was eight years old I was sent to a private school at Church Lane, Ridgeway. This was kept by a Mrs. Kathleen Fisher and she taught me (Miss Rhodes was to become a teacher herself at Frecheville School).

I had to help with the milking when I was about twelve. In the yard was a big stone trough and all the milk was put into it by buckets. I had to help lift the buckets in and out and it does take some lifting out when you have a bucket of milk in a trough of water. This was done to cool the milk. We used to make butter as well. We'd separate the milk and we had a big churn in the pantry and once a week we'd pour the cream into the churn and make it into butter.

My mother had a board, scales, a wooden bowl and a round print and she would make about 40lbs of butter and put it into greaseproof paper and then into baskets.

Every Saturday morning we used to set off in our horse and trap and go as far as South Street in Sheffield. (It was near City Road). We'd call in various houses selling butter and once when my father was in a house and I was left in the cart by myself, a man came by chewing a banana and after he'd finished eating it he doubled the skin and gave it to Nelly our horse. Of course she followed him pulling the cart and me along with her! Silly man!"

Threshing Day

The Rhodes' disliked threshing day. It was, they said, noisy, dirty and dusty. It was hated primarily because it spoilt the daily routine of the farm.

Earnshaws did the threshing for the Rhodes and in the olden days when there were plenty of men available they would come along with the machine and help but during the war years and after, there was an obvious manpower shortage and only three or four men would come along then so the labour had to be provided by the people on the farm.

Mr. C. Rhodes: "Threshing was done mostly in winter time. We'd all have to get our jobs done and be ready to start by 8.30 am. Before we had such a thing as a hose pipe we had to have a water carrier to supply water to the steam engine. Mrs. Croves, from Eckington Lees, was our water carrier and she was a big, hefty woman and she needed to be because she had to carry heavy buckets. She would carry two buckets from out of the water trough, down the yard, along the bottom and then up to the top of the stack yard. All day through. It was a hard job. Then they started using tractors to run the machine."

William, Henry Webster with his prize pig of 23 stones!
(Dennis Webster)

Farms near the Rhodes'

Eckington Lees (now demolished). Just a short distance from White Lane Farm, perched high on top of a hill, were until recently, the remains of what used to be a group of cottages called Eckington Lees.

Miss Rhodes: "Some people called Plant lived at Eckington Lees. Polly Marshall was Jack and Horace Plant's Mother's sister and they all lived up there. It was only a very little farm, more like a small holding. There were two houses up ther and Alf Croves lived in one. Mr. Elay lived there once too. It was then condemned and they all left. It was then that Eckington Lees and the land came under White Lane Farm.

Sunny Bank

A bungalow is situated on the site of Sunny Bank today but previously there had been four old cottages there. Elay (from Eckington Lees), Marshes, Bodsworth and Mrs. Wood were all tenants who lived in the cottages.

Birdfield Farm

Close to Sunny Bank is a farm called Birdfield. Once farmed by Henry Corker from Gleadless Town End (next to Hoylands). Mr. Corker bought the farm from 'Piggy' Ward. All the Corker family lived there before they moved out to Gamston. At one time the Woolley family also lived at Birdfield but after the Corkers left, it was obtained by the Rhodes family.

Teddie Hoyland's Farm

Miss Rhodes: "Hoyland's Farm was at Gleadless Town End. It was only a small farm and the Hoyland's had two sons and two daughters. One of the daughters was a teacher at Gleadless School and the other married a man called Milner and they lived in a house on Seagrave Road. Of the two sons Teddie, looked after the farm while his brother was the undertaker at Intake.

I remember at Charnock Hall Farm there was a big gate leading from the road and you went through the gate up the driveway to the farmhouse and the farm land stretched as far as Webster's field down Carterhall Lane.

Before Fidlers had Charnock Hall farm, it was owned by a family called Moody. Charlie Moody had two daughters and one of them called Winnie married my Father's nephew, John Rhodes who lived at the Herdings Farm. They later moved and went to live at Retford. We can't remember what happened to the younger girl, Cathy but the Moody's left Charnock when Fidlers bought the farm. Fred Fidler used to live in one of the houses at the back of 'Bagshawe Arms' at Norton before moving to Charnock.

The 'Old Harrow'

The 'Old Harrow' pub was just like your drawing. At the top end was a low kitchen and there was no upstairs above it. I remember it was a sweet shop where you could buy yeast and things like that. We used to go across and buy some yeast when my Mother wanted to bake. A big, plump woman used to bring the yeast from Sheffield and she drove a pony and tub.

View from the Nab (Fox Lane), 1920 (A. Jackson)
Above: Jaunty Lane is in the middle of the picture with the Vicarage set amongst the trees.
Below: Gleadless School on Hollinsend Road before the Middle School was built.

When we'd a penny to spend we'd buy some anniseed balls from the shop before we went back to school after dinner.

They kept pigs at the 'Old Harrow' and Maurice Taylor kept ponies there too. He had a fish round and he travelled as far as Cordwell Valley.

Lancasters were the first people I remember keeping the pub. Mrs. Lancaster's Father who was called Hardwick, lived at Gleadless and he had a green grocery round and Maurice Taylor helped with that too. The Lancasters left the 'Old Harrow' and went to the 'Sportsman's Inn' at Hackenthorpe. They had two sons and a daughter, Laura.

The cottages behind the 'Old Harrow'

There used to be some old cottages just behind the 'Old Harrow' and when I was a child some people called MacDougalls (who were printers) lived in one. They had a daughter and a son called Fred and when it was hay-making time in the big field at Charnock, they used to come across to our farm to play.

In those days hay-making was all done by hand and the corn had to be cut and turned and when it was dry enough they used to 'cock' it up with a fork. It was left loose until the time when it was put on drays and brought home.

The MacDougall children used to come and play hide and seek at this time and they would hide in the middle of these 'cocks' of corn. Nobody bothered them and just let them play.

Various families lived in the cottages. Stratfords lived in one and at the end house a family called Oxley lived there.

Polly Wainwright (see also 'Herb' chapter) lived next door to the 'Old Harrow'. I can see her now coming round with her herrings and kippers in a basket. She'd put her basket down on the step to show you what she'd got to sell. I remember one day when she came, our cat grabbed one of the fish but she just took it back, wiped it and put it back in her basket!"

Quieter days

In earlier days when White Lane was just a quiet lane, one could travel from Rhodes' Farm to Beighton without meeting anyone, so quiet and remote was the surrounding countryside.

Birley Farm house, is now a private residence, surrounded by the Birley Housing Estate. At one time Birley Farm's farming land stretched down Long Fields to Jaunty Lane and Miss Rhodes' Mother who was called Fox before her marriage, once lived there. However, when the Fox family retired they went to live at Mosborough Hill and let the farm to Jim Rhodes who was no relation to the White Lane Farm Rhodes family, in spite of the same surname.

One wonders if Fox Lane received its name from the Fox family who lived at Birley Farm or was it a place where foxes were common.

With the building of the Frecheville Housing Estate in the 1930's, a farm that was owned by The Sheffield Coal Co. and farmed by a Mr. Richardson, lost its farming land. Situated next to the Frecheville fishing pond (which was always a natural outlet for water), the farm was commonly referred to as The Birley Coal Co. Farm.

The 1947 Handsworth/Woodhouse Compulsory Purchase Order made it possible for the Sheffield Council to take the farm lands of Birley Farm and the Birley Estate was built.

Another farm, close to Birley Farm house, named Birley Wood Farm was as the name suggests, near Birley Wood. Once farmed by the Rhodes' Uncle, it has now been developed to house the Birley Golf Course.

When so many of the neighbouring farms have succumbed to housing development, Gleadless is indeed fortunate that White Lane Farm has survived, together with its beautiful farmland and one only hopes it continues to do so in the years to come.

White Lane Farm

1860	Joseph Rhodes
1881	John Rhodes farmer and coal owner White Lane.
1895	John Rhodes White Lane
1904	John Rhodes farmer White Lane
1922	William Rhodes
1928	" "
1932	" "
1936	John William Rhodes.
1941	" " "

Eckington Leys (Lees)

Eckington Lees were cottages that once perched on top of the fields that overlook High Lane and Birley Lane. These derelict buildings have recently been demolished.

1851 Census *(Eckington Leys)*

				Occupation	*Place of Birth*
William Rose		M	66 yrs	Annuitant	Eckington
Ann Rose	Wife	M	66 yrs		Norton
Emma Hirk	Serv.		17 yrs	Servant	Nottinghamshire

1871 Census *(Eckington Lees)*

Henry Marshall		40 yrs	Farmer of 18 acres	Bradfield
Harriet Marshall	Wife	29 yrs		Beighton
Harriet Ann "	Dau.	3 yrs		Eckington Lees
George Henry	Son	1 yr		Eckington Lees

Also Eckington Lees

Charles Nollett		M	31 yrs	Coal Miner	Birley
Elizabeth Nollett	Wife	M	31 yrs		Hansworth
John Nollett	Son		8 yrs	Scholar	Hansworth*
Elisha Nollett	Son		5 yrs		"
Henry Nollett	Son		2 yrs		"
Mary Nollett	Dau.		7mths		Eckington Lees

*Note the spelling of Hansworth

1881 Census. *Eckington Lees*

Henry Marshall		M	52 yrs	Carter & Farmer of 19 acres	Yorkshire
Harriet Marshall	Wife	M	39 yrs		Derbyshire
Harriet Ann "	Dau		13 yrs	Scholar	
George Henry "	Son		11 yrs	Scholar	
Mary E. "	Dau		2 yrs		

1895 *('Topography and Directory of Derbyshire T. Bulmer 1895')*

Eckington Lees. Henry Marshall

Carter Hall

Census 1861

Edwin Inman	Head	M	59 yrs	Steel Manufacturer Sheffield and Farmer of 140 acres employing 3 men and 2 boys.	Stannington, Yorks.
Elizabeth Inman	Wife	M	59 yrs		Rotherham, Yorks.
Ann N. Inman	Dau-in-law	W	30 yrs		Leeds, Yorks.
Tom Inman	Son	U	29 yrs	Traveller	Brightside
Rowland Inman	Son	U	24 yrs	Farmer	Brightside
Stephen New	Visitor	W	52 yrs	Printer,Master	Born Sheffield
George Aqne	Lab	W	48 yrs	Agricultural Lab.	Moss, Yorks
George Mumby	Serv	U	22 yrs	Farm Servant (under)	Willoughton, Lincs
Thomas Danit	Serv	U	21 yrs	Farm Servant	Belton, Lincs
Arthur Cliff	Serv	U	15	Farm Servant	Bramley, Yorks
Mary Brown	Serv	U	25	Servant Domestic	Hasland, Derbys
Frances Chambers		U	22	Servant Domestic	Welby, Lincs

Census 1881

Elizabeth Inman	Head	W	69	Farmer of 130 acres	
Albert E. Inman	Son	U	25	Farmer's son.	Eckington, Derbys.
Eliza Helliwell	Serv	U	49	House Keeper	Yorkshire
William Sharpe	Serv	U	25	Farm Servant	Retford, Notts
Thomas Rowsley	Serv	U	47	Agricultural Lab.	Co. Mayo, Ireland
Mary Helliwell	Visitor		15		Eckington, Derbys.

Carter Hall Farm

1754 The Carter Hall Estate belongs to Thomas Stott

1801 W. Fairbank's Map of Carter Hall Estate 1801 (Maps of Newton & Shawe Estate, S.C.Lib. Archives) shows the estate belonging to Wm. Cundliffe Shaw, Joseph Shaw and Harriet Yates. Other names on the map in the surrounding fields:
Lands of Thomas Clayton
John Mower
Samuel Roberts
George Booth
Thomas Hounsfield's land
Glebe land
Sitwell Sitwell Esq

1861 Edwin Inman Steel Manufacturer Sheffield and farmer of 140 acres. Carter Hall (Census).

1881 Elizabeth Inman (Census).

1895 Samuel Marsh — Carter Hall

1922/28/32 Frank Fidler

1941 Frank, Bertram Fidler farmer Carter Hall

Carter Lodge

1881 John Watmough

1895 Frederick Moore

1904 Ernest Moore farmer, Carter Lodge

1932 Wm Rodgers, farmer

1941 Mrs Mary E. Rodgers, farmer Carter Lodge

The local pubs in the White Lane area

The Phoenix Inn

1857 Charles Crookes The Inn Keeper

1860 Charles Crookes

1881 Samuel Marsh

1895 William Whitehead

1922 Henry Thompson

1936 Ernest Kay

1941 Ernest Kay

The Old Harrow

1841 Thomas Rose

1860 Thomas Rose

1862 Henry Ward (occupier)

1895 Thomas Henry Walton

1904 T.H. Walton

1922 James Fred Taylor

1932 〃 〃

1936 〃 〃

1941 Wm. Curtis (no 'Ye Olde Harrow')

An aerial view of Ridgeway Road in the 1930's before the Arbourthorne Estate was built. (Sheffield City Libraries)

Park House Farm

This farm once stood near the top of the Common where the Myrtle Springs School grounds are to-day. The Ward family who were the last family to live there before its demolition, had been tenants over generations since the 18th century. Mrs Hannah Ellen Ward who lived there with her daughter-in-law Mrs Thomas Ward, had lived at the Farm for 53 years. Her son Charles Ward who lived at Spring Grove on Hurlfield Road, was the actual tenant of the farm.

The Newbould family had resided there in the early part of the 17th century. One of the daughters married into the Ward family and when the Newboulds emigrated to America, the Wards took over the tenancy.

To indicate the age of the farm, the grandfather of the last tenant, Mr Thomas Ward, was born there in 1777.

Even at the time of the farm's demolition the Newbould family were still communicating with Mrs Hannah Ward, expressing interest in the farm that had close links with the early fortunes of their family.

In 1934, with Sheffield spreading to the outskirts of the city for building land, the farm was to make way for the 335 acres Arbourthorne Housing Estate.

The Earnshaws and the Birds — Threshing Days

Once the harvest was 'home' it still had to be threshed — to separate the corn from the straw; and winnowed — to remove the husks from the corn grains. The most generally remembered method of threshing was to call in 'the contractor', with his mechanical 'threshing box' or 'drum' and all its paraphernalia which was all powered by a mighty traction engine and presided over by a team of workers.

In Gleadless there were two families who were engaged in the threshing business. They were the Earnshaws and the Birds who were hired by the local farmers to do their 'thrashing'. From all accounts it was a very arduous task and the engine had to be 'fed' with water continually throughout the entire operation. As soon as the Harvest was 'fit' then the engine would be off chugging through the village, pulling the drum, the elevator and the chaff cutter, all coupled up behind one another to a neighbouring farm, much to the delight of mischievous schoolboys who would follow it in awe.

There were three machines in Gleadless; two of these being owned by the Earnshaws and one by the Bird family. The Birds covered the Ridgeway, Hackenthorpe, Beighton, Manor, Arbourthorne, Birley and Gleadless areas, while the Earnshaws covered more outlying areas such as Norton and Barlow. The Earnshaws, who lived on Smithfield Road and the Birds who resided at Gleadless Road, were families that were inter-related.

Jim Bird, whose father, William Bird, owned and worked the threshing machine for 20 years gave me the following information:

The Earnshaw's Traction Engine. "This engine was an 'Allchin' and the last one built was in 1925. Its name was "Royal Chester" and it is now kept in preservation order in Farnham, Surrey. The registration of the machine was NU 7483.

The Bird's Threshing Machine. The owner before and during the First World War was my grandfather, Thomas William Bird, who lived on Gleadless Road. My grandmother, Ada Bird was an Earnshaw who was sister to John, Tom and Ben. The Birds lived at No. 4 Main Road (now called Gleadless Road) next door to the Old 'Ball Inn.'

After the 1914–18 War ended, my father, William Bird, worked the machine in the village for 20 years before he moved to Mosborough and continued the threshing machine business there. The machine used to be seen 'parked' at the side of the 'Fitzwilliam' in Mosborough. The Bird machine was a Fowler engine and was called "Doris" after one of our relations."

The Earnshaw's Threshing Outfit, date 1924-29 (Photo Frank Cantrill, Australia) "On the engine is Tom Earnshaw (right) steering and John Earnshaw, the eldest, is on the left." Frank Cantrill's brother, Lewis, is in the centre on the ground. The man on the right is unknown but the one on the left may be called Fletcher who lived at the bottom of Smithfield Road.

4. OTHER INDUSTRIES

Apart from the previously mentioned occupations of agricultural work and mining, Gleadless had other smaller industries. Looking through the Census Returns one discovers a variety of 'craftspeople', blacksmiths, cutlers, an edge-fork marker, table-blade forgers and file-cutters working in the village.

Perhaps the most well-known family of file cutters was the Corker family who worked in their little file-cutting shop. Samuel Corker and his sons Tom, Harry, Richard, George, James and Sam all worked at the trade. George Corker however left the business to become a notable figure in local civic life as an Alderman.

The last outworker file-cutter in the Gleadless district was Richard Corker who until his death in 1908, had a file-cutting shop at the bottom of his garden in Grassthorpe Road. With his pony and trap, he used to travel to Sheffield to collect the blank files, work them and then return them. The small shop with its bellows and furnace has now been altered.

Going into 'Service' was another occupation,where a girl could help finance the family income and where she would often be provided for.

The village 'Bobby' was a community figure, being a well-known character he was as regular as 'clockwork' on his daily beat so that any would-be criminal often knew when the 'Bobby' would be walking past! Not that anyone can remember anyone ever being arrested by the village policeman!

Seagrave Nurseries employed several boys, who received an excellent training in the art of horticulture to become gardening specialists in their own right.

The following chapter gives us an insight into some of Gleadless' 'Other Industries'.

In Service

The rich man in his castle
The poor man at his gate
He made them high or lowly
And ordered their estate

'All things bright and beautiful'

During the first decades of this century, one in every three of all British women between the ages of fifteen and twenty were employed as domestic servants. So it was understandable that when a girl left school in the 20's and 30's she would find herself 'In Service'. In most rural areas, service was virtually the *only* occupation open to women. As a consolation, it was regarded as useful training for housekeeping when they themselves married.

If a girl lived 'out' when she was 'In Service', then it would help relieve her parents at home who (in cases of large families) then had one less child to clothe and feed.

Mabel Liversidge, who was born in 1902, relates her experiences of life 'In Service' beginning at the age of 14.

"I remember my first job in service. I was only 14 years old and I was just ready for leaving school when Mr Cawthorne, the old, road sweeping man who used to sweep the roads with his barrel, sweeping brush and shovel (he cleaned all the gutters) came to my Mother and said, "Mrs Hartley is Mabel ready for leaving school?"

So she says, "Yes."

"Well," he says, "I think I've got a little job for her. It's at the big house at the top of Hurlfield Hill."

So me Mother says to me "Go and see if you can get it."

Just like that! She never went with me. I got the job but I didn't sleep in straight away. I think I must have been there about two years before I did because my Mother had to work in 'munitions' so I had to go home and look after the kids. I slept in for the last few months I worked there. Otherwise I used to walk home from the big house (they called it 'Sylvainia'). It was a red brick house at the top of Hurlfield Hill (it is still there) and there was another house further back called 'Greystones'. We lived at Lane End (now called Hollinsend Road).

In 1916 when I worked at 'Sylvainia', a family called Clark lived there. They had one child called Harold Clark. They were nice people. Mr Clark was a traveller.

The house was beautiful inside. It had a lovely staircase. I did everything. All the housework. I was white washing ceilings at 14. I worked from 8 am until about 8 pm. I had to see to all the dinner pots before I could leave. There was only me there so I did all the work. I had to call them Master and Mistress and they were people who always had a lot of dinners in the evening. The next morning when I got to work I found that the table was left just as they had left it that night. So I had all the clearing up to do.

The house had big open fires in big grates and I had to make the fires and black lead the stoves!"

Mention black leading stoves to any lady of this era and she will cringe! It was a chore that was detested by all. The blacklead was applied while the range was cold and the polish was worked up as the range began to heat.

'To Clean a Range'. "Mix some blacklead with water, or better turpentine, to a paste. Apply this to the cold grate with a brush and rub smartly with another polishing brush until every part of the grate is black and bright . . . " (p.3 *The Victorian Kitchen*)

Mabel: "For my first job I got 2/6d a week. Mr Clark said, "We'll give you 2/6d (half a crown) a week Mabel," he says, "and I'm thinking of having some chickens. Will you clean them out for me and keep them clean?"

So I says, "Yes."

Then he says, "I'll give you 2d a week extra."

I had to wear a black dress and white apron when I was in service. My grandfather had two sisters (my Aunts) who were Governesses and one of them came to visit us. There was no room for her to stay with us so we put her in the 'New Inn'. It was the worst thing we could have done because she was teetotal! Anyway she said to me, "Mabel, I hear you're going into Service." So I said that I was.

She was a well-to-do lady and after she returned home to Malvern where she lived, a big basket arrived for me. We opened it up and inside was a black dress, two white aprons, two print dresses, a Bible and two nightdresses. These were all for me when I went into service. That's what she sent me.

I worked at other places — all in service. There was a farm next to the 'Heeley and Sheffield House' where the Robinsons lived and I worked there. I used to help take the milk out. They had cows and the fields stretched down Hollinsend Road.

During the war I worked at Charlie Richardson's house. Mr Richardson had been in the forces. Then I worked for Mr & Mrs Lineham who had moved into the Clark's old house and I went back there. Later I helped Mrs Lineham when she opened a shop in the village.

It was hard work in service. All the washing and ironing and everything, but I must have done my job well because when I married and my son Jack was born Mr and Mrs Clark came to see me (and I hadn't seen them for years) and they brought me a baby's hat and christening veil and they said "Mabel, this is for your baby." Wasn't that lovely!"

Kathleen Cupit's experiences of life in service were on a somewhat grander scale when she was employed as a Housemaid in a stockbroker's house. There were just the stockbroker and his wife (their three children being away at school) but they had ten servants to look after them. It was a disciplined life but one which Kathleen enjoyed before the war broke out and ended her life in service.

"My Mum decided that I ought to go into service because I would get kept and get a wage as well.

The first place I worked at in service was at Mr Skelton's (he lived at the top of Gleadless Road) but I only worked there for a short time before I moved on. I would be about 15 years old then, this was in the 30's. I was the Kitchen Maid there, washing up and doing the vegetables for the Cook. The Kitchen Maid only did the work for the Cook — preparing it all for her. We had a Cook there and another girl who was about four years older than me.

Then I went to work for Geraldine Crossland (Rev. Crossland's daughter). She had a Private Residential Hotel on Clarkegrove Road. The people who stayed there were people in good positions. There was a Headmistress, a chief draughtsman and a chief architect among her guests.

There were three of us in staff. Helping to make the beds, waiting on at the tables and seeing to the dining room work.

I worked there for a couple of years before I heard of a better job which offered more money (that's what I was after really for me Mum needed more money) so then I went to work for a stockbroker who lived at Millhouses Lane.

There were ten of us in staff there, a much bigger place. I was the Housemaid. There was the Kitchen Maid, the Cook, the Housemaid, Parlour Maid, Chauffeur, Head Gardener and three more gardeners.

My job was doing all the beds and that sort of thing and helping the Parlour Maid to clean all the silver which took us two days. Everything was solid silver. The cutlery, finger bowls and turreens and it wasn't just plain silver, it was all beautifully decorated. It took some cleaning because we had to clean into all the nooks and crannies of the designs. On the dressing tables the brushes and combs were all backed with solild silver — Sheffield made.

I had to take the Parlour Maid's job when she was off. This meant I had to wait on at the table. That's what the Parlour Maid did. She was the main one really. She got more money but she had more responsibilities and she came in contact with the Lady more than I did.

A Housemaid's duties

I used to get up at 6 am and go round the room seeing to the fires. I had to make the fires in the rooms and prepare for the breakfast and set the table before the family came down. In the dining room I would go round with the vacuum (not like they are today!). While the family were having their breakfast,I used to be upstairs seeing to the beds and the bedrooms. Then I'd go and give the Parlour Maid a hand.

I used to wear a blue dress in the morning with a white apron and white hat. Then in the afternoon I used to have a black dress with a little lace apron and white lace cuffs.

After lunch when we'd all washed up we had two hours free time. We had a little sitting room of our own where we could sit and read or knit and sew or you could go out into the grounds. We had our own staircase to our bedrooms. We didn't use the family one. We had to share our bedrooms, with one or two of us sharing.

The grounds were so big that they were let off. People could come and look round them when all the daffodils were out because they were daffodil woods. They also had their own boating lake and tennis courts. They used to charge 6d and all the money went to the Royal Hospital Linen League. The grounds have all been built on now and there's all new houses there.

I had one day off a week which was on a Sunday and I used to go home to my Mum to give her my money. She lived on Honeymoon Row which was a group of houses near the 'New Inn'. She used to give me my tram fare and enough fare to go home again the following week. I didn't keep any spending money because you were kept. I received 7/- a week, but I enjoyed it. It was another life.

The family at Millhouses also had a big house in the Lake District and they used to go and live there for six months of the year. What used to happen was that half the staff used to go with the family to the Lake District while the other half used to stay behind to do all the Spring cleaning while they were away.

Then of course the War broke out and we had to go in the works to help the war effort so I went into a Staff Canteen and later I got married and I never went back into service after that."

As a matter of interest here is an extract from *Mr Beaton's Household Guide*, 1901, suggesting what should be done daily in an ordinary, small household. It was to be done in the following order:

"The shutters and windows must first be opened, then the kitchen range must be brushed and cleaned, the fire lighted and the kettle put on. Next comes the room in daily use to be got ready for breakfast; the rug must be rolled up, the table cover shaken and folded, the room swept (using tea leaves), the grate cleaned (if in winter) and the fire lighted, and then the room must be dusted and the cloth laid for breakfast. Next in order comes the hall; which must be swept, the door steps cleaned, and the brass handles of the door polished. Boots and knives must also be cleaned before the breakfast is cooked. Directly breakfast is over, beds should be stripped and bedroom windows opened. Then will come the clearing away of breakfast things and the washing up; then the slops should be taken from the bedrooms, jugs filled, the beds made and the rooms tidied and dusted; and between the time that this work is finished and the midday meal time, the cooking can be done, and the cleaning of whatever rooms arranged for on that day accomplished .... Where there is a general servant, she is not expected to change her gown till after she has washed up and tidied her kitchen ...."

Great emphasis was placed on cleanliness as cleanliness was considered "next to godliness". As Mrs. Beeton stated, "a dirty kitchen was a disgrace to both mistress and maid." Even the simplest household task followed a systematic sequence of events.

The greatest demand for maids came from the rising middle classes of the large towns, for whom the keeping of a servant was an absolute essential and was perhaps a symbol of emergence from the 'great unwashed' and the addition of domestics proved one's progress of upward mobility!

Seagrave Nurseries

"There's Senc. there's Ike, there's Alan, there's Bill and there's Joe. Are we downhearted? No, let them all come ...." (Song).

One of the other 'industries' in Gleadless was Seagrave Nurseries. Mr. S. Seagrave lived down Seagrave Road and he started his nursery business there. Later he acquired land in the Kirkby Road area and moved his business there. The large greenhouses were a familiar landmark in Gleadless and covered a large area of land where the 'Kirkby' houses are today.

On Mr. Seagrave's death the business was left to Isaac Harrison who was already working there. He had two daughters. Doris and May. Hubert, Isaac's son, sadly, had been killed in the First World War. May Harrison was to marry Alan Corker and Doris, Sensical Boul. On the death of May the Nurseries passed into the hands of Doris and the Boul family. Isaac's sister Charlotte Lancaster ran the funeral side of the business until she died. Seagrave & Co. are florists in the Castle Market, today.

The Nursery land in Gleadless was sold for building land losing an area which was once a haven of peace and horticultural beauty.

Stan Taylor began working at Seagrave Nurseries when he left school, preferring gardening to his alternative job of working down the mine.

Stan: "I started work in 1928 at Seagraves and the staff at that time were Ike, the boss who ran the business in the market shop at No. 12 Dixon Lane and also a stall in the old Norfolk Market Hall. The Nursery foreman was Joe Harrison who was Ike's brother and his other brother Bill was the van driver and he took the plants out and the flowers down to the nursery.

The rest of the staff were Herbert Hall, who was the Head Gardener, Jack Cook, Arthur West, Dick Helliwell, Horace Coe, Albert Richardson, Tommy Salt, William Kitteridge and Horace Ellis. Sammy Gill came about six months later and as much as I can remember, that was the complete staff at that time.

The Seagrave Nursery workers during the 1926 Coal Strike.
(Photo Albert & David Jackson)
This photograph was taken duringthe Coal Strike. They were digging in the Kirkby Road for coal to use in the Nursery boilers. *Back row:* Albert Richardson, Herbert Hall, Richard Hallewell, Harold Hallewell, Albert Jackson and Joseph Harrison. *Mid row:* Arthur West, Horace Coe, Bill Kitteridge and Cyril Lancaster. *Front row:* Tom Salt, Horace Ellis (Mussel), and Lewis Harrison.

We started work at 6.00 am till 8.00 am then went home for breakfast at 8.30 am. Then worked till 12 noon then home again for lunch then worked from 1.00 pm till 5.00 pm or 5.30 pm, six days a week, although we finished earlier on Saturdays, as most of us had connections and played with the local football or cricket teams.

When the young workers had gained experience they were expected to join the older workers on a rota system of 'weeks on' which meant taking responsibility of a boiler. First watering plants in greenhouses and all duties appertaining to the maintenance of the Nursery from Saturday lunch to Monday morning when normal work commenced.

The week's duties didn't finish altogether because in winter you had to attend to the three Coke Boilers which meant going back late evening to stoke up for the night. In summer you went back late evening to shut the greenhouse ventilators and cover the garden frames etc., all for the sum of 4/- (20p today). This carried on till some one else took over the following Saturday.

I well remember one year we had a period of hard frost and when it was my turn to do my 'week on', I had to go back every two hours from finishing work at 5.30 pm till 4.00 am the next morning, then report back for work at 6.00 am to keep the three boilers going full tilt as frost protection. This lasted nearly all week. Good job we were all local lads and lived near by!

There were happy and no complaints. The training paid dividends in later years for nearly every one of us seemed to get quite a good position when we left."

Sam Gill began working for Seagrave Nurseries in 1930. He left school at 14 and when they were looking for two or three boys to start work there, his Mother who worked at the Harrison home said her son might be interested. Indeed he was and as Mr. Gill says, "I became a gardener because my Mother worked at the Seagrave Nursery house!" He continues:

"I first started work at Seagrave Nurseries in 1930. Isaac Harrison had it together with his brothers Joe and William. Then there were his two son-in-laws Sensicle Boul and Alan Corker. We used to sing a song at the Nurseries and it went, "There's Senc, there's Ike, there's Alan, there's Bill and there's Joe. Are we downhearted? No, let them all come . . . ."

Bill used to make wreath rings, starting right from the ball of wire. He also erected the boilers. That's why I knew so much about gravity feed boilers because as a kid I'd laboured for William erecting these Britannia boilers. All the sections were put together and then we used to put flow and return 4″ pipes right to the top 'house' which was at the highest point. Then we'd put a tank up there. There was no water laid so we had to fill these tanks and when it was your weekend duty you had to keep them topped up with water.

Joe Harrison was the horticultural brain and Herbert Hall was one of the best plantsmen I've ever known.

We used to grow for market. There were three big 'houses' 100ft long. We had sweet peas in one surrounded by stocks. We cut the heads off the white stocks for wreath work. In the other two houses we grew tomatoes in the Summer season. Then the following year we moved the sweet peas into the other side. We'd rotate them. We grew pot plants and roses so we learned the job really well. We grew thousands of herbaceous plants and planted them out on the land.

The Kirkby area was all Seagraves. They even rented half of Corkers land. The Nurseries covered about seven acres and we had to dig it all with a spade. It took four or five of us to do it. There were no cultivators then.

Seagrave Nurseries from the top of Gleadless Road. (A Jackson)
November 29, 1926. The Gleadless Independent Chapel is in the centre of the picture.

I left Seagraves when I joined the Army in 1940. I was captured and held as a prisoner of war until the war ended."

Mr. Sam ("Sammy") Gill did not return to work for Seagraves when the war ended but he did continue his life in gardening. In 1951 on the retirement of H. H. Grace he was appointed in charge of Norton nurseries and occupied the position of nursery supervisior until his retirement in 1976.

Seagrave Nurseries produced some excellent gardeners and many left the nurseries to become top gardeners in their own right.

The Village Policeman

It seems that the only method needed to keep the peace in Gleadless was having a local "Bobby". Walking 'the beat' by the regular policeman was such a routine occurrence in the village that nearly everyone knew exactly what time of day he would be passing their houses!

This was of particular interest to the village children, especially the would-be footballers who timed their disappearance from 'the football field' (the road) to coincide when the local "Bobby" was due to appear.

One must understand that at this period in time, the only traffic likely to disturb the tranquility and peace of the village, was a horse and cart and not any heavy good vehicle pounding its way along the main road!

(The late Reg. Cartledge)
The Policemen's lodging house – Hollinsend Road.
(Taken in 1897). This was the home of Mr. and Mrs. William Harrison (Issac's brother) where the policemen lodged.

The adults in the photo are: Arthur Corker (at the door), Emma Corker, Mary Anne Harrison (older lady) known as Polly and William Harrison.
William Harrison was Reg. Cartledge's grandfather and Reg. told me that the initials seen above the door (WH 1874) signified that either his grandfather or his father before him, both of whom were called William, built the house. The Constabulary badge is noticeable above the door.

Reg: "We used to have two village policemen. One that was 'on duty' and the other that was 'on relief'. We all knew the exact time they would be coming round the village. 10.00 am in the morning and 3 in the afternoon!"

Football in the road

Mr. Robertson: "There were only three "Bobbys" (policemen) in the Gleadless area and they worked in shifts. I remember "Bobby" Renshaw, Scratchley and Marr. Before "Bobby" Marr there was "Bobby" Little who used to live on Intake Road (now Mansfield Road) just opposite the Cemetery. The other two lived on Stanhope Road.

After "Bobby" Little retired, "Bobby" Marr took over his shift. "Bobby"

Marr married Miss Hoyland who was a schoolteacher. The Hoyland's had a farm at the top of Gleadless Road (where the Banks are today) and there were all stables there.

We usually played at football on the road. We couldn't play in the fields.We weren't allowed. We'd generally know what time the policeman was coming round so we'd stop then before he could see us. If he did see us playing football on the road, he'd never run after us but the next time he saw us he'd give us a clip at the side of the ear with his gloves and say, "You know what that's for don't you? Don't let me see you doing it again!"

We daren't go home and tell our Mum and Dad because we'd get hit some more."

5. SHOPS AND TRAVELLERS

. . . . 'I can almost cheat myself into a fancy that I have heard the shop-bell again on the street door and that a village customer has come in.'
(George Bourne. William Smith, Potter and Farmer)

Those whose memories go back far enough tell me that the village shop often had a pleasant odour of groceries compounded of, bacon, tea, tobacco and paraffin which formed a permanent background with overtones of apples, brussels sprouts and spring onions, according to the season. Yet groceries was not all the shop held. Glass jars contained sweets, acid drops, pear drops and other children's delights. More often than not the customer walked straight in from the street to be faced by a wooden counter, with scales, biscuit tins, loaves and other odds and ends on it.

The social background to shopping, however has changed beyond recognition. Before 1914 the important thing for any shopkeeper of a rural area was to get the custom of the 'big house' or rectory. This would assure the shopkeeper's income. Frequently the retailer would call at the houses of his important customer. If he had left them to call at his shop, they might have gone elsewhere, for the idea that anyone should carry his purchases away with him, was unheard of. Delivery was part of the tradesman's job. So in Gleadless, commercial travellers journeyed to Norton and the surrounding area, where the gentry resided, in order to find out what their potential customers required.

However, to the ordinary Gleadless folk, the village shop was a way of life, where gossip was exchanged and the time of day passed. To enter a village shop one usually entered the shopkeeper's home where more often than not he was a good friend.

Shops

Richardsons — the Butchers

Nora Richardson remembers: "I believe my Grandfather, John Richardson, started the butcher's shop and my Father, Tom Richardson, took it over from him, long before his Father died because my Grandfather lived to be 89 years old, which was in those days a very remarkable age.

My Father carried on with the Butchers shop on Gleadless Road, until he died in 1934 when he was 57 and then the Websters came into it. They rented it from my Mother who was Ruth West before she married.

We lived in the white-fronted cottage which was near the shop. My mother and I lived there until after the 2nd World War and then they started building houses down Hollinsend Road (on the top at the right hand side, now a cul-de-sac). These houses were built on our land and we went to live in one of them and so we moved from the big house at the top.

Websters didn't move from Carter Lane to live in the house but some people bought it from my Mother and that's how we disposed of it.

Originally, the butchering trade was centred around the Richardson family and I think I'm right in saying that they were the first butchers in Gleadless. They didn't do their own slaughtering. You bought whatever carcasses you wanted and went to the slaughter house for them. I can't remember where that was. I remember near Pond Street, was a place they called the 'Ice House' and my Uncle Charlie (who was Sally Marples' husband) used to work there.

We always knew when a pig was being killed in the village because we could hear the squealing. We had pigs but I don't remember them being killed.

We had a horse too because we had a horse and trap to deliver meat. We delivered as far as Beighton, Handsworth and Ridgeway and even down City Road where my Father had several sisters. He was one of a very big family of about twelve, I believe.

My Grandfather, John Richardson was buried in the graveyard at Christ Church and his grave can be seen against the church wall."

The West family

Nora Richardson: "The Wests started as farmers. Next door to our house (the Richardsons) was a long field that stretched right down to Lane End and next to it, away from the road, was one of the fields that the Wests had and they lived in an old house at the top. Their land was parallel with ours. My Mother's Father was called Tom West.

They had some cows and because they wanted more land they rented some opposite the Old Toll Bar (Norton Ave.) These fields were across from the road there and were called the Birchitts. They rented the fields for pasture land and it was my Mother's and her two sisters' job to take the cows there and bring them back again for milking purposes.

The Drury family lived in the Old Toll Bar but I never remember it being used as a Toll Bar but I do the one at the top of Hurlfield Hill. I even remember the Toll Bar charges on a board which hung there.

My Mother, Ruth West was born in 1881. When she was a girl she had to fetch water from the well near Gleadless Road. The well was at the end of Ashleigh School's grounds. I remember it being there although we didn't fetch any water from it but my Mother, her sisters and brothers did. It was drinking water and she used to talk about fetching the water from the well and she'd say how much things had improved now!

My grandmother West outlived my grandfather and she went into the Post Office and kept that for a few years. My youngest Aunt, who was called Lizzie (Elizabeth Hall when she married) lived there with her.

There were eight children in the West family. My Mother Ruth was the eldest and then there was (not in order) Sarah (Sally), Lizzie (Elizabeth) and the five boys, William, Tom (Thomas), Cyril, Arthur and Eric who was a postman. He lived at the Post Office for some time. He suffered a terrible injury in the war and received a complete disability pension but he was able to do a postman's job. My Uncle Arthur (West) worked at Seagrave Nurseries. That was a lovely place, just like an oasis of calm and quiet.

Along Gleadless Road

Near Wests' farm was Corker's Yard but there were cottages in between. There was West's farm, then three cottages standing further back, next was a big house where Stubbs the milk people lived and at the end of their garden was a row of five cottages. Now Henry Corker lived there (later he moved to Birdfield) and Gladys Virgin and the others, I can't remember their names now.

Then I believe the stack yard started there and behind there were two more cottages where my cousin Winnie Haddock lived and next door to them were some people called Froggatt. Beyond there was Charlie Bell who lived in the next cottage and then there was Corker's Farm and then Teddie Hoyland's farm and that was the end there.

Mrs Marples had a little shop and she had two children Sally and Billy (William). She looked after the shop and Sally helped her. Sally married my Uncle Charles, Edward Richardson and they lived in a cottage behind the shop. There were two cottages there and in the next cottage lived a lady called Miss Annie Mather."

Websters — the Family Butchers

One of the main focal points in the old Gleadless village, was Websters Butchers' shop which stood on Gleadless Road. In the centre of the village, it was surrounded by the daily 'bustle' of everyday life.

Websters took the shop over from Tom Richardson and rented it from the Richardsons. When William Henry Webster came into the Gleadless shop, he already had a butchers shop at 66, Main Road Ridgeway, and both shops were kept going throughout the War.

The Websters 'came from' Carter Lane, with Dennis being born at the small holding down there. His two brothers, William and Harold, together with sisters Lilian and Connie, all helped in both shops. Dennis came into the Gleadless shop after the 2nd World War and Harold went into farming.

Their Father, William Henry, retired in the 1940s and when William died, Dennis and Lillian continued working in the shop together.

Although Websters did not slaughter the animals on the premises, there were slaughtering facilities inside the shop which shows that this practise must have been undertaken there in the past. In the 30's it was not such an uncommon sight to see a herd of animals being 'driven' along the road from nearby farms to be taken to the Sheffield Abbatoir on Cricket Inn Road.

Finally, this quaint little shop, that had served the Gleadless community from the early 19th century, was closed for the last time in the 1970's due to road widening and was subsequently demolished. Websters then moved to their present shop on White Lane.

Today, Richard Webster who works there with his father Dennis, is continuing a long family tradition by following in his 'Father's footsteps'!

The old Websters' Butchers Shop on Gleadless Road (1950's) (D. Webster)

Miss Shipston's Kirkby Road shop

At the top of Kirkby Road stands a very unusual house. Unusual because of its narrowness. It is now a private residence but at one time it was one of the village's 'little corner shops'.

Miss Shipston had the shop for ten years and it was then known as 'H. Shipston, Grocer', on 2, Kirkby Road.

Miss Shipston: "I started at the shop in 1950. Mr Pashley had it before me and his Father, old Mr Pashley, lived at the back of the shop. It was a lock up shop and I was only the tenant so we lived in Seagrave Drive. I remember that the top floor of the building was sloping and the house was so narrow. In fact it was only one room wide and we had to leave by the side door.

Miss Shipston and Winnie Higgins outside the Kirkby Road shop (Miss Shipston) 1950's

It was still rationing time when I had the shop so to begin with I could only have customers who came to me with their ration books. I could only buy stock according to the number of coupons I received from people's ration books. Every month I had to take these coupons to the Food Office and they would give me a permit for the quantities of goods so when the traveller came round I could only buy as much as I had on this permit. It was only by gradually getting customers to bring their ration books to me that I was able to build up the business.

It was the corner shop convenience. There weren't the supermarkets like there are today. I sold butter (pre-packed) cheese, ham, bread and confectionary goods. The cheese used to come in large pieces and we had to cut portions off when people needed it. We had whole hams and we'd put them on the machine and cut them as they wanted it. It wasn't put in piles in the window.

The shop hours were from 9 am to 5.30 pm with one hour for dinner. I worked on my own but on Fridays and Saturdays, Winnie Higgins came and helped me.

I finished with the shop in 1960 and went into the Civil Service. All the stock was sold and after that the property wasn't occupied for some time, until somebody bought the property and did it up and re-opened it as a drapery shop. That didn't last long and then it finally became a private house."

Other village shops

The old Fish and Chip shop

Nora Richardson: "On Hollinsend Road (across from the "New Inn" but further up on the left hand side) was a little wooden fish and chip shop and a chap called George Lomas ran it. He used to stoke it up every night. We loved going there for 1d worth of chips and a 2d fish . . . oh they were so nice! But it used to take him such a long time to get going though because he only cooked with coal. In fact everybody in the village used to say that he used to cook them with a frying pan over a candle because it took him that long! There used to be queues right up the road. That was the only Fish and Chip shop in Gleadless then."

"After Mr Lomas, my Aunt Emma (Harrison) had the little fish and chip shop which was up the Lane End." (The late Reg. Cartledge.)

"I remember there was a lean to sort of a shop which was the first chip shop we had in village. I believe my Grandad Taylor had it before Aunt Doris who was married to Arthur Dawes who had returned from being a prisoner of war in 1914 - 18 War. Through his wounds he couldn't return to pit so he opened a chip shop instead, at the side of road when the other old one was demolished, this they kept until about 1926 when they moved to Cleethorpes to carry on in the fish and chip business till they retired." (*Stan Taylor*)

"There was a fish and chip shop at the bottom of our garden. They was a wooden one at first. They had a supper room with a table and forms in and you had 1d or 2d worth of chips. I remember once falling down while fetching a woman some beer and they took me into shop and poured some iodine over my cuts. Oh, it was painful!" (*Mrs Liversidge*)

The Ice Cream Lady

"Dolly Moseley used to sell ice-cream. I remember a very funny thing about that old girl. She lived on Church Row which was near the Church and her ice-cream cart was one that had been home built wi' carriage wheels on and you had to lift it down steps into the bottom yard. Of course we used to 'elp 'er when we were young lads and one day it uptipped and poor old girl, everybody got a free ice-cream!" (*Stan Taylor*)

Sally's little shop

"Sally Marples (Richardson) had a little shop which was near to the old Post Office. She baked home made bread and sold all that and she sold sweets and things as well. She was a lovely person and it used to be lovely going in there. It was like going into her front room. You used to walk in doors and you'd see bread with pancheons 'round stove and then she'd say, "Just a minute." Then she'd come and serve you at this tiny little counter, whatever you wanted. Little odds and ends." (*Mrs Layden*)

Annie: "At the Marples' shop they used to sell flour and you took a white pillow case when you wanted to bake bread. They had flour in a big bin and they had a scoop to scoop the flour out and they weighed you a stone of flour. We bought yeast as well from there when Mother wanted to bake bread."

May Hartley: We used to buy our coal from Marples' shop. They had loose coal at the back of the shop. They'd sell it you in half-hundredweights. I fetched the coal in an old fashioned coal cart with iron wheels made out of an old wringer wheels. I'd pull this barrow up the hill and fetch ½cwt of coal for 1/-." (Old money — 5p to-day).

Jack Sellars — the first Newsagents in Gleadless

"The first newspaper man in Gleadless village was a chap called Jack Sellars. He originated from Heeley before he came to Brierley Terrace and took a little house there. Linehams had it before him as a Drapery Shop.

When Jack got this shop he opened it as a newsagency but they couldn't deliver *The Star* papers to Jacks at night so we 12 year old boys had to go to Robinsons at Intake and pick up 'The Stars' from there.

We used to go with a little barrow and deliver the papers right up Hagg Lane, past Gleadless Common, down to the Brick Yard (on Hurlfield Hill) where there were two cottages I delivered papers to. Then I'd come back and go round Myrtle Springs, and down Zig-Zag (near Hurlfield Hill) where there were a lot of railway waggons and people lived in them. Down to the bottom of Bartle Road, then pick some more 'Stars' up from the shop and then deliver those all round Gleadless Town End, all for 6d (2½p to-day).

I used to do that every night and before I went to school in the morning. I'd get up at 6.30 am or 7 am. I was at the shop lifting all the papers in, put my own papers up and then deliver them for 3d. At night I used to work from 5 pm to 7.45 pm. I still hadn't finished on a Saturday. In the afternoon I'd go round and collect the money for Mr Sellars. I'd collect as much as £5 or £6 for the week and he'd give me 6d (2½p) for doing that!

For doing all the lot for the week, I'd get 5 shillings and that I had to take straight home to my Mother and she'd give me 6d (2½p) back to keep. That's what you used to do in those days." (*Walter Gill*)

Shops in the village

Mr L. Siddall: "Majarissons' shop was at the top of Kirkby Road. Hollands owned the shop before them and on the building it says 'Holland's Terrace'. Hollands later moved to Intake and carried on a shop there.

At the corner of Honeymoon Row (a group of cottages passed near the

'New Inn') was *Birtles* corner shop.

Oscrofts shop was up Gleadless Common (where Leadbeater Road is to-day) and Schofields took it over from Mrs Oscroft.

Close to *Richardsons* (later Websters) Butcher's shop was Marples little shop. Sally Richardson and her brother Billy Marples ran this shop.

Simpsons had the shop at the bottom of Smithfield Road (now Waites) before they moved to live in Ridgeway Road with Nurse Anderson."

The corner shop at the top of Thorpe (now Grassthorpe) Road

The late Reg. Cartledge: "At the top of what is now Grassthorpe Road was a shop run by Mr & Mrs Mellors. In those days they had to go to Sheffield for their groceries and they had a little pony and trap and the only way to get from Gleadless to Sheffield was either to go up the hill and down Gleadless Road or up the Common down Hurlfield Road and on to Intake Road as it was then, City Road as it is now. Nobody liked to go with a horse and cart down Gleadless Road because Hurlfield Hill was very, very steep."

The old corner shop at the top of Thorpe (now Grassthorpe) Road.
(Photo B. Thompson)

This corner shop was quite a 'land-mark' in Gleadless. Once owned by the Skeltons and Mellors it was also occupied by the Palmers. Jack and Dorothy Palmer only had the shop for 18 months before they had to move out due to receiving a Compulsory Purchase Order for Road Widening.

Dorothy Palmer told me that when they first moved into the shop it was decorated in dark brown varnish and in the weekend before they were due to open on the Monday they quickly re-painted it all white.

They sold wood, fertiliser, rustic fencing and gardening implements. The shop closed in March 1959 and they left Gleadless to live at Ballifield.

The old Gleadless Post Office

For many years the Post Office at Gleadless was situated on Gleadless Road and catered very well for the small village community. Many residents remember the late Artie Elliott, the sub postmaster at Gleadless, with affection, and it was Artie who had the present Gleadless Post Office built on White Lane.

The Closing of the Old Gleadless Post Office

(from *The Star*, Friday September 17th, 1954)

The closing of the old Post Office at 795 Gleadless Road, caused sufficient interest for it to be reported in "The Star" newspaper. "The last Post after Century of Service" was the headline and the report continued to inform the reader that "the last stamp will soon have been licked, the last pension paid and the last parcel sent on its way from the century-old Post Office at Gleadless Sheffield."

With the continued housing development in the area it meant that the little Post Office could no longer accommodate the growing population of the Gleadless residents so Mr Artington (Artie) W. Elliott, had the new P.O. premises built.

"The Post Office", he told 'The Star', "had been in the family group for about 50 years." The first person in the family to run the Post Office was Mrs Annie West, the Mother of Mr Elliott's brother-in-law, who passed it on to her son, Mr Eric West, the village postman, who kept it for about ten years before handing it over to Mr Elliott's Mother, Mrs Ada Elliott. In 1945, Artie Elliott took over the Post Office from his Mother.

The Old Gleadless Post Office
Situated at 795, Gleadless Road.

(The late Mrs West)

The report informs us that many years ago the old premises comprised of three cottages, "in which the occupants had to climb up a ladder to get into the bedrooms, and when finally settled for the night, had to draw up the ladder after them."

Later the premises were altered and made into the Post Office.

At the new building, on White Lane, Mr Elliott will stock sweets, tobacco and stationery and the article continues, the old post office will remain, "as a fruit business run by Mr Elliott's nephews."

(Ronald Ward)

An envelope showing the Opening Day of the new Gleadless Post Office (20th Sept. 1954).
The envelope shows the signature of the then Sub-Postmaster, the late Artie Elliott.

Gleadless Postal Services

1848 — *Mrs Elizabeth Kay* appointed receiver at Intake in March, 1848, referred to as 'Sub-Postmaster' in 1860.

Sheffield Post Office 1867. Messenger at 6.30 am weekdays only.
Joseph Dunns, to Intake and Hackenthorpe.

1867 — *Luke Carr,* shopkeeper. Letters from Sheffield through Intake P.O. now Mrs Elizabeth Kay receiver.

(From Kelly's P.O. Directory of the W.R. of Yorkshire, pub. Nov. 1867.)

1876 — *(White's)*
Gleadless Post Office, Martin Simmonite, Intake. Leters via Sheffield.
Mrs Ellen Carr, shopkeeper.

1871/2 & 6 (White's) Nearest Post Office for Gleadless at Intake. Letters via Sheffield.
Martin Simmonite, grocer and receiver. Letters arrive 8.30 am despatched 6.10 pm by foot post via Sheffield.

1881 — Ellen Carr appointed Sub-postmaster/mistress on July 25th, 1881 (P.O. Records) Gleadless.
Hollinsend Wall Box erected 2nd August 1881 (P.O. Records)

1884 (Whites) Gleadless P.O. Mrs Ellen Carr. Nearest Money Order Office — Intake.
Nearest Telegraph Office at Handsworth Woodhouse. Letters received 9.30 am despatched 6 pm. Wall Letter Box Hollins End cleared 6 pm weekdays only.

1889/90 (Kelly's) Gleadless P.O. Richard Rowe, receiver, grocer and tea dealer. Letters arrive from Sheffield at 9.30 am despatched at 5.45 pm. Nearest Money Order Office is at Intake and Telegraph Office at Heeley. Hollins End Wall Box cleared at 6 pm.

c. 1890 P.O. Records. Rural Postman Sheffield 7 White Lane. 17/- per week: annual increment of 1/- rising to a maximum of 21/-. Rural Auxiliary at Intake 10/- weekly.
A 'Mail Car' was contracted for on 1st March 1890 from Sheffield to Woodhouse and Intake (weekdays) at a cost of £70.
Left Sheffield at 5.40 am arrived Woodhouse at 6.37 am and Intake at 7.10 am returning empty to Sheffield due to arrive back at 7.30 am.

1890 Contractor John Stones, 7 Thorpe Road, Highfields, later 20 Russell Street Sheffield. All crossed out presumably when contract terminated.

1893 Gleadless P.O. John Radley Liversidge, grocer, receiver.
Letters arrive from Sheffield at 8.45 am, despatched at 5.45 pm.
Wall Letter Box, Hollins End, cleared at 6 pm.

1895/6 John Radley Liversidge, shopkeeper, general dealer and postmaster.

1896 (White's Directory) Gleadless P.O. Mrs Elizabeth Emma Stacey.
Letters arrive 9.15 am, despatched 5.45 pm via Sheffield.
Wall letter box Hollins End, cleared at 6 pm weekdays only. Intake is nearest Money Order Office and Sheffield nearest Telegraph Office.

1901 (Kelly's) Mrs Elizabeth Emma Stacey, Shopkeeper and sub-postmistress. Postal orders issued but not paid. Letters arrive at 8.55 am and 6 pm and are despatched at 5.15 and 6.20 pm via Sheffield. Wall letter box at Hollins End cleared at 8.45 am, 5.35 and 6.40 pm weekdays only. Intake nearest Money Order Office and Heeley nearest Telegraph Office (3 miles).

1904 (Kelly's) Mrs Elizabeth Emma Stacey, Post Office. Postal orders are issued but not paid. Letters arrive at 8.55 am and 6.15 pm and are despatched at 5.20 pm and 6.25 pm via Sheffield. Wall Letter Box at Hollins End cleared 8.45 am, 5.35 and 6.40 pm, weekdays only.

1912 (Kelly's) Post Office, Mrs Annie West, Postmistress and shopkeeper. Letters arrive via Sheffield at 8.45 am and 6.30 pm and are despatched at 5.20 pm. No Sunday delivery. Wall Letter Boxes at Hollins End cleared at 9.30 am and 5.35 and 6.40 pm weekdays only. Lane End at 5.20 and 6.25 pm. Intake nearest money order office, Heeley nearest Telegraph Office (3 miles).

Extracts from Sheffield Post Office Records covering the 1890s

(from Ronald Ward)

1896. Post 25 Section dealing with HANDSWORTH SUB OFFICE.

Handsworth S.O.	6.45 am depart	9.0 am arrive

This section omitted here as it went as far as Woodthorpe Hall by Foot Post with the Night Mail Delivery covering 2½ miles.

Day Mail

Handsworth S.O.	3.30 pm	6.0 pm

This covered the same ground with the Wall box at Handsworth Church emptied and also the Station Service, Delivery, &c Time 4½ hours.

Darnall Station	arr. 4.10 pm	Weekdays
	dep. 4.30 pm	S.O. Postman
Handsworth Rd	arrive	
Handsworth W.B.	7.30 pm	
Richmond Lane		Day Mail delivery
Richmond Park		tested 13/8/1897
Richmond W.B.	7.10 pm	

	Richmond Hill			This Postman waits at
	Intake S.O.	6.55 pm	5.10 pm	Gleadless S.O.
	Hollinsend	6.40 pm	5.25 pm	30 mins.
	Gleadless	6.25 pm	5.55 pm	
Post 51A		*dep*	*arr*	
	Sheffield	6.00 am	10.00 am	Foot Post 8 miles out.
	Manor			2¾ miles in, weekdays.
	Elm Tree W.B.	9.10 am		Rural Auxiliary
	Intake S.O.	9.05 am	7.15 am	*Intake S.O.*
	Hollinsend W.B.	8.45 am		Night Mail Despatch
	Four Lane End	omitted		see POST 52
	Birley Vale Colliery	" "		Salary £16.4.0
	Birley Vale	" "		
	Intake on return		9.00 am	

The Handsworth postman conveys the day mail correspondence to the Sub Office and a delivery is made to callers at 5.30 pm (Intake). A collection is made by the Handsworth S.O. Postman at 6.55 pm.

Post 52		*dep*	*arr*	
	Sheffield P.O.	6.00 am	6.45 pm	Foot Post 12 miles out,
	Deep Pit Colliery			4½ miles in, weekdays.
	Elm Tree Hill WB	6.00 pm		
	Windy House	omitted		Rural Postman
	Stand House	" "		Tested 2.11.1892
	Elm Tree			
	Intake S.O.	5.55 pm	omitted	
	Hagg Lane	omitted	see POST 51A	*Gleadless S.O.*
	Paddocks Farm	" "		
	Myrtle Spring	" "		
	Myrtle Hill	" "		Salary £7.14.0
	Hurlfield	" "		
	Hollinsend WB	5.35 pm		
	Gleadless Common	omitted		
	Gleadless S.O.	5.20 pm	8.55 am	
	White Lane End	5.05 pm		
	Birley	omitted	10.00 am	

20th Century Postal Records

1914. (White's "Sheffield & Rotherham Directory)

P.O. Mrs Annie West. Letters via Sheffield arrive 8.45 am and 6.20 pm and are despatched at 12.20 and 8 pm. No Sunday delivery. Intake nearest Money Order Office. Wall Letter Boxes. Lane End cleared 12.20 & 8 pm. White Lane cleared 12 Noon & 7.40 pm weekdays only. Hollins End cleared 9.30 am, 12.35 & 8.05 pm weekdays.

1915 No change

In 1921 The Sheffield Corporation Act Extension Order brought in Handsworth, comprising the villages of Handsworth, Gleadless and Woodhouse and the hamlet of Richmond. Effective 9th October.

1923. (Kelly's, formerly White's Directory)

Gleadless P.O. listed as at 13, Heeley Road, Gleadless, in 1926 - 27 as Eric West, sub-postmaster, 795 Gleadless Road.

1927 (Kelly's) and for several years:

Post Office at 795, Gleadless Road. Then Eric West, shopkeeper. No mention as sub postmaster. The box at the Gleadless Post Office could be opened from both inside and outside, when at 795, Gleadless Road. When transferred to Town End, pillar box erected.

GR Wall Box No. 312 Hollinsend Road — Gleadless Common. This was in the Chapel Wall (United Reform Church) and moved in 1966 further up Hollinsend Road, the replacement being an EIIR Pillar Box. For several months in 1966, No. 312 was in the box at the corner of Woodholm Place and Woodholm Road, Ecclesall.

1931, The population was 4,814.

Mrs Ada Unwin Elliott, sub-postmistress. Post, Money Order and Telegraph Office. Letters through Sheffield.

1945 Mr Artington Ward Elliott was appointed sub postmaster. Mr Elliott took over the Post Office from his Mother, Mrs Ada Unwin Elliott.

1954 *18th September.* The old Gleadless Post Office at 795, Gleadless Road was closed. *20th September.* Opening of the new Post Office in Gleadless at the junction of Briarfield Road and White Lane. Mr Artington W. Elliott, had the new premises built.

1974 Mr 'Artie' W. Elliott, sub postmaster retires from Gleadless Post Office.

(My grateful thanks to Mr Ronald Ward F.R.P.S.L. for his assistance with the Gleadless Postal Information.)

On April 1st, 1950, the creation of a new postal district — Sheffield 12 — which covered Intake, Gleadless and Frecheville came into force with residents being asked to use "12" from now on. Mr H.J.E. Still, Sheffield's Head Postmaster said that the creation of "12" "was decided on in order to bring the outlying areas into line with the rest of the city."

Rita Berney: "I worked on the Post Office for about 18 months when I was 16. I went to work at Norton with Lizzie Cook. She delivered post at Norton.

I started my round at the top of Seagrave Crescent then onto Gleadless Road, Lister Crescent, Carson Mount, Base Green Avenue, then Drive and White Lane. Then I'd cross over to Charnock and then down Carter Lane to Rodgers' farm, and Websters then to Fidlers right down at bottom. I'd walk all that way all for 14/8d a week. I started at 6 am until about 8.50, six days a week and I loved it. Billy Marples was a postman at Gleadless as well and I worked with him.

I remember when I got married Artie Elliott sent us a telegram. We liked Artie and his wife."

Mary's Store, Gleadless Road

Brian Cregand: "The old Post Office building had been closed for some years when Mary and myself took over the shop in 1961. It had been empty before then. We sold socks, bootlaces and fruit and anything that would show a profit but it was mainly fruit. It was a little gold mine.

We had plenty of orders and there was only Mary (my wife) and myself in the shop and a part-time girl who helped us out when we were really pushed, mainly at the weekends.

Les Simpson had the main fruit shop at Gleadless Town End and his shop was massive. He sold wet fish and mussels etc., as well as fruit.

At the time we had the shop, the Gleadless Valley Estate was being built and we had to close the shop in 1972 under a Compulsory Purchase Order which came under road-widening and not slum clearance or anything like that, even though it was a really old building.

It was a large place inside and round the back was a building like a big barn which had been neglected. Previously it had been a farm.

Websters Butchers' shop closed before we did and Guymer's shop across the road closed due to Compulsory Purchase Order, though not for road widening like us. We were the last shop to close in that little area on Gleadless Road."

Lineham's Shop

At one time Mrs Lineham occupied the shop that had once been the 'Ball Inn'. *Mrs Liversidege:* "The Linehams went to live in the house where the Clarke family once lived and I went to help the LInehams there. One day this shop in the village came empty and Mrs Lineham says, "Mabel we're thinking of starting a bit of business and our Jack thinks that we ought to have a farm of some sort — a pig farm."

Well I cleaned the pigs out and did everything. I had to do. Mrs Lineham opened a grocery shop and a Drapery Shop in two rooms. One was a Grocery and the other a Drapery. I used to bake for the shop. I used to bake up six stone of flour a day. I was up before 6 am and I'd make it in a great, big bath. I had to be up early to get bread ready for shop.

I never drew a wage but she used to clothe and feed me but I never got any money.

Travellers used to come to the shop. We had Carrs, the biscuit man, Hebblethwaites, then sweet travellers and Balm people.

Mrs Lineham had a shop on Brierley Terrace before she had the 'Ball Inn' place. Then Sellars got the Brierley Terrace shop. It was in one of houses and they made a paper and sweet shop out of it."

Guymer's shop on Gleadless Road

Guymer's also occupied the premises of the old 'Ball Inn'. Mrs Rita Berney together with her Mother Lily Guymer, ran the little shop that was a familiar landmark in the village.

"I went to live in the shop in 1935, when I'd be about eight years old.

There was my Mum and Dad, my two brothers and myself. It was my Mother's shop for my father, Bob, had a bad heart and he died in 1940. My Mum lived there until 1963 when they decided to knock it down. It was in an awful condition and wasn't fit to live in. There were cockroaches and it was very damp.

We sold general groceries, vegetables, potatoes, cheese and bacon. I was brought up to look after the shop from being big enough and I was only 13 when my Father died. When I left school I didn't go to work but stayed and helped Mum in the shop.

Delivery to our shop was by van. We had our own little van and in a corner we had our name written on. We had three deliveries of bread and a delivery of Danish bacon. Butter came in barrels and we used to weigh it out in tubs. We'd tip it out of barrel and with a big butter knife we'd cut it up the best way we could. Cheese came in big blocks and we'd cut that up with a knife. We had a little wooden till to keep our money in.

When you came into our shop you saw a counter but there was another narrow counter where we used to have the bread. All the deliveries came through the front door. Sugar came in sacks and we'd weigh it out into lbs and put sugar into blue bags which weighed a 1lb or 2lb. We had a little scoop to dip into sack with. Kids came for 'aporh and 'pennorth of sweets and we'd put sweets in 'corner' bags.

We only lived in the bottom part of our house because we had two flats upstairs. Little Billy Kidger lived in back one and Mrs Ward and her niece, Emily Drury who worked at Charnock Hall, lived in the front one.

There were stairs up the middle of the builidng and they (the flat dwellers) couldn't get through our part and we couldn't enter their part. Not many of the houses were in good condition. They were very damp but somehow people lived to an old age!

Mr & Mrs Winters had our shop before us and when my Mother left, the shop was demolished to make room for the road to be widened. We were the last people to live in the old house.

Now the house in 906, Gleadless Road (that is what our number was) was built in our garden before the old house was knocked down. The person bought the ground for the house to be built before we left and we used to call it the Ranch House because it was built in the garden but that's why I know exactly where our old house used to be. I was upset when I left Gleadless. It was a lovely little village when we lived there."

Shopkeepers in Gleadless

The following lists show the number of shopkeepers in Gleadless during the 19th and early 20th centuries. Only those that have been termed 'shopkeepers' by the Directories have been included here. It is unbelievable to imagine that Gleadless has progressed from four small shops, listed in 1833, to a wide range of shops in the area to-day. In 1833, the shop was where people lived and was not by any means a specially designed, purpose built shop.

One can hardly comprehend what our local Gleadless shopkeeper, living in 1833 would have thought of Gleadless shopping facilities to-day, complete with its supermarkets!

1833

Jon Clayton, Lane Ends
Simon Jones, Commonside
James Searls, gardener & shopkeeper
Jas & Jph Skelton, shopkeeper

1841

Wm. Carr
Simon Jones
Job Searls
James Skelton

1845

Wm. Carr
Simon Jones
Job Searls (Gardener & c.)
George Martin

1849

Simeon Jones
George Martin
Job Searls

1854

George Martin
Wm. Carr (S. & table blade forger)
John Rawlins (S & Nurseryman, used to be a woodman)
Job Searls (S. & nurserymn)

1856

Wm. Carr
James Drury
George Martin

1860

Wm. Carr
George Martin
William Martin

1871

Mrs Ellen Carr
Benjamin Jones
William Martin (lived Commonside, owned house & shop)
George Rogers

1879

Mrs Ellen Carr
John Holland, tailor
Mrs Eliza Jackson
William Martin
Frederick Robins
George Rogers
Henry Salt (Exors. of)

1881

Job Searls is now listed as a private resident
Mrs Ellen Carr
Abel Daniel, grocer
George Jackson, Lane End
William Martin
Reuben Roper
Tom Simpson

1883

Mrs Ellen Carr
Abel Daniel
William Martin
Reuben Roper
Tom Simpson
Geo Holland, tea dealer & tailor
Richard Rowe, grocer & tea dealer
Joseph Skelton, grocer & tea dealer
Ellis Ward, grocer & beer retailer

1889

Abel Daniel, grocer
William Martin, shopkeeper
Geo Holland, grocer, tea dealer & tailor
Richard Rowe, grocer & tea dealer & POST OFFICE
Tom Simpson, shopkeeper
Joseph Skelton, grocer & tea dealer

1890

Abel Daniel, grocer
Geo Holland, grocer, tea dealer & tailor
William Martin, shopkeeper
Richard Rowe, grocer & P.O.
Tom Simpson, shopkeeper
Joseph Skelton, grocer & tea dealer

1891

Abel Daniel
George Holland
Leonard Marples, grocer & clerk
William Martin
Richard Rowe, shopkeeper & postmaster

1893

Abel Daniel
Geo Holland
Jn. Radley Liversidge, grocer & Post Office
William Martin
Tom Simpson
Joseph Skelton

1895/6
Abel Daniel
Mrs Mary Holland, shopkeeper
Charles Horner, shopkeeper
John Radley Liversidge, shopkeeper, general dealer & postmaster
Frank Marples, grocer
William Martin
Tom Simpson
Joseph Skelton

1900
Arthur Holland, greengrocer
Mrs Mary Holland, shopkpr
Frank Marples, grocer
William Martin
William Henry Neal, shopkeeper
Tom Simpson
Joseph Skelton
Mrs Elizabeth Emma Stacey shopkeeper & Postmistress

1902
Henry Bellamy, shopkeeper
George Hatton, fishmonger
Arthur Holland, greengrocer
Mrs Mary Ann Holland shopkeeper
William Linacre, shopkeeper
Frank Marples, grocer
Thos Moseley, greengrocer
Wm Henry Neal, shopkpr
Connor Pashley, shopkpr
Mrs Sarah Simpson, shopkpr
Joseph Skelton
Mrs Elizabeth Emma Stacey, shopkeeper & Postmistress

Cottages on White Lane (Mrs Hullah)
Barker's Garage is on the left, while the cottages on the right are where the Vet's Surgery is today!

Traders in Gleadless Town End/White Lane area

1922 Samuel Cox, shopkeeper, 39 Town End
Fred Simpson, shopkeeper, 45 Town End
John Earnshaw, Thrashing machine proprietor, Smithfield Road, Town End.

1928 Mrs Florence Simpson, shopkeeper, 45 Town End
Mrs Mary Watson, shopkeeper, 35 Town End
John Earnshaw (T. Mach)

1936	Bert Nichols, shopkeeper, 45 Town End
	Mary Watson, 35 Town End
	John Earnshaw (T. Mach.)
1936	Mrs Ethel Barker, Petrol Station, Town End
	John Earnshaw (T. Mach.)
	B. Nichols, 45 Town End
	Jn. Fred. Frost, shopkeeper, White Lane
	Mrs Emily Richards, fruiterer, White Lane
	Willie Sandsford, draper, White Lane
	John Reginald Sellars, Newsagent, Lane End
	Frederick Taylor, boot repairer, White Lane
	Ernest Ward, butcher, White Lane
	Mary Watson, 35 Town End
1941	E. Barker, petrol
	Edwin Oswald Barber, insurance agent, 24 Base Green Road
	Willie Bell, boot & shoe repairer, 108 White Lane
	Ronald Brown, fried fish dealer, White Lane
	Jn. Christopherson, fruiterer, 61, White Lane
	Mrs Catherine Earnshaw, Thrashing machine proprietress, 11 Smithfield Rd
	Harry Hardwick, shop White Lane
	Joseph Mappin, chimney sweeper, 168 White Lane
	Tom Merchant, decorator, 165 White Lane
	Edward Price, fruiterer, White Lane
	L & H Ryder, coal merchants, 152 White Lane
	Harold Ryder, plumber, " "
	Willie Sandford, draper, White Lane
	J.R. Sellars, news
	Leslie Herbert Simpson, butcher, 63 White Lane
	Joseph Smith, builder, 30 Charnock Hall Road
	Miss Mary Walker, shop, 45 Town End, and grocer, White Lane
	Mrs Irene Ward, ladies hairdresser, 129 White Lane
	Jas. Hy. Watson, 35 Town End shop
	Ernest Wills, teacher of music, 4 Carson Mount
	Alec Wiseman, insurance agent, 6 Charnock Hill (Hall?) Road

'Pop' Watson's corner shop at Gleadless Town End (D. Higgins)
In the cottages on left lived Williamsons/ Browns/Sam Corker/ & Oxleys. 'Granny' Cox lived in the end cottage after the shop.

Baker's Garage, Gleadless Town End

Although in the 20's and 30's, very few Gleadless people possessed a car, there was a little petrol station at Gleadless Town End. It was started by Mr Horace Baker who originally came from Duke Street where he had a hardware business. When he moved to No. 40, Townend, he brought his hardware business with him.

In the 1920's and 30's, Horace Baker, was what we would term to-day, a commercial traveller. Driving a splendid car he would tour the neighbouring villages of Norton, Greenhill and down to Lightwood with his 'travelling shop'. Everything from pots and pans to brushes and vinegar was sold from this travelling 'Aladdin's Cave'!

Mr Baker's brother-in-law, Herbert Nichols, who lived at 38 Townend, also worked as a commercial traveller and drove his goods around in a most striking vehicle that would to-day make any vintage car enthusiast green with envy!

In 1932, Mr Baker sold his hardware business and sunk a pump outside his home (No. 40 Townend) to start a petrol station. Trade came from the nearby villages, Intake, Ridgeway and Norton. In the immediate area there were only two petrol pump stations at this time which were situated at Intake and Ridgeway.

Baker's Garage, Town End. Mrs Baker is pictured. (Mrs Hullah)

Shortly after the opening of the Townend petrol station, Mr Baker died and his wife Ethel took over the running of the garage. At the side of Baker's garage was a piece of land where Earnshaws kept their threshing machinery. Later Reginald Sellars had a house built on the land for his newspaper business and it is familiar to us to-day as the G.T. News Shop.

Competition to Baker's garage came when Flemings had a garage built on waste land opposite the Gleadless Methodist Church. Eventually

Flemings sold the station to a big petrol company and when the Charnock Estate was built, a bigger station with more pumps was 'sunk'. To-day, this is the BP Petrol Station on Ridgeway Road, at Town End.

However, the Bakers, with daughter Vera, continued with their business until 1962. Today, the garage is White Lane Service Station.

Travellers

Every village in the early part of this century had its 'commercial' traveller. These travellers, who must have journeyed many miles, were characters in their own right and everyone looked forward to seeing these travelling salesmen.

Stan Taylor:

'Pot Jack'

'Pot Jack' (the only name he was known by) was a traveller who visited the village periodically with his pottery. He sold cups, saucers and plates etc., which he carried on his head in an old fashioned wicker clothes basket which he balanced perfectly without using his hands.

When his days work was done, which was usually opening time at the nearest local pub — which would be either Charlie Bryant's "Red Lion", Totty's "Heeley and Sheffield", or George Lomas' "New Inn", he would go into pub and spend nearly all his takings. Then as a very good mouth organ player he would earn a few more extra pints and a few coppers to take him back home in a cab or tram according to his finances and condition!

Mr Wortley

Mr Wortley was another regular visitor in the early 20's. I think he was a tailor and came from one of the cloth mills at Huddersfield. He usually came in a three wheeler Morgan car with his suit case full of clothes.

Many local children, like myself, were provided with their new Whitsuntide suits from the few shillings our Mothers paid him on his fortnightly visits. In fact if you wanted measuring for anything he would have it made and brought back the next week as requested.

Dolly Worrall:

George Ibbotson

"One of the best men who helped Gleadless was called George Ibbotson. He came round with a very big, strong Shire horse and cart, four wheeled, like what you might call a dray and he sold everything.

He came from the Infirmary area. On Thursdays he went around Intake and on Wednesdays he'd come to Gleadless. He even sold paraffin for lighting because we didn't get electric lighting until the 1930's.

We had iron bedsteads in those days and I remember my Mother once saying to George (remember there wasn't any water toilets at this time), "Mr Ibbotson," she said, "I wonder if you could get me some enamel jerries instead of pot ones because when you put them under the bed the handles get knocked off with the iron bedsteads?"

"Well," he says and he was a country man and spoke slow, "I can get ye some ye know Mrs Wattam but they're very musical!"

Herbert Nichols

Herbert Nichols, commercial traveller with his travelling shop.

Later Mr Nichols took over the corner shop at the bottom of Smithfield Road (now Waite's). What a fantastic car!

6. RELIGION

Victorian England (1837 - 1901) was a deeply religious country with a great number of people who were habitual church or chapel-goers, attending church at least once and probably twice every Sunday. This was particularly true in smaller towns and country villages. To most Victorians they had no doubts about the truth of their version of the Christian gospel, whether it was High Church, Low Church or Chapel. The Bible was widely and frequently read by people of every class. The earliest school in Gleadless was a Church School which was established primarily to 'instruct the poor children of Gleadless' to read 'the Holy Scriptures'.

Strict Sunday observance was the rule and a day on which work was forbidden and pleasure condemned. Sunday was set aside for church-going and Sunday Schools. Later ages have perhaps criticised this era and yet to Victoria's people it was a real and deep observance in their daily lives. This organised religion in the Victorian age has had its critics but on the positive side it made people hardworking and filled them with a strong sense of duty.

After Queen Victoria's reign, changes in English life began to alter the religious opinions of many people. However, organised religion in Gleadless began in 1822 when the Rev. Mark Docker and the Rev. F. Dixon of Sheffield, first preached Christianity in the neighbourhood. They were joined by Messrs. Bower, Turner, Parkinson, Rhodes, Woodcock, Hallam, Leader, Slater and Wolstenholm. At first their preaching met with very little success but their perseverance finally won through and in 1828 a small Chapel was built, part by subscription and the rest by a loan (which was later re-paid) from the Rev. Dickson. The land was given by Mr Hugh Parker, J.P. of Woodthorpe Hall and on May 6th 1829 an organised Chapel led by the Rev. Mark Docker was created.

Such was the beginning of the Bethel Chapel later the Gleadless Independent Church (Congregational) and now the *Gleadless United Reform Church.* By 1834 the little Chapel was too small for the growing congregation and so it was pulled down and another one was built which is the present one today. As before, Mr Parker gave the land, on condition that one shilling should be paid as an acknowledgement. Subscriptions met part of the money and £100 was lent by Mr William Smith of Gleadless.

The chapel continued to prosper but in 1839 the Anglican *Christ Church* was built. This was a problem for the Chapel for the Ministers of Christ Church said that the Independent Church had no right to worship God

Gleadless United Reformed Church

Gleadless Methodist Church (Mr & Mrs B. Thompson)

but only in their Church and to believe what they believed. There was a distinct opposition of opinions.

This matter was brought to a head when in 1840 the Chapel members decided that they should have a Sunday School. At first they met in one of the cottages at Lane End where Josiah Trotter and his family lived. However, this proved to be very inappropriate and so it was decided to hold the Sunday School in the Chapel. Opposition to this resulted in Justice Parker being informed and consequently one of the Chapel members had to appear before him. Mr Parker asked them to return to the cottage for their meetings which they did but eventually they returned to the Chapel again.

Three times they were advised by Mr Parker not to do this until finally Mr Parker was told that, "In the name of the Lord, they meant to go forward teaching in the Chapel," so they were left alone after that.

Conflict with Christ Church continued throughout but the Congregational Chapel members grew in numbers. Many fine Ministers have given their services to the Chapel and in 1893 the Rev. Crispin Gretton Holt became the first Pastor of the Church. He gave 21 years service to the Chapel before retiring through ill health in 1915. Local roads, Crispin Gardens etc., bear his name.

In 1921 the Chapel Field was acquired by the Chapel at a cost of £1,050. These 5 acres were for recreation and for the benefit of the Chapel and Sunday School. Alderman George Corker J.P. and Mr Richard Rowe were great workers in acquiring the field. A portion of the field was reserved for any extension of the Church premises and the building of a Manse. A Pavilion was also erected in the field. The Chapel Field (now the site of a new housing development) was to be an essential place for village leisure activities and Whitsuntide events.

Christ Church

Gleadless did not have its own separate Ecclesiastical District until 1881 and when Christ Church was built in 1839* it was intended as a Chapel of Ease to Handsworth where the Rev. J. Hand, who was the Rector of Handsworth Church, officiated any Anglican matters that were undertaken in Gleadless.

The Parish Registers at Christ Church began in 1839 and the Communion cup which was presented to the Parish of Handsworth by the Rev. J. Hand is inscribed with the date 6th August 1839. In 1843 the Church was consecrated.

* According to the 1851 Ecclesiastical Census, Christ Church is referred to as Gleadleys Church of 1838. The church had sittings for 322 people of which 250 seats were free.

Situated near Ridgeway Road, the Church is built in the Early English Style and was sited there because it was halfway between the Parishes of Norton and Handsworth. Previous to Intake Cemetery being opened, Gleadless peoples' resting places were either in Handsworth or Norton graveyards, if they did not wish to be buried in Christ Church's cemetery.

Christ Church has had various alterations over the years.A complete restoration was undertaken in 1889, with the erection of a new chancel, organ chamber, vestry and the removal of a gallery at the West end together with the replacement of high and rented pews to make way for free and open benches. The glass window representing the Crucifixion was placed in the East end. In later years more alterations were to follow.

Across the road from the Church is a fine Victorian building which until recently was the Vicarage. Built in 1859 at a cost to the parishioners it was later enlarged in 1896. This imposing, stone building has housed various clergymen over the years. Perhaps of all these *Rev. Cyril Crossland* is the most eminent, who certainly left an immense impression on his parishioners. Even today the older villagers recall him 'trotting' around the village in his pony and trap wearing a long black cloth coat and a shallow, topped bowler hat. He was part of the village and if he called on wash day then work would stop, tea would be made and conversation flowed. Artist, antique collector and violinist were just a few of his attributes. The Rev. C. Crossland was a most prominent leading figure in the villagers' lives.

Before Rev. Crossland came to Christ Church in 1887, the *Rev. William Henry Booth* was the Vicar. More noted for being the Vicar of Woodhouse for 30 years or so, he was for five years the Vicar of Gleadless beginning in 1882 until 1887. He received the nick-name of 'Fanny' Booth being a small and dainty figure who always wore a frock coat, and shovel hat which he held down with the crook of his umbrella! In St. James Church, Woodhouse is a stained glass window in his memory.

After the death of Rev. Cyril Crossland in 1923, Rev. Robert Gregory became the next vicar of Christ Church and served the parish for ten years. Rev. Gregory's successor was Rev. Bernard Sharp who spent 37 years at Christ Church before retiring in 1971. In comparison, the Rev. Roberts who arrived in 1972 seemed to stay for only a short time of 7 years before moving to Norfolk.

1980 saw the arrival of the present vicar of Christ Church, Rev. David T. Thomas, who before coming to Gleadless was at Salford in Manchester and was the Vicar of St. Thomas', Pendleton, as well as being the Chaplain to the Salford College of Technology.

Above: Christ Church, Gleadless
— without the clock in the tower. The clock was erected in Rev. Crossland's memory.

Below: The Crossland Family
Standing: Gladys/Eric.
L/R Norman/Mrs C. Crossland/Rev. C. Crossland/Christabel/Tom
Geraldine/Sylvia/Kathleen

Methodism — Hollinsend

As we have already noted the Independents, later known as the Congregationalists, were active in Gleadless before the first Anglican Church was built in 1839. Methodism, which seemed to thrive in poor and mining areas especially, began to make its presence felt, firstly through Hollinsend before later spreading to Gleadless.

In 1822, Intake Colliery was the scene of an explosion which tragically claimed the lives of seven of its miners. This pit accident was the subject of a whole sermon given by the Minister of Garden Street Chapel in Sheffield, who described the miners as "godly men".

Whether this accident completely revolutionised 'the life of the village' as was suggested in some writings, is debatable but a religious upsurge certainly took place and with the demand for a place of worship, cottage meetings were begun at 139 Hollinsend Road, the pioneers in this being John Almond and William James. Later these men were joined in 1842 by Henry Needham and his wife. Methodism outgrew the house meetings until in 1857 the idea of a Chapel took a tangible shape. The invitation to come and help met with a hearty response from the young men of the village who dug the foundations and carted the stone and generally paved the way for the builders. By 1858 the foundation stone was laid and the Chapel opened in the following year with the sermon being preached by Mr Richardson who enjoyed the unusual nickname of the "Lincolnshire Thrasher".

The pulpit, pews and fittings originally belonged to the Chapel at Norton which once stood within the grounds of Norton Hall almost exactly opposite 'The Grange' at Bunting Nook. The Chapel was demolished in early 1853 and part of the woodwork was used for Hollinsend Chapel with the window frames remaining just as they came from Norton. The last Minister at Norton Chapel was Henry Hunt Piper (1805 - 43). The Nonconformists of Norton held regular meetings at Norton Hall for nearly a century.

Gleadless Methodist Church, 1865

Methodism had been preached in Gleadless long before the Gleadless Society was formed in 1859 when it is recorded that the first meetings were being held in the cottage home of Skeltons. However, when the accommodation proved too small, Mr W. Smith offered the use of the 'Mangle House' in Smithfield Road and here in 1862 the first Sunday School was started. Messrs. Daniels and Vardy were appointed in charge of the Society and being so well supported it soon became evident that an extension was a matter of urgency.

It is perhaps interesting to note that the response to the call for a new Chapel met with instant and enthusiastic response by the village Methodists. Gleadless was a working class district, composed for the most part of farm workers and colliers, whose hours were long and whose wages were small, but their hearty response knew no bounds when their interest was roused in such a worthy cause. Mr W. Smith gave the land, Mr Thomas Rhodes of Charnock Hall and Mr Joseph Rhodes carted all the material free and in no time at all the foundation stone was laid and the new Chapel was well on the way to completion. This was during the year 1864.

The opening took place in 1865 and one must mention here the occupants of Charnock Hall who opened their apartments for religious services during the erection of the Chapel and allowed the use of their 'front park' for outdoor functions, especially at Whitsuntide and for Sunday School Anniversary Services, when a barn was used, as the new building was not large enough.

In the course of time another extension had to be planned and in 1890 work on the present Chapel was started with the opening services being held in the following year. The cost of this building was £1,300 which was a formidable amount of money for such a small village society to raise in the late 19th century.

To the right of the church gate one notices the memorial cross, erected by public subscription, to the memory of Elizabeth Sharpe wife of John Sharpe (see also 'Herbs and the local Doctor' Chapter).

1957 saw another milestone in the history of Gleadless Methodist Church with the signing of a contract for the building of a new Sunday School Hall to be erected on the site of the demolished cottages in Chapel Yard behind the Church. The Hall which cost £7,000 was opened on the 15th March, 1958.

More recently a porch was added to the Church in 1982 and it is certainly an indication of rising prices when one considers that this extension cost over £9,000!

Over the years many prominent figures have featured in the development of the Methodist movement in Gleadless and although it is unfair to record names, people like Abel Daniels, Andrew Vardy, John Sharpe and the Plants whose early efforts were an inspiration to the formative years of Gleadless Methodist Church, can justfiably be included here.

St. Peter's Church, Basegreen

St. Peter's Church at Basegreen is comparatively a new building compared to the other churches in the Gleadless area. It was dedicated in

1955 and stands almost on the exact site of the old Base Green farmhouse (for further details see 'Life on the Land' chapter).

Previous to St. Peter's being built the Anglican community in the Basegreen district had to hold their services in a tiny Nissen hut on White Lane. At one time the Church authorities had hoped to convert the Basegreen farmhouse into a church but the building deteriorated so much due to the delays in handing over that the scheme had to be abandoned.

In order to raise money for the building of the church, bricks were 'sold' with the purchasers of the bricks being allowed to write their names on them for inclusion in the building of the church. Bradley, the family who once occupied the farmhouse,w as one of the first names to be written on the bricks.

In 1954 the foundation stone of the new church was laid by Maj.-Gen. L.C. Manners-Smith who used a silver trowel. The service was conducted by the Vicar of Ridgeway, the Rev. Edward Sketchley (the new church was in the parish of Ridgeway) and the lesson was read by the Rector of Eckington with the sermon being preached by the Archdeacon who said in his address that St. Peter's should be the centre of the community and that 'it is not our fault if houses are built in such vast numbers in new districts before you can say 'Jack Robinson' but it is our fault as Christians if we do not see that the centre of the community is the House of God.'

The following year on the 29th June, 1955, the church was dedicated, having cost £12,000 to be built. The Bishop of Derby led the Dedication Service and the church was packed to capacity. As part of the ceremony, the cross bearer Mr Howard Bradbury and the choir, walked along White Lane from the old Nissen hut which had been the church for the past six years and which would continue to be used by some of the Sunday School children.

Built in an 'L' shape, the church is finished in light stone. Inside, sliding screens enable the Hall to be separated for social purposes and the church can be 'halved' for short services.

The Rev. Roger Atkin is the vicar of St. Peter's Church today and works closely with Christ Church and the rest of the religious bodies in the area. Indeed Gleadless has never enjoyed as much close, friendly liaison between all the various religious bodies in the area, as it does today. Gone are the days when friction between the Independents and Christ Church led to disharmony. Today's religious organisations in Gleadless work alongside each other in co-operation, which is an admirable situation for the whole area.

7. SCHOOLDAYS

Education in Gleadless

Most schools in the country were National or Church Schools. Although these schools had been Government assisted since the foundation of the "National Society" in 1811, voluntary assistance played a great part in the founding and the running of a school, sometimes contributing twice as much money to the school's upkeep as that obtained from the Government grant.

A similar situation existed in Gleadless. The earliest record of a school for poor children in Gleadless was in 1815. The school being built by subscription on the site of the present Conservative Club on Hollinsend Road. Hugh Parker, who resided at Woodthorpe Hall, gave the land on which the school was built.

Although there is no firm documented evidence to prove it, the older local residents have told me of an old lady who used to teach children in her home situated near Gleadless Road. Dame Schools, as they were called were very common up to the 1870 Education Act. These Elementary Schools were run by women, the usual fee being 3d or 4d per week.

The Old Gleadless Church School (Irene & Brian Thompson)
Now the Gleadless & District Conservative Club

An important point to remember is that although the 1870 Education Act provided for schooling of every child to the age of thirteen, education was not free until 1891. Until this time children attending Gleadless Church School or as it became later, a Board School, had to pay 1d for their education.

In the Myrtle Springs area, Dr. Flory's Boarding School provided an education for middle class children who came from the Sheffield area. Gleadless children were not educated there.

My first book on Gleadless* deals more fully with Dr. Flory's school and Gleadless Church of England School and how they came to be formed.

During the 19th century, the idea gained ground that an uneducated and uncivilised working class might be more dangerous than one which had been to school. Not that one can suggest for one moment that the children of Gleadless were ever dangerous! However, the majority of children in the early nineteenth century grew up unable to read and write.

Nationally, there was some desire to set up some form of educational system. There were three factors governing this desire:-

1. To instruct the poor in religion, for which purpose they should be able to sit and read the Bible.
2. There was a growing need in business for people who could read and write.
3. The granting of political power to working class people; 'We must educate our masters,' said a leading politician in 1867.

However, in Gleadless in 1844 Rowland Hibbard of Saint Hill, made in his Will, a bequest of £105 ot the trustees of Gleadless School. The Rector of Handsworth (at this time the Rev. John Hand) gave an additional £25 plus legal expenses which culminated in a total of £130 which was to be laid out on the land. From this £130 the Gleadless School Trustees were asssigned a piece of land which contained over 2 acres, which had previously been part of Gleadless Common together with another area of land where Gleadless School then stood and which also formed part of the Common.

A further bequest came when in 1845 Thomas Weldon bequeathed in his Will "half the dividends on the sum of £400.", which amounted to the school receiving £6.9s.2d. per annum. Thomas Weldon on leaving this money to the school wished, "for the instruction of poor children belonging to Gleadless, in Reading, his great object being that every child should be taught to read the Holy Scriptures."

*'*Gleadless from Village to Suburb*'

With these Bequests, the old school was pulled down and in 1867 a new building was erected on the same site. Today, the building is no longer in use as a school but now houses the Conservative Club.

Before, the 'new' school (now the Gleadless Nursery and First School) was built further down Hollinsend Road, in 1898, all the children in Gleadless attended this little school. We know from the early school log books that the conditions at Gleadless Church School had reached a serious breach of overcrowding.

An entry in the log book dated 21.3.1892 states: "Immediate attention should be called to the serious overcrowding of the Infants. The accommodation is for 50 and the following numbers show the crowding to be habitual" . . . The numbers are shown to be in the 80's.

Some eighteen months laters, conditions are becoming critical at the school and Mr. Roberts, the Headmaster writes after a meeting of the Managers in 1893, "It was considered that from £300 to £400 would be required to carry out these improvements (*i.e.* the improvement of the closets, provision of lavatories etc.) and there seemed very little hope of this amount being raised in the parish." Arrangements were therefore being made for transferring the school to the School Board.

Board Schools were established after the 1870 Education Act and were the first local authority-run schools. School Board districts were devised with the boards being empowered to build new schools in areas of poor provision or otherwise to absorb existing schools. Unlike the Church schools, these board schools were secular and undenominational.

Locally elected School Boards were given the power to levy rates to pay for them. Previously, the old Church School received a lot of help from the Church and in particular the Minister of the Parish. So from the 1st June, 1895, the School Board took over the charge of Gleadless School.

From the earliest photographs I have of Gleadless schoolchildren, they can be seen displaying a caption in front of their school photo 'Board School'. It was not until 1902 that the Board Schools became Council Schools. The school then became known as Handsworth Gleadless Council Mixed School.

So on the 19th April, 1898, the new school building, which we now call Gleadless Nursery First School, was opened to the children of Gleadless. Intake children who had applied for entry were refused.

The old school continued to be used as an Infants School with Ada Garrick being the Headmistress in 1895 before Miss Waite took over the post from her and continued until 1915. Miss Bayns-Smith of whom many older Gleadless residents remember, became Headmistress after Miss Waite until 1928.

Gleadless Board School 1899

Later the old school was used as a Sunday School room by the children who attended Christ Church then as business premises before finally being used by The Gleadless & District Conservative Club.

Before 1921, Gleadless was under the West Riding Education Committee until on the 8th November, 1921 when the Handsworth Urban District, which Gleadless was a part of, came within the area of Sheffield and the school was then transferred to the Sheffield Education Committee.

It seems that overcrowding had always been a problem at Gleadless. Reading the entry from the School Log book dated the 8th June, 1936 we find that the majority of classes have nearly 50 children in each.

Class 1	Standard VII & VIII	Roll 50 Mr. Staton
″ 2	″ VI	″ 48 Miss Hardwick
″ 3	″ V & VI	″ 46 Miss Sisk
″ 4	″ IV & V	″ 48 Mr. Bradley
″ 5	″ III & IV	″ 48 Miss Rodgers
″ 6A	″ II	″ 40 Miss Jones
″ 6B	″ II	″ 20 Miss Raiford PT
″ 7	″ I	″ 45 Miss Holland
″ 8	″ Class 1 Infants	″ 43 Miss Mander
″ 9	″ ″ 2 ″	″ 42 Miss Oxley
		No. on Roll 439

By 1953 the children attending the school had risen to nearly 600 with poor Mrs. Bartlett who taught Junior 1 having 52 children in her class! While in 1954, it was suggested that the 'transfer of many Secondary children to Hurlfield Secondary Schools when completed, would result in considerable reduction in the numbers in the School . . . .'

This transition did come about, with the Senior Girls attending the Hurlfield Secondary Modern Girls' School and later, in 1955, the Senior Boys were all transferred to Hurlfield Secondary Modern Boys' School. Afterwards in 1956 there were alterations to the school building, resulting in indoor toilets, a new staff room and a Headteacher's room etc.,

The Middle School

May, 1968 saw the proposal that Gleadless School was to be re-organised as a "First School 4 - 8 years, probably in 1972 and that a new "Middle School" was to be built on the land at the side of Jaunty Lane and opposite the 'First School'.

The older type of Junior School was established after the 1918 Education Act but was not prevalent until after 1926. Junior schools were for children between the ages of 7 - 11 whereas the earlier elementary schools had catered for children from 7 - 14 years.

Plans went ahead for the new Middle School and when the school re-opened after the Summer Holidays in September 1972, Gleadless had been split into two schools.

From the School Log book entry 4.9.72

'School opened and is now organised into:-

(a) The new Open-Plan Middle School Building across the road from the old building – 8/11 years

(b) In the old main building and huts – 5/8 years.'

It was not until March of the following year that the Middle School was officially opened by the Lord Mayor and Lady Mayoress.

Over the years Gleadless School has continued to grow and a provision has now been made for the very young children in the opening of the Gleadless Nursery which is housed in part of the older school building.

Today, Mr. C. New is the Headmaster of Gleadless Nursery First and Middle School, a school which began as a Church School with its primary intent of teaching the poor children of Gleadless to read the Bible.

Gleadless Schoolteachers

Gleadless, "a school was built here in 1815, by subscription."
(*White's Directory* – 1833)

1833	Adam Eaton, schoolmaster
1841	
1845	
1849	Joshua Barraclough, schoolmaster.
1854	William Beet, master of National School
1856	William and Mrs. Beet National School
1860	" " " " " "
1867	The Church of England Endowed School was rebuilt, together with a master's residence, at a cost of £800
1871	John Methley & Mrs. Ellen, teachers, Church School.
1872	John Methley and Ellen, teachers, Endowed National School.
1879	George, William Rook & Mrs. Eliza, National schoolteachers.
1881	Church of England School (mixed) Joseph Garside (Master) Mrs. Elsie Lamb Garside, Infants' Mistress.
1884	Mrs. M. C and Frederick P. Twyst, National Schoolteachers
1889	William Roberts, Schoolmaster
1890	" " "
1891	" " Church of England, schoolmaster.
1893	" "
1900	" "
1902	William Roberts, Board schoolmaster. "The Church of England Endowed School was rebuilt in 1867, together with a residence for the master, at a cost of £800, but is now only used as a Sunday School, the attached house being occupied by the master of the Board School." (White's Directory 1902)

Gleadless Teachers, 1916 - 1965

1916

Standards	7 & 8	Mr. Roberts (Headmaster)
"	5 8 6	Mr. Staton
"	4	Mr. Ennis
"	3	Miss Drewry
"	2	Miss Hoyland
"	1a	Miss Rodger
"	1b	Miss Nutt

1953

Senior Group	1	Mr. S. North
" "	2	Mr. R. Hamley
" "	3	Mr. R. F. Pashley
" "	4	Miss M. Hardwick
Junior	4	Mr. N. Iosson
"	4/3	Miss Hill
"	3	Miss Lester
"	2	Mrs. Haynes
"	2/1	Miss Parkin
"	1	Mrs. Barlett
Infants	2	Miss Carpenter
"	2/1	Mrs. Wilks
	1	Mrs. Lowe
Reception		Mrs. Bell

1965

J4	Mr. N. Iosson
J4/3	Mr. A. Batty
J3	Mr. B. Dyson
J3/2	Miss B. Metcalfe
J2	Miss K. Dale
J1	Mrs. P. Foster
J1	Mrs. C. Gregory
I2	Mrs. K. Taylor
I2	Miss K. Poultney
I2/1	Miss R. Varney
I1	Mr. J. Farrell
I/R	Miss B. Abson
I/R	Miss V. Hobson

This information has been taken from the School Log Books and lists the former Headteachers at Gleadless.

Headteachers of Gleadless Church School/Handsworth Gleadless Council Mixed School/Gleadless Junior and Infant School/Gleadless Nursery First & Middle School.

1884 - 1917	Mr. W. Roberts
20/6/17 - 19/6/18	Mr. F. J. Hinchcliffe (Acting H.T.)
19/6/18 - 17/1/19	Mr. J. R. Hodgson
20/1/19 - 31/10/35	Mr.F. J. Hinchcliffe
2/12/35 - 31/1/44	Mr. J. H. Hawkins
1/ 2/44 - 2/11/64	Mr. J. B. Spir
2/11/64 - 30/3/65	Mr. B. H. Dyson (Acting H.T.)
1/4/65 - 22/7/66	Mr. R. Barlow
6/9/66 - 22/7/83	Mr. D. H. Barratt
1/9/83 -	Mr. C. H. New

Headteachers of Handsworth Gleadless Council Infants School

31/8/94 - 17/5/95	Ada Garrick
18/5/95 - 31/3/15	A. S. Waite
1/4/15 - 26/7/28	H. Bayns-Smith
26/7/28 - 31/10/35	Mr. F. J. Hinchcliffe
31/10/35	As on other list.

Headteachers of Gleadless Temporary Provided School

15/10/06 - 29/3/12	Ada Drewry
29/3/12 - 20/6/17	Mr. W. Roberts
20/6/17	As on other list

Handsworth Gleadless Council Infants School and Gleadless Temporary Provided School eventually merged with the main school.
(Above extract from *"A History of Gleadless School"* pamphlet).

Schooldays remembered

These are just a few comments I received when I asked the question "What do you remember about your schooldays?" Readers will probably have a lot more to add to this collection of memories!

Stan Taylor: "Sam Staton was a teacher at Gleadless School and he was a bit of a character. He had one daughter and I believe they called her Gretel. She married a pal of mine called Jim Jackson. Sam used to live at the bottom of Grassthorpe Road.

I started going to school in 1919 and a Mr. Marples was the caretaker. There wasn't a caretaker's house at the school then, so he lived up the Croft at Hollinsend.

The Headteacher at that time in the seniors was a chap called Mr. Hinchcliffe and the Headteacher in the Juniors was Miss Baynes-Smith who lived in the first bungalow at the corner of Hollinsend Road and Ridgeway Road. Another teacher was Mrs. Biggin, she was a little old lady, Mr. Hopkinson was a character. He wore thick glasses and when he was writing on the blackboard and had his back to you, he'd know what you were doing. Somehow, he could see you by the light reflecting on his glasses. I remember 'im now writing on the board and somebody at the back would be doing something silly and he'd turn around wi' chalk and throw it at them!"

Dolly Worrall: "I was at school in 1909. When we were in the Infants we went to what we called the Lower School (Gleadless First School now) but when we got to Standard 1 and 2 (there were just two Standards in the top school) we'd go back up to the old school (now the Conservative Club). The house next door was the Headmaster's. Mr Roberts was the Head and he was a very stern man but a very, very good man.Everybody had to behave themselves.

There were two Miss Drurys who taught at the school. They were sisters and one was tall and slim and the other was small and plump. They were good teachers though and they lived at Mansfield Road, Intake.

We went to Intake School for cookery lessons. We had to come from Intake School by walking across the fields and there was a pathway down the side of the Church and we crossed the road but it wasn't a road then it was a field (now Ridgeway Road) and we'd come out against the old school.

The School House

During the first World War, there was an Institute where the Conservative Club is now and there was a family called Fisher who lived in the School house. Mr Fisher could play the violin and Mrs Fisher was a very good pianist. It cost 1/6d to go so we used to go there, have a dance and a sing-song with Mr Fisher playing the violin and Mrs Fisher playing the piano. It was a nice get-together.

Mrs Biggins

Little Mrs Biggins was ever so good. She used to make cocoa for the children, ½d for a cup of cocoa. There wasn't school dinners then but you could stay if you wanted. You could take sandwiches and she would make cocoa. She was a smashing little woman. Her husband got killed in the First World War. They stopped women teachers when they got married but they never stopped her because they thought she'd made enough sacrifices with her being a War widow.

Mrs Scattergood

I remember Mrs Scattergood who taught me. Little woman with her hair done in a coffee-pot bob on the top of her head and she asked me if I'd wash the pots because they'd had dinner. So I said, "Yes". But me, whirlwind as usual knocked spout off the teapot. What a calamity! Oh, she was ever so cross. Well, I never remember me Mother ever going down to school either before or after but she went to school.

Mr Roberts said, "Now, Mrs Whattam can we help you today?"

So she said, "Yes".

He said, "Is there something the matter with Dorothy?"

Me Mother said, "She came home and she was very, very upset and it was Mrs Scattergood who upset her!"

"Oh, I'm sorry about that," says Mr Roberts. So he says I'll send for her. So Mrs Scattergood came in and me Mother says, "Now Mrs Scattergood, I don't mind my daughter washing your pots, we have a maid at home to wash ours, but I don't want her upsetting if she has an accident. She was very, very upset." Which I were.

Mrs Scattergood says, "Well, it won't happen again."

Class photo, Gleadless School — 1924 (Mrs Layden)

Front row: Eric Robinson, Tom Ward, Ernest Shaw, Norman Ketridge, Cecil Higgins, Clifford Wakelin, Ernest Staley. *Next row up:* Charlie Patter, Tom Hobson, Lewis Ryder, Ernest Gill, John Deakin, Eric Shaw, Jim Whittaker, Tom Salt. *Next up:* Violet Crouch, Kathy Wattam, Doris Drury, Elsie Simpson, Kathleen Mirfin, Alice Savage, Ada Crouch, Edna Barker, Lilian Froggatt, Lydia Crop. *Next:* Harold Biggin, John Cadman, Eric Lowe, Stanley Allen, Albert Pashley, Cecil Nicholson, Colin Taylor, Richard Stubbs, Albert Broadhead. *Back Row:* Winnie Harrison, Cissie Maxfield, Phyllis Mansell, Mabel Taylor, Elsie Samson, Ethel Blood, Connie Kayly, Lizzie Pearson.

Gleadless School Infants — 1932 (Mrs Freda Cooke)

Front row: Gilbert Gould, Harry Heslop, Frank Corker, Jean Coe, Arthur Crookes, Billy Bennet, Alec Robertson, ?, Alan Robbins. *2nd row:* Charles Shaw, ?, Arthur Corker, Ken Parker, Rosie Burkinshaw, ?, Eileen Torr, Elaine Hotchin, Billy Corker, ?, Agnes Davies, Kenneth Barlow. *3rd row:* Ken Warner, ?, Joyce Eaton, ?, ?, ?, Bob Burger, Billy Burgin, Bette Sayles, Jeff. Lee, Billy Knapton. *Back row:* Molly Pallet, Dorothy Boul, Sensicle Boul, Connie Harding, Brian Cooke, Walter Nettleship, Eddie Finnon, Nellie Maynard, Marjorie Kangley, ?, ?.

Stanley Crofts:

School Discipline

"Sam Staton used to teach the Standard 6 which was the last Standard before you left school. We used to call him a 'tarter' because he kept discipline with a firm hand. He seemed to have eyes in the back of his head because he would be writing on the blackboard with his back to us and suddenly he'd turn round and throw the chalk and hit whoever he wanted to hit. He was a dead shot with the chalk! You'd have a chalk mark on your hair and you daren't go home and tell your parents because they held a teacher as being in their shoes whilst you were at school. In other words they thought that if the teacher had hit you then you must have been doing something wrong, so you deserved to be punished. Nobody complained.

Although the discipline was very hard, at the same time the education we received was marvellous and I'm certain that you couldn't have got a better education than you did at Gleadless Council School. I think Sam Staton and Mr Hinchcliffe's method of teaching, starting from the Infants with Miss Scattergood was brilliant. Sam Staton was a great teacher and so was Mr Hodgkinson who taught Standard 4 (I believe). He came from Hunters Bar to Gleadless. The teachers were all disciplinarians.

School Football Team Pride

At playtime some of the teachers used to play football with us and we'd try and tread on their toes! We used to have pride in playing for the School Football Team. Our shirts used to be green with yellow cuffs and collar. We didn't have a school football pitch so we had to play all our matches away.

I was delighted to have been chosen for a West Riding Council Football Team to play against North East Derbyshire District on Woodhouse Town's Football Ground, where we won 7-2. My Mother had to pledge my elder brother's suit so that I could have some new football boots to play in the match. I have played many representative games since but none so satisfying as that boyhood one when I scored 3!"

Mrs Pass:

School Punishment

"When I first started school a chap called Roberts, Councillor Roberts, was the Headmaster. In the Infants we had a Mrs Biggin and a Miss Scattergood. I didn't like her. She used to hit you. Miss Baynes-Smith was the Infants Headmistress and she used to push your sleeve up and smack you on your arm. Lads used to be stood there waiting to get the cane. Both boys and girls got the cane. There was no playing about. You weren't even allowed to talk in class. The teachers would throw rubbers, books and pieces of chalk at you if they saw you talking.

One of the teachers called Bob Ennis had a voice like thunder! You could hear him shouting at the lads at the "Heeley and Sheffield House"!

At school kids were hit across there behinds with a cane. I liked Sam Staton even though he was keen because whatever you'd got in you he would bring it out.

School Dress

You could wear anything to go to school but we always wore a pinafore and the boys wore short trousers, not long ones. They'd be about 16 before they got long trousers and even baby boys weren't "breeched" until they were about four. They used to wear dresses and when the boys were going to be put into trousers they used to say, "He's going to be breached."

We used to wear black boots called "wrinkers" and then we'd wear button boots which were buttoned with a button hook. Lads used to wear those little short boots and clogs and if they'd no shoes then they didn't come to school. Then the "School Bobby" used to come to your house. They called him "Bobby" Errin who was a big, plump man with a little belly and we used to dread him coming. People would get into trouble if they didn't send their children to school and he would come round to see why you hadn't been to school.

School times

We started school at 9 o'clock in the morning and finished at twelve for dinner. We had two hours dinner time and for those who lived at Ridgeway they needed that time to get home and have dinner and come back again because they had to walk all the way home. School would start at 2 pm in the afternoon and then we'd go on until 4 o'clock."

Mrs Martin:

Best Attendance

"If our class had made the best attendance during the week we were very pleased. We had a red banner that came to a point and had a gold fringe on and it used to say, "Good attendance". We'd hang this red banner up in our class. I think we used to get a half day holiday on a Friday afternoon or we could take a story book to read."

Sweets

If we ever had any money we'd spend it on sweets. I liked Tiger Nuts. These nuts were so sweet and we'd "locusts" as well. These were long and flat in shape and we'd get so many for 1d (old money) and ever so often they'd be seeds in them. They were lovely! We had coconut chips and Rileys Toffee Rolls. Rileys were in Sheffield and their Toffee Rolls were beautiful. You got six Toffee Rolls for a ½d."

Kath Cupit:

"Mr Hinchcliffe was so immaculate. He was a wonderful man and was tall and very straight. He had short, white hair and he always had beautiful, shining shoes. I remember he wore spats and he always wore a handkerchief in his pocket. He used to take us for singing. I don't ever remember him losing his temper.

Sam Staton who I was terrified of, had one daughter who went to Private School. Miss Haigh lived in Granville Road and Miss Drury was an Intake woman who lived in Mansfield Road. Miss Doris Oxley lived at Deep Pits and her family owned a garage called "Oxleys Garage". She took the Infants. Miss Baynes-Smith, the Headmistress was little and dainty but she was very nice.

The main things we did at school were the 3 R's. Reading, Writing and Arithmetic and we didn't have P.T. but we had what we called 'drill' in the yard."

Sam Gill:

"I started school in 1921 and went to Gleadless School. While I was there the teachers I remember were: In the Infants — Miss Baynes-Smith (Headmistress) Mrs Biggin and Miss Oxley. In the Juniors were Standard 2 Miss Rodgers, (3) Miss Revill, (4) Mr Hodgkinson followed by Mr Spir, (5) Miss Millicent Drury, (6) Miss Haigh and Standards 7 & 8 (one class) Sam Staton. "Gaffer" Hinchliffe was the Headmaster over the Juniors. I think there was a Pupil Teacher in the Infants as well.

Miss Rodgers was a 'tartar'. She had a red face and she was always giving you the stick. Miss Drury used to take your 'spice' off you and eat it while you weren't watching. When we were eating spice she used to take it off us then she'd eat all your banana split! Then she'd say, "I'd better give you 2d for some more!"

I used to run errands for Miss Drury. She lived with her old Mother on Mansfield Road and I used to have to run across there with messages now and again.

Swimming lessons

We used to go to the baths with old Sam Staton with our ½d token for car (tram). We went to Park Baths at the bottom of City Road. When you first went you had to stand on the side of the baths and someone shouted, "Anyone that can dive, dive in." Two or three dived in but we'd never been before so we didn't. So we had to stand with our arms raised then a big fella, called Bladderwick used to come behind us and push us in the back and as we fell forward he'd get hold of our ankles and we dived in! We didn't realise that we had dived though! That's how they taught you to swim!

When we went the following week everyone dived in straight away!"

Memories from Frank Cantrill, now living in Australia

"I was not born in Gleadless but my first recollection was the day I started school on the 1st April, 1906. I was not quite four for my Birthday was in July but it is as plain to me as to-day, for I remember Liza Carr, a few years older than me taking me to school. Kids started school at four in those days.

Miss Ellen Ward, "Piggy" Ward's daughter was my first teacher and she was a stern disciplinarian and Miss Waite was the Head Mistress. She was later married to Councillor George Corker for his first wife died. Miss Ward married and became Mrs John Sizer.

"Gaffer" Roberts was the Headmaster and couldn't he use the cane. For years two classes met in the top school and Mrs Scattergood, not being able to send the boys to the Headmaster, used to get the boys to bend over the desk and the dust did fly from the boys' pants. It was a good job we wore corduroy pants as they did take a lot of the sting!"

Gleadless Teachers

Unquestionably, teachers leave a lasting impression (whether good or bad!) on children who carry with them, memories of their teachers into adulthood.

We are often told that "Schooldays are the best days of our life." However true that statement is relies on how much one enjoyed school! For the children of Gleadless growing up in the 20's and 30's, discipline was both strict at home and at school. As one elderly gentleman informed me, "If I told me Mam that I'd been caned at school she would have given me another 'clip' because she thought I must have been doing wrong in the first place and so I deserved it! So I always kept quiet about it if I'd been punished."

Talking in class, untidy work and dirty shoes were just a few examples of how children 'qualified' for caning!

"Sam Staton used to come round every morning and ask if you'd cleaned your shoes. If you hadn't, then it was upstairs for the cane! We couldn't afford a tin of polish and we had to spit on them to try and get them clean!"

Some teachers were over zealous in their discipline as one entry in the School Log Book illustrates:

(1894, written by the Headmaster) "Spoke to Mrs Richardson about the complaints I have had from parents with regard to her striking the children.

Several children have been sent to other schools because of it. I have warned this teacher before and have now informed her that on no account is she to strike or beat any child in her class."

And again in 1900 we discover that one Edith Thorpe had been sent to Intake School because she had informed her Mother that she was afraid of being in Mr Ennis's class as he had struck her twice and dragged her out of the class.

"I (the Headmaster) have spoken to Mr Ennis on the matter but he denies having struck the girl at any time . . ."

Although life at Gleadless School was strict, many children had a true respect for their teachers. Many of the older residents speak of the respect which they had for them and apparently the stricter the teacher the more admiration he gained from his pupils.

"They may have been strict but they always brought out the best in you."

One teacher who is remembered with affection was Miss Emma Haigh whose untimely death brought sadness to the village.

Emma Haigh

Walter Gill: "One of the teachers who taught at Gleadless School, used to live on Gladstone Road (now Ridgeway Road). Mrs Haigh who baked bread and tea cakes lived in a cottage there with her daughter Emma.

Emma Haigh taught me at Gleadless School and I would only be about 5 years old but I remember her saying to me, "Walter come and take this book to the Headmistress."

She always asked me even though I didn't like to go to the Head.

One day she went to town on her bicycle and she got under a steam waggon and it killed her. I think she'd be about 25 or 26 years old. That was in 1915 when it happened."

R. Martin: "Miss Haigh was killed when she was only 18, I think she'd be. She taught the Infants. I shall always remember as they came past with the coffin we all came out of the school, all the children did. We were all crying because we liked her that much. It was a terrible tragedy. She'd gone to town on her bicycle and had an accident. She was buried in Intake Cemetery."

Miss Haigh's accident happened on the 1st September 1915 and the entry in the School Log Book written by the Headmaster, Mr Roberts reads as follows:

2.9.1915. 'Miss Haigh, a teacher in the Infant Department, was on her bicycle in Sheffield last night, when she was knocked down and killed by a motor lorry. Miss Haigh had been at the school for twenty years, as scholar, pupil teacher and Assistant. She was a great favourite with both scholars and teachers and her death has cast a gloom over the whole school. I was in Sheffield most of the day, trying to secure the return of her two brothers from France. Miss Haigh leaves a widowed mother of whom she was the mainstay.'

A more detailed account is given here by a Sheffield Daily Telegraph reporter:

Emma Haigh's Funeral

From Sheffield Daily Telegraph (Sheffield Local Studies Lib. microfilm)
Monday Sept. 6th 1915.

Villagers' Grief

Sheffield Teacher buried at Gleadless

Amid many manifestations of grief the funeral took place at Gleadless, yesterday afternoon, of Miss Emma Haigh, of 19, Gladstone Road, Gleadless. Miss Haigh was the victim of a collision that occurred in Abbeydale Road, Sheffield last week, between her bicycle and a heavy steam lorry, which ran over her, death being instantaneous. The accident is the subject of an adjourned inquiry.

The whole village of Gleadless now mourns her loss, for Miss Haigh was born there 25 years ago, attended at the Gleadless Council Schools until the age of 14, when she became a pupil teacher in the school, and continued as such until the day of her death. Possessed of a very winning personality, her influence was very strong in the infants dept. where she taught. Hence it was that the tiny tots of the school were in prominent and pathetic evidence at the closing sorrowful scenes.

Assembled round the graveside, under their headmistress, Miss Baynes Smith, each child paid her last respects to "Teacher" with a spray of flowers. Lining the path to the church doors the other depts., of the school paid a similar tribute; while the headmaster, Mr W. Roberts, read the lesson at the impressive choral service that was conducted in the quaint old parish church by the Vicar, the Rev. C.T. Crossland. One of the hymns sung was, "Peace, perfect Peace," and at the close of the service Chopin's "Marche Funebre" was played by Mr G.C. Ricks, the organist. The church was crowded with the villagers.

The chief mourners were Mrs Haigh (her widowed mother) the Misses C & A Haigh (sisters) Mr & Mrs Taylor (brother-in-law and sister-in-law) Mrs M. Haigh (sister-in-law) Mr & Mrs W. Hamilton, Mr Harry Thompson and Mr and Mrs F. Haigh (uncles and aunts) and several cousins of the deceased. Councillors Atkin, Corker and Herring represented the Handsworth Education Committee and Councillor Potts of Intake was also present. The floral tributes were numerous.

Two of Miss Haigh's brothers are with the Coldstream Guards in France and could not get leave to attend the funeral.

Sam Staton

Sam Staton spent his entire teaching life at Gleadless School. Sam, it seems was 'part of the building'. Everyone I spoke to had something to say about this most unforgettable teacher! Although a fierce disciplinarian, the children had a deep respect for him. This respect was shown on his retirement from school when his service to 'his' school was recognised. I quote from the School Log book the entry when Sam (sorry I mean Sir) retired!

Sam Staton retires

21.12.49. "Mr Sam Staton retired from the Teaching Profession. The children presented him with a fountain pen and pencils, an autograph album containing several hundreds of signatures of scholars past and present and members of staff, colleagues and ex-colleagues, and a collection from parents, teachers and friends resulted in the presentation of a cheque for £25. A fitting recognition of great service and a tribute to Mr Staton's loyalty and devotion to duty. Sam Staton started his career at Gleadless as a pupil teacher in 1905."

Mrs R. Mottershaw

(ex Gleadless Schoolteacher)

"I believe I started teaching at Gleadless School in 1939 or 40. The school where I had been teaching was blitzed. I was at Gleadless School eight years and I left in 1948 to go to a new school at Charnock and Mrs Mundy went there too.

I was there another eight or nine years until 1956 or 57. Then I got a transfer because my daughter Margaret was going to take the Sheffield scholarship exam. and in Derbyshire of course they were training them for the Derbyshire exam. but because we lived in Sheffield she would have to take the Sheffield exam so I brought her back to the little school, the church school and then we found our holidays were different. That's when I applied for a transfer to Hemsworth and I was at Hemsworth another eight or nine years. I retired from Hemsworth in 1960.

Class sizes

Miss Mander was at Gleadless for years and she had the reception class and I do remember when she had classes of 90! Some of them were on another register because she wasn't allowed to have them all on one register. I don't know how she managed!

At school then we went on ability and not age. Children would go up to the next class not by their age but by their ability. I don't know that

I particularly remember this at Gleadless but when I was at school, when I was in Standard 2 we would have some school leavers amongst us. They hadn't managed any better than that. At Gleadless though some children remained behind in one class for about one year but no longer, but they were always a year behind.

When I was in Standard 7 we had Standard 7 & 8 together and we had 60 in the class. We were sitting three at a desk to get 60 children in. At the end of the year the teacher had a nervous breakdown!

The Merit Certificate

On top of that in those days was the Merit Certificate. Mr Sharpe was the Director of Education in Sheffield and he brought in what was called a Merit Certificate Exam. so you had an exam. in Standard 7 where you either did or didn't gain merit and one in Standard 8 and she (the teacher) had two lots together in that class, some training for Standard 7 merit, some training for the Standard 8 so it wasn't just plain straightforward teaching and of course in those days you only took a scholarship exam if you intended going and you actually went to that school you wanted to go to, to take your scholarship exam. I went to the Pupil Teacher's centre and I think we had about two days exams. and I took my exam there."

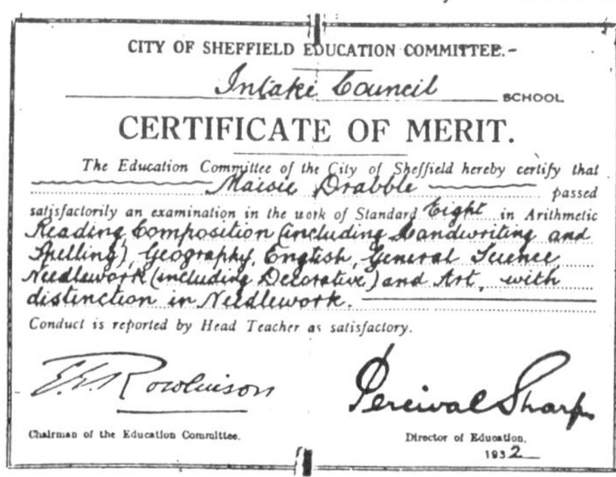
CITY OF SHEFFIELD EDUCATION COMMITTEE.

Intake Council SCHOOL

CERTIFICATE OF MERIT.

The Education Committee of the City of Sheffield hereby certify that Maisie Drabble passed satisfactorily an examination in the work of Standard Eight in Arithmetic Reading, Composition (including Handwriting and Spelling), Geography, English, General Science Needlework (including Decorative) and Art, with distinction in Needlework.

Conduct is reported by Head Teacher as satisfactory.

F. W. Rowlinson — Chairman of the Education Committee.

Percival Sharp — Director of Education.

1932

The Merit Certificate
This was no bigger than an old driving licence.

Stanley Crofts recalls: "I left school in 1926 with a red Merit certificate with a Distinction in Mathematics. The said certificate was of no use, as boys were all destined to work in the Pits and your only recommendation was your father or brothers, who were already working there."

Mrs Mottershaw continues:

The Headmaster's room

"In the early days of course there was no Headmaster's room on the top corridor. Tht was built up out of the corridor when Mr Spir came, I believe. He had that done. The Headmaster used to take a class and before he had his own private room he used to have his things in his classroom.

We didn't have a staff room at all so we had to sit in a classroom. In fact after the Head's room had been built on the top corridor, we used to sit in the classroom which was next to mine and Mr Bradley's and we'd sit and talk in that room at dinner time. There was no staff room.

School dinners

School dinners started while I was at Gleadless. Before that the children either brought sandwiches or went home and if they brought sandwiches, of course they just sat in the classroom and ate them and there were no provisions made of any sort.

There wasn't a dining room. The staff brought sandwiches and some of them used to send out and have a hot dinner, a person made them and they were brought in but not many did that. No, mostly we took sandwiches and of course the staff toilet was across the yard, in one corner.

The children

Gleadless School was a much smaller school than it is now. One thing I remember was that one child who was in school was what was known as a blue baby. She had some heart defect and when she was about seven years old she was taken to London to have what was then a very, very new operation to counteract this heart trouble.

When she was at school we had to watch her because one of her favourite tricks was climbing walls and chasing around, even though the child's heart was so bad that she could have dropped dead at any time but when she returned from London the blue had gone and everybody was thinking that she was well on the road to recovery but she had a sudden relapse and died. Well, when she was dead all the neighbours and children were invited in to look at her in the coffin, this was an old custom.

She was in the room where she lived which was one of those little cottages further down Hollinsend Road below the school and most of the children had been inside the house and seen this child, which seems terrible to me but they came back with stories about, "Oh well she's not blue now Miss." They never worried about it. You know you were 'Miss' no matter whether you're married or not. But this was the custom, to go in and see the person who died. I suppose it was paying your last respects.

The Hollinsend and Gleadless children were pretty much alike in that they were all country children. Gleadless had been taken into Sheffield by the time I was at the school but the children all mixed with each other. Perhaps the Hollinsend children were, shall we say, from poorer homes and they had no hot water and things like that, but so were some of the Gleadless children.

Mostly, their parents would be colliers or farm labourers. You see they'd started building on Gleadless Common in those days. There was a difference that some were better dressed than others and perhaps not quite as rough but the Hollinsend children were quite a nice set of children. They'd roughed it more perhaps but on the whole we didn't have the nasty children.

Jaunty Lane was of course our favourite nature walk; there were all sorts of wild flowers and things down there which of course have gone forever now.

Gleadless schoolchildren outside the old school, 1890/95 (Mrs Mottershaw)
William Hallam is on Miss Richardson's immediate left.
The teacher was aged about 16 years old.

Gleadless School in the Nineteenth Century

When my Father William Hallam was a little boy (he was born in 1876) he went to the old school which is now the Conservative Club on Hollinsend Road. There were only two classrooms there. The Headmaster took the boys in one room and a Miss Richardson (not Nora Richardson already mentioned) took the girls in a classroom at the other side. Miss Richardson (when out of school) was never given the name of Richardson, she was always referred to as Butcher Richardson's daughter because her father kept the little old fashioned butcher's shop along Gleadless Road.

The Militia

Once a year, at the old school, the Militia used to come. They exercised in a big field opposite the school. There's some houses built there now.

They came in their usual red coats and you know clay pipe and trousers etc., and to the children that was a very great day but they weren't given a holiday so the little boys used to offer to carry the forms inside for people to sit on who came to the display and they 'forgot' to come out again!

My Father told me that when he was absent from school, Miss Richardson herself used to come to the cottage where he lived to enquire why he hadn't been to school and he said that very often he would see her coming down the lane and he'd pop out through the window at the back and across the fields before she came so he wasn't there!"

Mr Vincent Bradley, O.B.E.

(ex Gleadless Schoolteacher)

Mr Bradley spent 23 years teaching at Gleadless School before leaving to take a Deputy Headship at Nether Green School. From early childhood he was always interested in music. His Father played various musical instruments, including the violin and organ, while his grandfather, Frank Bradley made cellos.

At an early age, Vincent began his musical career by playing the violin. His life reflects the deep love he has for his music and anyone who has spoken to him cannot but be impressed with his outstanding knowledge of music. For many years he produced a Music Programme for "Radio Sheffield", while his Music Appreciation classes, run by the W.E.A., continued for 22 years! His many achievements were recognised when he was awarded the O.B.E.

I was fortunate to talk at length to Mr Bradley, about his work as a teacher and his musical interests. The two, as his teaching life developed, became inter-related. Mr Bradley relates here, his time spent as a teacher at Gleadless School.

Early Days

"I first went to Gleadless School as a Pupil Teacher which was the year you did before you went to College, possibly to find out if you were suitable for the job. The Pupil Teaching year was spent in school. I was a Pupil Teacher in 1930 and the Head then was Mr F.J. Hinchcliffe. At the end of my P.T. year he said that when I came out of College, if I wanted to come back to Gleadless School, then to let him know.

So I went to College and when I'd finished I got in touch with Mr Hinchcliffe and returned to Gleadless School where I stayed until the war.

After my war service I returned to the school. It was a jolly good school and I liked it but I was told if I wanted to get promotion then I would have to move. I was reluctant to leave but when the chance of being Deputy Head at Nether Green School came, I took it. Later I became the Head of Darnall Church School and then Hucklow Road School, which was known as the Music School! I finished my teaching career there when I retired.

Time Table

I introduced recorders and music to the children at Gleadless. Also I was the first teacher to attempt project work with the Senior 4th year pupils. They were the extra year pupils and I did a project on "Sheffield" with them. This was 1947-48.

However, the Time Table was formal under Mr Hinchcliffe. There was a time table framed and you had to keep to it or else! If your time table said History and you went over five minutes into the English lesson, then you were in trouble. Mr Hinchcliffe used to come in and point out that you'd run over your time in History.

It produced results. The children could read, write and spell and knew their tables. It was geared to the 11 + exam. I think Mr Hinchcliffe's object in life was to get as many children through the exam. as possible. To give them a chance of a Grammar School education.

Mr Hinchcliffe

I saw three Headmasters when I was at Gleadless. Mr Hinchcliffe was a strict disciplinarian. Not only did the children quake in their shoes when he did his rounds but the young teachers did as well!

You had to stand up to teach and not sit down on a chair. You daren't wear a pullover because if you weren't properly dressed, Mr H. would gently point out that you looked as if you were off for a round of golf! You wore a suit with a jacket and a waistcoat.

After Mr Hinchcliffe, came John Spir who was tragically killed in a car accident.

Discipline

The discipline at Gleadless was like an iron rod. You had a cane which you waved! Some teachers used it of course but I very rarely did. We had a high desk and a high chair (I believe they're in Museums now aren't they?) so that the teacher towered above the children. Some teachers' opening gambit was to put the cane on the desk just as a warning and it worked well.

Sam Staton

Sam was part of the building! He was a 100% disciplinarian. The kids liked him but they daren't move a finger out of place when Sam was taking the class. They had to have absolute silence and 100% concentration on what he was talking about. He was one of the strictest disciplinarians that I've ever come across but he got results. I think the kids appreciated him. There was no messing about in his lessons.

Sam was a Pupil Teacher, then went to College and after returned to Gleadless School and stayed there until he retired. He spent all his life in Gleadless School! He was synonymous with the School. The kids were scared of him but yet they respected him. He was a jolly good teacher but a tough disciplinarian. That was what he was noted for. When he walked into the room, there was a deathly silence and he got on with it. He used the cane if it was necessary. When you're faced with sixty kids as we were, you had to show them who was boss. If you were a bit weak then the kids would take over.

Gleadless School Teachers. Date prior 1949 — around 1946 (Mrs Smith)
Back row: Miss Taylor/Richard Pashley/Miss Abrahams
Middle row: Cyril Lancaster (caretaker)/Rose Mottershaw/Rob G. Davie/Vincent Bradley/Normal Iosson/M.D. Matthews
Front row: Miss Mundy/Miss Hardwick/John B. Spir/Sam Staton/Miss Elsie Mander/Mrs Lowe.
Mr Spir was killed in a road accident on 30th October, 1964. Sam Staton retired from Gleadless School in December 1949, after starting his teaching career at Gleadless as a pupil teacher in 1905.

Class size

It used to be the teacher against sixty children. My first class was 59 at 21 years old. I was lucky because I didn't get 60. That's why you had to have discipline. When it's one against sixty, you had to show them who was boss. It was "Sir", "Yes Sir" or "No Sir".

Lesson notes

There were eight lessons a day. Four in the morning and four in the afternoon and I had to write notes on each of those eight lessons. Every day I had to put these notes on Mr Hinchcliffe's desk before 9 in the morning and he would come and sit at the back of the classroom and listen to them. Your speech always had to be grammatically correct.

Rural School

When I first went to Gleadless, it ws a very rural school. Not like a city school at all. It was out in the wilds, surrounded by fields. A nice little school with the emphasis on work. They were some very bright pupils there. I've met some of them since and they've won Honours Degrees and the like.

What was a bit shattering to me, was when a kid came up to me and said, "You taught my Mum!"

I was there long enough to have done that, having started in 1930, leaving for the war and returning in 1946 before leaving in 1953.

Twenty three years I was at Gleadless School. I thought the first one who comes and says, "You taught my Grand-Dad," I'm going!

But that never happened!"

Empire Day

Empire Day was a National event which was not only celebrated by Gleadless schoolchildren but the rest of the country too.

When in 1906 Sheffield held an Empire Day Pageant at the Bramall Lane Football Ground, huge numbers of schoolchildren took part. They were drilled and rehearsed for weeks before the event and formed a tableaux representing the colonies.

"One girl had the special honour of acting the part of Britannia and entered the arena on a cart drawn by 120 boys in sailor suits and escorted by another 300: 3,360 boys in appropriately coloured clothing made up a huge 'real' living, moving, speaking Union Jack; there were four military bands in full review order; hymns written specially for the occasion were sung; and inevitably the ground was packed to capacity." (P. Harvey Book 1, p. 16.)

That excellent description portrays the lengths the children had to go to, to celebrate Empire Day for that was a very special day when everyone showed their patriotism to King and Country.

Gleadless children showed the same enthusiasm.

"On Empire Day we used to march and sing. We'd sing songs all about wars and the teacher would play the piano." *(Mrs Pass)*

Empire Day Celebrations at Gleadless School, 24th May 1917 (?) (Mrs Pass)
Two children on far left unknown. Esmond Hinchcliffe (with flag), Harold Ryder (kneeling), Ethel Gill (now Pass), Doris Cadman (Britannia) now Mrs Frank Fidler, Boy kneeling unknown, Margaret Kenion (now Hanley) Eric Wilson, Raymond Wattam, Emma Dawson (now Bellamy) and Janet Layden.

Mrs Martin recalls: "We used to celebrate Empire Day at school and we were preparing for it for weeks. We held the celebrations in the school yard and it always seemed to be fine weather in those days! Empire Day was always held on 24th May and all the girls wore a sash. Some wore a white one, some a blue and some red and we used to have drills and sing:

'What is the meaning of Empire day
Why do the cannons roar
Why do they cry God Save the King
Echo from shore to shore

Why does the flag of Britannia float
Proudly from mast to main
Why do they cry God Save the King
On glorious Empire Day
On glorious Empire Day

On our Nation's scroll of glory
Ever more we homage pay
To our banner proud
That has never bowed
And that's the meaning of Empire Day

On Empire Day, so many soldiers who had been wounded in the First World War, were invited to the school. They came from Wharncliffe Hospital and they had their tea in the school yard. I remember that they wore pale blue uniforms which were like a coat and trousers."

The games children played

Games are inevitably an essential part in the life of children and to the children of Gleadless playing games was a welcome relief from the hard times they lived in.

There was no special time for children to play certain games. Weeks would go by with everyone at school skipping madly until one day some child would come to school with a bag of marbles or a whip and top and then suddenly everyone else would do the same.

Many games had been handed down from earlier generations, ring games and ball games with rhymes to accompany them, although some of the words would have lost their original meaning.

Some of the games needed more than one child to play them but it was nothing to see a small solitary child, pig-tailed and pinafored, skipping. Mothers would have disliked the skipping craze because it wore out so much boot leather but skip the children did. In some better off areas, children possessed proper ropes with nicely shaped wooden handles all painted red and blue, but not in Gleadless, for poor children had to be content with any old bit of thick rope they could get hold of which was usually 'orange' rope. Skipping games often started with a slowly spoken jingle, 'Salt, mustard, vinegar, pepper', before being speeded up to finish with a 'one hundred'.

There was quite an art in skipping. Some children progressed to skipping backwards and if they could jump in the air while the rope twirled twice under their feet then they were really happy!

Whip and top was another popular game. This time the art was in keeping the top going by just thrashing it with a whip. Of course there was marbles or 'mabs' as they were referred to. Both boys and girls played this game but it was really considered more of a boy's game with the 'mabs' being carried in flannel bags secured tightly at the top with a thread of tape.

Hop-scotch was played too and 'beds' would be marked out with a piece of rough stone. The 'bed' consisted of six large squares joined together and in each square a number was written. The art of this game was to slide a small, flattish stone from one square to the next by hopping on one foot and gently kicking the stone along with the other so that it landed right on the number. The stone landing on a line or sliding too far meant that the player had to start again. The winner was the one who completed the game without any faults.

Of course the children's free time wasn't all games; very often away from school there were errands to be 'run' and jobs to do. Of the games mentioned here, only a few are played today either by Gleadless children or children elsewhere. In an age which was free from sophisticated toys, children of yesteryear just had to make do with any odds and ends they could turn into a toy or make into a game. This they managed to do admirably — together with a good helping of a child's imagination!

Mrs Thorpe:

Skipping

"We used to skip with what we called 'orange ropes'. These were the ropes that were tied around the orange boxes that had come from abroad. They were like plaited ropes and very strong and very long because they wrapped them round the orange boxes for handling purposes. We used to go to all the fruit shops and say, "Have you got any orange rope?"

If you were lucky you'd get one. The ropes were so long that two girls held the rope (one at each end) and about five or six of us could skip in the middle. We had a really good time doing that. At home we'd play in yard skipping and if you had a small piece of rope you could skip on your own."

Mrs Pass:

Football. A pig's bladder

"When a pig had been killed we used to wait for its bladder so we could use it as a football. That's the only type of football we ever had. We used to blow up the bladder and kick it.

Down Hollinsend Road, was a fruit shop called 'Flowers' and we had to wait while the fruit man came and brought a box of oranges and then we queued to try and get the rope that tied the boxes. The rope was then used as a skipping rope."

Rose Martin:

Tied 'Snecks'

"There was no vandalism then. I think the worst thing they did was to tie (the houses were in rows) the 'snecks' of the doors with a piece of string together (with the next door) and then knock at each door and wait for the people to come and try and open them.

But when it was dark we had to be in. There was no wireless or T.V. then and one of the games we played was called Cherry Stones.

Cherry Stones

"We'd save cherry stones and then get a shoe box. (Shoes came in boxes then. They didn't put your shoes in a bag when you bought them). We'd make holes in the lid and number them one to ten. We played by throwing the cherry 'wabs' (we called them that) to try and get them in the holes. If a stone went in number ten hole then you had to give the person you were playing with, ten cherry stones. We carried on playing like that. A few of us would play at that game.

'Mabs'

We also played at 'mabs'. They were made out of glass and we used to say, "Up your longs". There was a long run up to the hole in the ground, about six yards it would be. There were three holes and we had to try and get the mabs into the three holes. We'd go up and down playing these three holes and when we were on our last hole we used to say, "I'm on my 'lolls'" (last). The person who finished all the three holes first, won. This was really a boy's game.

"Peggy"

Lads or young fellas played at "Peggy". For this they had a piece of wood shaped and they placed a stone on it. Then they'd hit the stone with a stick and it went up in the air and whoever knocked the stone the furthest won. They'd mark it on in strides. That was another game that's gone now."

Another version of "Peggy" is related by *Mr Robertson*. "We used to have a big stone and stand it up and put another stone on top of "Peggy" stone. We had some wooden balls (the ones from the fairground which they used to throw at the coconuts) and then we'd try and knock the stone off."

Rose Martin:

Whip and Top

"Girls used to play with a shuttlecock and a 'battleboard' as well as playing with whips and tops,as did the boys. The boys used to have a peg which had a sharp point and they'd wrap cord round it and throw it. At the bottom of the top was a steel peg.

The girls had tops that were flat in shape and they'd set it spinning and it would spin for a long time. They'd even get the top onto their hand and drop it down again while it was still spinning."

"We used to put a penny on the ground. Spin a top, pick it up on your hand and then knock the penny out of the ring." *(Mr Robertson)*

Peg Tops

"We'd play at rounders, skipping and whips and tops. The lads had what we called Peg Tops. It was a top with like a peg in the bottom and they'd wrap a cord round it and throw it. Then it would keep going by itself." *(Mrs Pass)*

The Champion Shuttlecock player!

"We had shuttlecocks. Some had four feathers but the 'posh' shuttlecocks which the 'posh' kids had, had a lot of feathers and they were rubber at the bottom or cork and had fancy little pictures stuck on. Mine was only common wood!

We'd knock the shuttlecocks up and hit it with a 'battleboard' (a bat).

Auntie Maggie was a Champion shuttlecock player! She used to win the Shuttlecock Competition which was held at the bottom of Gleadless Common. To be Champion it was for how high you could knock it up and how many times and she won it." *(Mrs Pass)*

Mr Robertson:

Dollies

"Dollies were marbles but they were like iron and we'd put so many dollies in a ring then stand back and try and knock so many out of the ring. We'd roll our "dolely" up and those we'd knock out of the ring we'd keep in our little bag. We'd all take it in turns trying to knock them out so that we could win some other people's marbles."

Some games like marbles, skipping and peg tops could be played at school or at home but there were some that were definitely played away from school. One such game was called "Da le Vo".

Playing on the road was not allowed and farmers frowned on any youngsters daring to play in their fields. Apart from the backyard then the woods would probably have been the best available 'playing ground' for Gleadless children.

However, children being children, they did find exciting places to hide away from one another and have their fun and as *Mr Robertson* relates:

De le Vo

"We used to make two dens on the road. There were two teams that could play 'da le vo'. There were six on each side. One side used to go and hide in the fields or under the rhubarb leaves or anywhere they could find, while the other team stayed in the dens (the dens belonged to just one side). Then they'd come out and try and catch you and if they did you had to go and stay in one of the dens.

If you could get to the den without the other side seeing you then you could go in the den and release the others who had already been caught. When all the players on one side had been captured then we changed over and the other team went out and got hidden and we had to find them then. That's when the 'Bobby' (the policeman) gave us a 'clip' for playing 'de le vo' on the road."

Singing Rhymes

Children usually had a jingle or a chant that they would sing while skipping or bouncing a ball and one such little song went as follows:

"There came three Jews across from Spain
To ask you for your daughter Jane
But your daughter Jane is far too young
Go away we cannot stand you song."

Walter Gill: "That's how we used to sing when we were playing. One game I do remember playing was called *"Duck Stone".* We'd play in the pinfold (the pinfold at this time was not where cattle were kept but was a depot for heavy stones etc. which was used by workmen). We'd stand a big stone upright (like a kerb stone) and the person who was 'on' put their stone on top of this and we'd all try and knock it off by throwing stones at it. If we managed to knock it off then we all had to run and try and pick our stones up and come back with them before the person who was 'on' could put theirs back on."

Many of the games played by Gleadless children in the 20's and 30's have failed to survive today. Marbles and football are still played but only recently there was a National Campaign to try and encourage children to skip again in an effort to make them fitter.

There were, however, more unorthodox games indulged in and certainly NOT to be played! Like taking your sister in an old pushchair and pushing it to the top of a tip, then letting go and hoping that the person at the bottom would manage to 'save' (stop) the pram. As one participant of the 'game' confessed, "The pram didn't always finish the right way up!" Such brotherly love!

But as they say, "Children will be children!"

8. LEISURE

In theory, at least, the people in the period mentioned in this book would have had less leisure in their lives than we do today. The hours people worked were a great deal longer but nevertheless Gleadless people seem to have found time to enjoy more things in life than work.

For most people living at this time possibly the pressure of work itself was less intense and in a country village, which Gleadless was in the twenties, it was possible to pause for a while and pass the time of day with a neighbour who happened to be walking by. There seemed to be no lack of entertainment in the village but it was made by the villagers themselves. Perhaps it is fair to say that our grandparents were much better at providing their own entertainment than we are today. The Church provided an outlet for leisure activities as well as fulfilling the villagers' religious needs with both the Methodists and Independents fielding excellent football and cricket teams!

The miner, apart from visiting his 'local' and racing his pigeons, was often a keen gardener too. Everybody did their garden whether to grow produce to eat, or to cultivate flowers to show at the local Flower Show.

Excitement was in the air when it was 'Feast Week', when nearly all the villagers would hurry down to Hollinsend or Intake to enjoy 'all the fun of the fair'. This travelling Fair was eagerly awaited, especially by the children who would try and 'lend a hand' to the fairground people so that they would be offered free 'goes' on the many rides, in return. Usually, the 'Feast' week was in August, every year and the noise and brightly painted roundabout horses provided a kaleidoscope of colour to the area.

If the men enjoyed their football and cricket what did the women do? Apart from joining the Church activities, such as the ladies sewing circle, there seems to have been very little leisure time for women. The demands on them with their large families, cooking, baking bread, washing and ironing, left them with no real time for leisure pursuits. Any free time would have been taken up earning some extra money. Jobs such as pea and potato picking and taking in washing, were quite common amongst women at this time.

The celebration of Whitsuntide was always a prime event in the village with the sun always seeming to shine then!

Hetty Hobson remebers that on, "Whit Monday we would go round singing with the Chapel and then come back to the Sunday School afterwards and a meal would be provided for us. We would go in Charnock

Hall field (where the Supermarket is today) and play games. They would bring our food in baskets and bring it into the fields so that we all ate in there and then after we had eaten we played competitions. When all the Charnock fields had been taken for building land we then had to go as far away as Clumber Park because we'd nowhere really to play."

Dolly Worrall: "Charnock Hall Farm was lovely. When the Wesleyan Chapel had a do on Whit Monday they always held it in the field. I remember there was a pond in front of the Farm and we used to race round it and once I won. Do you know what the prize was? A penny! Oh, it was a good prize."

The late Reg. Cartledge: "The highlights of the village life in those days for kiddies and for teenagers even, was Whitsuntide with the Whit tea and fun and games. Same at Bank Holiday Monday and 'o course we 'ad Norton Show. A lot of the locals used to take their produce there and during the winter nights it was socials in the Sunday Schools or concerts. We 'ad our own little concert parties and all that and well, frankly they were the only things that there was to do in the village then. There wasn't even a wireless. We hadn't even got a local cinema (The 'Rex' was to come later). Eventually they built the Manor Cinema at the top which is now a supermarket. They built that in the 1920's and there used to be a great big snooker hall underneath."

Dolly Worrall: "They used to have a Show at Gleadless, an agricultural show in the fields near Gleadless Hill. The Show was held in there and they all used to be competing, who's got the biggest onions, who's got the best cauliflowers? It was really a matter of life and death. If you didn't win at Gleadless Show you were a poor thing."

Walter Cook: "What I really looked forward to was the 'Field Day'. That was held in fields opposite our cottage at Lane End. There was one field that belonged to Charlie Richardson and then the next field which were Arthur Shaws. They had sports for kiddies and one marquee for the big vegetable show. Intake Jazz band and Intake Prize Band used to come and play. Everybody in area had some sort of show though."

Stanley Crofts: "I even remember Gleadless Chase. It was a running race and our Arthur came second in it one year. They used to start off somewhere near Teddie Hoyland's place.

I always liked boxing and down Bartle Road was a family called Linley. Mr Linley was an old boxer and he decided to teach his boys to box and then he encouraged some of the boys in the village to go down and train to box.

But what was a great treat for the children of Gleadless was when they used to run race trips from the 'New Inn'. They'd go to all the race meetings, like Doncaster and York. The men and women used to go in Sedgewick's charabanc but when they came back they would bring their kids butterscotch and Pontefract cakes. But the kids' biggest treat was when Mr Sedgewick used to put all kids in charabanc and take them all for a run round. That was great!

At the 'Red Lion' on the back window was a verandah where Charlie Bryant used to sell meat. They had a bowling green and pigeon cotes behind the pub as well. Charlie Bryant timed a pigeon in a day from San Sebastian and he won a gold medal for pigeon racing. He'd plates with beautiful paintings of pigeons on."

Hetty Hobson: "We used to think it was a long way when we travelled to Baslow in the horse and cart (waggonette). We had a charabanc and a waggonette and who ever went in charabanc came back in waggonette so that it was fair!"

Football and Cricket

Every village had its football and cricket teams and Gleadless and Hollinsend were no exception. It was often said that if the visiting football team playing at Hollinsend won, then invariably they would be chased out of the village! Teams usually met and changed at the local pub, as there were no specially designed Sports Pavilions in those days. The earliest Gleadless Football Team photograph shows the team outside the 'Heeley and Sheffield' house complete with Manager and Trainer! Just below the 'Heeley & Sheffield' pub was the field that was used as the local football and cricket pitch. The Chapel Field (now the site of the new Gleadless houses and bungalows, just off the Common) was another field used as a recreation ground by the independents.

The games were played with tremendous village rivalry and produced some excellent footballers who would have played well in any 'Professional' football team.

Stan Taylor:

Tom Critchlow

"Tom was one of the older members of a large family that lived on the Common. He was a big, strong and rough but great hearted miner and a member of the local football team which was formed from members of the 'New Inn' pub. The pitch was a field near the top of what we knew as Gleadless Hill and as there were no stripping accommodation on it, the teams had to use a room in the 'New Inn' and then walk the few hundred yards on the main road to the field, dressed in full soccer kit and heavy studded football shoes.

Tom never liked this because it hurt his feet and many times, when the match had only been in progress a short time, you would see him take his shoes off and play in his stockings! He was so strong and fit he could still kick the ball harder and further than most members of the team."

Gleadless Football Team outside the 'Heeley & Sheffield' pub (The late Mrs West)
Standing: Bob Hotchin, Billy Marples, Harry Hardwick, Jim Marclew/?/?/Tom Urton/?/?/?/?/Tom Critchlow, Fred Elliott.
Sitting: George Elliott, ?/?/Billy Coe/?

It was also said of Tommy that he was so good at football that all the teams wanted him to play for them but it all depended on what mood he was in before he decided! Football was played with great vigour — too much sometimes and occasionally accidents and injuries did occur. Billy Marples sustained a bad accident whilst playing football and never fully recovered from it. But games were played for sheer enjoyment and a relief from the dark, dismal mines.

The late Reg. Cartledge: "I've seen the days when we (The Independents) had two football teams, two cricket teams and tennis courts going on there (In the Chapel Fields). We played football and cricket on there and across in Hollinsend Park as it is now. By the way the Hollinsend recreation ground was opened about 1930 and in 1931 the bowling green was opened. The bowling club was formed in 1932. Well, they held a boy's tournament in 1931 and I've still got the medal."

I mentioned earlier that some of the men who played in the local village football teams were good enough to be professional footballers. One such man was **Joe Sykes**.

Stan Taylor: "Joe Sykes used to live in a cottage at the side of the 'Old Harrow' and when we were lads he used to come home in the summer months. Of course we were football fanatics and we used to really delight in going and listening to old Joe tell us about his career. We'd only be about eight or nine but I can see Joe now. He used to sit on an old seat at top o' what we used to call Long Fields which went from side o' the church right up to the back of the 'Old Harrow' and old Joe used to tell us kids all about his footballing career.

He played at centre-half for Sheffield Wednesday but then he went to Swansea Town and biggest part of his career was with Swansea, and he was made Captain there. It would be in the 1910's when Joe was playing. He had a tremendously long career in football."

Hollinsend Rovers F.C. (1934) (Photo Jack Marriott)
The team outside the 'Noah's Ark' pub, Hollinsend.
Back group: Jim Barraclough (sec.), M. Harris/?/Mr Spottswood, Charlie Beatty, Lawrence Beatty, Johnny Potts, Ernest Shaw, Ernest Lanes, Henry Briggs.
Front row: Frank 'Nut' White, Arnold Parker, Jack Heaton, **Jack Marriott**, Sam Marriott, Leonard Heaton and Jack White.

Jack Marriott was another local man who played football professionally. He played football in Hollinsend with a team called 'Hollinsend Rovers' but began his footballing career as an apprentice at Bramall Lane in 1936.

Jack Marriott (Centre Forward/Inside Forward)

Football career details:

1936 Bramall Lane apprentice
1943 Doncaster Football Club. Played 5½ - 6 years as a professional footballer there.
1949 - 51 Transferred to Southport.
1951 - 53 2 years at Boston United.
1953 - 55 2 years at Scarborough Football Club, then retired.
Played Cup matches Northern Section 1947 Championship.
(1945 - 46 season scored 7 goals.)

'The Humbug' at Gleadless Town End

Opposite the 'Red Lion' was a piece of waste land that once acted as a pinfold where animals were kept while farmers refreshed themselves in the pub while on their way to either the market or slaughterhouse with their livestock.

Later a wooden hut was built on this land and was used by some of the locals as a meeting place either for socials, whist drives or for the occasional Saturday night dance (This was before the 'Azena' ballroom was built). Mrs Cox (known as 'Granny' Cox) lived in the little cottages at Town End and supervised many of the dances held there.

The 'Humbug' or 'Bug Hut', Gleadless Town End (Mr & Mrs H. Hobson)

Referred to affectionately as 'The Humbug' because of its black and white stripes or 'The Bug Hut' (no explanation needed!) this little hut was a favourite with both young and old as *Ted Higgins* writing from Canada indicates. "My first recollections of Gleadless go back to about 1934/5 when as a child I used to accompany my parents to the weekly whist drives, held in the wooden hut known as 'The Humbug'. It was aptly named due to the black and white decor of its exterior surface. Vertical stripes, as I remember it. I have no idea of its 'raison d'etre' other than a sort of community or social centre.If my memory serves me well, I think the whist drives were held on Friday evenings and whilst the parents pursued their card game, we the kids, used to buy sweets and pop, from the shop at the bottom of Smithfield Road."

Later this otherwise social attraction had drawn attentionto itself by being left in a state of disrepair and a comment written to 'The Star' in 1955 by a correspondent described the hut as, "This area of depressing dirt — with a shack in the middle of the road." Something should be done said the writer and indeed it was. The 'Shack' was demolished and in its place Public Conveniences were built!

Another important part of a mining village was the colliery brass band. Although I have not found anything that supports the diea that Gleadless had a specific brass band, some of the local miners played in the Woodhouse Brass Band. Each village was very proud of the skill of its band which always played on festive occasions such as Gala Days..

During lesiure time boots were repaired, clothes mended amd gardens were tended. Relatives were visited and on Sunday the church and chapels were attended. The beautiful surrounding woods and fields which now houses 'The Gleadless Valley Housing Estate', once echoed to the sounds of children playing and walks to Cat Lane Woods at Heeley or to Lightwood at Norton were a delightful pastime in summer.

Mr F. Cantrill: "There was those wonderful walks on Sunday nights to Ridgeway along White Lane and Norton and the rambles as kids through the Little Woods down Carter Hall Lane through Inman's Woods. All the surrounding places and then farther afield when we got a bike."

Children made their own sports such as football, played with an empty tin can or flew kites, played marbles or just sub-bathed.

Leisure time was a relief from the hardships of everyday life and for some families, from the constant worry of finding food for the next meal.

9. CHARACTERS & TRADITIONS

"There was a character in every house!"

Apart from Christmas, Festivals and Feast Days and the annual Gleadless Flower Show, life in Gleadless followed its normal daily routine but the village was full of characters; people who had that individuality that brought humour and colour into everyday life. People were more dependent on their neighbours and as such they knew one another very well. Consequently, whatever one did in the village was always common knowledge to everyone else. This closeness of individuals brought with it a certain story telling and repartee between the village folk. Some of the stories I include in this chapter must have begun with, "Do you know what I heard the other day?"

"Nay, what!"

"Well, do ye know old Yorkie?"

"Oh, ay. What's he been up t' na?"

And so the story would begin and be passed on to the next willing ears. Come to think of it, do you know the one about old Yorkie?

Yorkie, whose real name was Jack Huff, lodged with Mrs. Barber at Lane End cottages. She was well known for her pies and peas and her dandelion and nettle beer but even more "famous" in Gleadless was her lodger who was nick-named Yorkie after he had set off from York to walk to London but had only reached Gleadless when he stopped and decided to stay.

This comedian of Gleadless, was a 'poorly' man with a bad chest and he used to cough and say, "I'm ready when he's ready aboon (above)!"

He was fond of telling jokes at the expense of himself and perhaps the humorous stories he told were just "tall" ones, but they have been well remembered by Gleadless residents.

A typical Yorkie story ran as follows:-

Yorkie, "One neet, a bloke came t'our 'ouse an' our cat wor' laid theer."

Bloke says to Yorkie, "Tha's got a fine cat theer."

"Ah," Yorkie replies, "he's a good mouser."

And just as he said that a mouse came out and

Bloke says, "Whey! He's not touching it! What's up we 'im?"

"Oh, it's all reet," Yorkie quickly replies, "that's one o' ours!"

Yorkie's cat had sat that long in front of the hearth that its fur had received brown scorch marks.

When someone remarked, "Tha's got a reet cat theer Yorkie. It's got no fur on!"

Yorkie immediately replied, "Ah, mice have pulled it all off!"

When Yorkie was engaged as a navvy, he was digging a hole when the boss shouts down to him, "I want wanna yer awt t' theer!"

Yorkie looks up and shouts back, "Whey, there's only me down 'ere."

"Ah," boss answers, "either thee or muck. One of thee out!"

One of the strangest stories I find difficult to believe, yet many of the locals related this incident to me, was the day that Yorkie's house caught fire. Whether it was a big fire or not no one seems to know but it was disturbing enough for someone to call out the fire brigade. The firemen complete with their fire engine duly arrived and had reached the bottom of the Common when they stopped to enquire the way. Yorkie (I am told) cooly went up to them and directed them the wrong way!

"Let it get a goin' a bit!" he said as he watched them drive off.

As Sam Gill comments, "He was that type of fella, old Yorkie!"

Perhaps it was because times were hard and mining accidents and illnesses were common place that the villagers laughed when they could and were philosophical about the bad days.

Bob Critchlow was another character who went into the cobbler's shop with his shoes and said, "How much are they for heeling?"

And the cobbler replied, "Half a'crown."

"And how much are they for soleing and heeling?" Bob asked.

"Seven and six", said the cobbler.

"I'll leave 'em," Bob replied and then quickly added, "Heel 'em up t' toe!"

Sam Gill: "There used to be stories about the old characters like 'Pod' Watson, 'Jakey' Plant and Walt Cadman. They used to go to "New Inn" then go on to Fair. For a bit of fun they used to ride on roundabout horses and wouldn't get off. The Fair men got to know them well and didn't mind because they used to draw the crowd and gain custom so they never sent them off.

They'd be riding round on horses and one in front used to turn round and shout, "I'm beating thee na' Jakey!" For they were pretending it were a horse race on roundabout!

One particular time, 'Pod' Watson went to Ice-cream man who was in Fair ground entrance and he said, "All you kids come 'ere!" Then turns to Ice-cream bloke and says, "Na gee all kids a cornet!"

So this Ice-cream chap's ever so busy giving out ice-cream to all kids but when he finished and told 'Pod' how much it would be, 'Pod' said, "Oh, no, I only said, gee 'em one!"

And he got away without paying him!
These were some of tricks they got up to.

"I thought I would tell you about a true story of two men of old Gleadless," wrote *Stanley Crofts* who is one of the 'Mush' Crofts. "One was **Tom Critchlow** the senior and the other Ike Caley (senior). They had been and had a few drinks in the "New Inn" one Sunday lunch and got into a debate about the ferocity of Fox's bull which was loose in a field across from Oscroft's shop. The same bull had jumped over the wall near the gate twice, first injuring a woman and then it broke old man Fox's arm.

Our two heroes decided that they were not frightened of it and went to the field where one held the bull whilst the other one rode it and then vice versa. Some wit in the "New Inn" made a lead medal for this distinguished event but I have no idea where the medal is now."

'Piggy' Ward.

One of the most talked about characters of old Gleadless was a gentleman called 'Piggy' Ward who lived in the cottages next to the Gleadless Methodist Church (now 'Tea time at Angela's'). One of 'Piggy's' daughters married a Sizer and so the Sizer family then live there. *Fred Stubbs* who was born in 1885, remembers the Ward family and relates a few stories for us here

'Piggy' Ward had the farm next to the Methodist Church at Gleadless Town End. He had three daughters called Mary Ellen, Ethel and Lizzie and a son called Billy who was my pal and we used to go rambling together. He later married Tom Kaye's daughter. Tom Kaye had a furniture fitting business in Gleadless. 'Piggy' had cows and pigs and he used to deal in them.

'Piggy' had a pony and trap with a sort of bar across the front that he used to hang rabbits on and he'd ride standing up in this trap. Well, once when 'Piggy' was in his trap he passed this man called Walter Fox who was going to work so 'Piggy' shouts to him, "Get in Walter, I'll give you a lift!"

But Walt shouts back, "Nay, lad. I'm late na!"

Another time 'Piggy' was coming along in his pony and trap carrying just a bag of chaff which was small hay all chopped up. That's all he had in his cart.

He was trotting on by when a voice shouts, "Can I have a lift Mester Ward?"

"Oh, nay lad," says 'Piggy', "I'm ladened!"

Speaking of characters, **Fred Stubbs** was born in 1885 at Newhall, Burton on Trent and was 100 years old when I spoke to him about his early life in Gleadless.

"There were four houses in a field called Victoria Road with a footpath right the way through our fields. These four houses stood in the field and our house was the bottom one.

I came to Gleadless when I was three years old and my father was a butcher. We'd used to go around killing farmer's pigs. We had three or four cows and my father was a pig killer for the local people as well as for the farmers.

We had a pony and trap and we went around the Gleadless farms and Lightwood and Norton area and we used to kill for the Bagshawes."

Although this story is not related to Gleadless, it is perhaps interesting to learn that Mr. Stubbs, as a boy, watched Queen Victoria officially open the Sheffield Town Hall which she did on the 21st May, 1897.

Queen Victoria's Visit to Sheffield

"I remember Queen Victoria coming to Sheffield. My father took me down from Gleadless to see her come. She sat on a high stool, so people could see her, for she was only a little person and we saw her in her carriage.

The road was all decked up and there were soldiers all the way down the Wicker. They were so close they were touching one another and they were wearing busbies.

I saw Queen Victoria come to open the Sheffield Town Hall gates with a golden key. They put a red carpet down on the road right up to the gates. I saw her very close and I'd only be about 12 years old.

They had forms (benches) on both sides of the road, in the Wicker for people to sit on and wait while she came. It was decked with buntings and flags and everybody was cheering. It was a sight to see!"

John, Thomas, Siddall

"Lewis Siddall's Father," relates *Stan Taylor*, " was a valuable and respected member of the village. He not only dealt in Insurance but was the local agent for the National Deposit Friendly Society of which most of the villagers were members.

I remember him having a room in the Independent Chapel building where we used to take our small subscriptions which provided a medical benefit as well as a holiday club. The medical part provided cash when anyone was off work ill and for Doctor's visits (there was no such thing then as Nat. Insurance) and the holiday cash was usually drawn out for the third week in August which was the recognised Feast Week when a large Fair was held at Intake. All the local pits shut down that week and most villagers went either to Cleethorpes, Blackpool or Derbyshire for just day trips or a week by the sea.

If any of the locals had any worries financially or otherwise, it was usually said, "Go and see Tommy Siddall and he'll know what to do."

Mr. Siddall was a first class musician and singer, as was all his family and he was choirmaster for the Chapel for numerous years."

'Pop' Sizer

A house still standing at the corner of Ridgeway Road and Gleadless Road near the Gleadless Methodist Chapel, reminds me of 'Pop' Sizer. I believe he was an important member of the Wesleyans but to most people he was the local representative of The St. John's Ambulance Service and you could see him in full uniform at nearly all the sports games and local gatherings. It was said if you suffered any injury or was suddenly taken ill, go and see 'Pop' Sizer before calling the Doctor. I believe 'Pop' had two sons, Stan and Jack."

The reader may have noticed the presence of 'nicknames' while reading through this chapter; Yorkie,'Mush' Crofts, 'Piggy' Ward and 'Pop' Sizer. In Gleadless, as in most places at this time, the use of nicknames was quite common. Familiarity, seemed to have given people the right to attach a nickname to their neighbour or "workmate". Whether the recipient fully appreciated his or her nicknme is debatable but one thing was for sure, once you inherited a nickname, you were very often 'stuck' with it for the rest of your life. Indeed some people's correct names were never actually known by the rest of the community.

Nicknames were usally derived from either a person's physical appearance or from a characteristic feature peculiar to themselves. One could spend some time guessing how the following received their nicknames; 'Chucky' Fox, 'Pod' Watson and 'Jakey' Plant but twins, Tom and Arthur Plant were known as 'Tomato' Plant, due to their names being spoken fast (Tomarthur) which resulted in a 'Tomato' sounding word!

Stan Taylor "A family called Kirks lived near the part of Gleadless Road that the locals called "The Irish Channel". One of the youngest of the Kirks was known to everybody as PUNCH. However, there wasn't any resemblance to the Punch, of Punch and Judy fame.

My recollection is of a small, bow legged lad who was a very good soccer player but who had a very short temper which usually got him into trouble with the referees because of his fighting attribute. Perhaps this was the reason?"

These people were just a few of the characters of old Gleadless. There were many more too numerous to mention here, for as one local remarked to me, "There was a character in every house!"

Mrs Ethel Mulford (nee France) B.E.M.

Mrs Mulford is the daughter of the late Arthur and Ethel France of Town End, Gleadless. During the Second World War, Ethel joined the W.A.A.F. and became a Flight Sergeant being stationed at the Norton Balloon Barrage for 18 months before moving to Cardington and later to London.

As Flight Sgt. France she broadcast on several occasions and was awarded the B.E.M. for devotion to duty. She received the award from King George VI and later in the evening a big reception was given her at the R.A.F. Station, Kensington Gardens.

She had charge of an exhibition in London, consisting of balloon and parachute exhibits and it was while she was there that she met and talked with Lady Welsh, Director of the W.A.A.F.

Gleadless indeed was not without its celebrities!

Traditions

At certain times in the year traditions played a part in the villagers life. Christmas time must have been a very bleak time for the poor families but most joined in by entertaining themselves. Monologues and songs (a few of which are included here) were just a small but important part of family entertainment. *Dolly Worrall* recalls what Christmas time was like for her family:-

"At Christmas time you always had to do something at our house. It didn't matter whether you liked it or you didn't, you had to and needless to say we all enjoyed it. We were never bored.

I played and sang and me Father would say, "Now Doll, play us 'Ole Pal'."

Me Mother used to say, "Tom, it's a public house song that. We don't want to hear that."

"Well, I like it Em. Go on Doll play it," he would say.,

Then we used to say, "Now go on Mother it's your turn."

Mother used to say, "Well, I've said it many a time."

But we'd say, "Well go on say it again." So she'd recite:-

This is the tale of a maid who was loved and deceived at the age of eighteen
And ever since then a man-hater she'd been
She adopted a babe from a neighbouring fold
Whose mother had died so the tale is told
She decided that no man this girl should see until she was 21 years old
But at last the day came round
Mamma and the carriage came round too with the lovely horses high-stepping pace

She said, "Ma, what is that that walks with such grace?
And Ma, he's hair on his face."
That is a man, a man monkey my dear and when you've seen the world and all the things in it
You'll shut these men from your mind this minute."
They drove to the jewellers, the milliners and the other fine shops
But that young maiden's eye left the costliest gem to roam o'er the counter and o'er to the men
And she said, "Ma, how handsome they are I should like one to live with shouldn't you?"
Ma uttered a groan, ordered the coachman to drive quickly home
But that night in her prayers the young maiden said, "Dear Father in Heaven are these men all alike?"
Deliver us from evil and so her prayer ran that the handsomest thing in the world is a man.

She'd say all the old Yorkshire ones, like, 'The lad that lives next door'.

'That lad as lives next door.'
I've nought agin me neighbours
And I wain't 'ave it said I'm cross and nazzie
I'm not I'm kind and mild instead
But there's an end to patience
Even Job knew that I'm sure
But 'e ne'er 'ad no dealings
With that lad as lives next door
'e's never out 'o mischief
And 'e never stops 'is din
'e's no sooner out o' one scrape
Than he's another in
If 'e were mine I should thrash 'im
While skin cum off 'is back
I'd lern 'im to tie t'door snecks
And then gie door a knack
I'd learn 'im to draw shape o' me
Wi' chalk on lavatory door
And make mud pies on our front step
And leave 'em there by t'score
But 'eres 'is father coming
He's looking trifle sad
I should be sad an' all

If I'd getten such a lad
What de ye think little Jimmie's very ill
They think 'e will not live
I've ne're out agenst 'im ye know
I liked that lad I'm sure
Please God be merciful
And spare that lad as lives next door.

And then there was another one, 'Some neet when tha's nowt to do'. It was about a woman telling her husband what he could do some night when he's nowt to do like:-

'Come home soon and spend a night with me, our Jack and Freddie
And I shall think it ever such a treat and I shall have t'white wash ready."

She's telling him all the jobs he's got to do. Honestly, there's enough work to last 'im a month!"

Songs and monologues were 'made up' about everyday situations and were performed either for family fun or at the local 'pub' as this next little song illustrates:-

Sam Gill. "They'd been out on a little boozing party somewhere in this cabby coach and coming home it hit a lamp post. Well, somebody on the cab was good at making verses and made this little song:-

The Gleadless Bus Song.
(The 1st.verse only)
Sailing merrily home in a cab
As happy as happy could be
The cab it did stop
The lamp it did drop
Someone shouted
"Oh, dearer me!"
Bob Robins, he thought he'd been killed
He shouted, "Oh, wier is me stick?"
Jud Staning looked gay
When he came the next day
His muscles were far to pick."

'Treacle Sop' was a monologue recited by Arthur France either to entertain his family or at concerts given at the Chapel. Not only was this 'entertainer' good with his monologues but he played the mouth organ too.

During the 20's and 30's, treacle was delivered to the local shop in casks ('treacle cast') and it was quite common to take an empty jar to the corner shop to have it filled with treacle.

Treacle Sop

Once in a little country town, a grocer kept a shop,
And selled among 'is other things, prime treacle, drink and pop,
Tea, coffee, curry, cocoa, soft soap and powder blue.
Preserves, pickles, cinnamon, all spice and pepper too.
And other things as such a' came
as figs, currants, raisins, spice too numerous to name.

One Summer's day a wagon stood just opposite his door
And childa all gaped round as if they'd never seen ought afore
An' in it was a treacle cast, it were a woppa too
To get it out they both were fast which ever way to do

But while they stood and parleyed there t'old horse gave a sudden chuck
And out it flew an burst, it flew all treacle into muck
Then childa laughed and clapped their hands, to them it seemed rare fun
But grocer nearly lost his wits when he saw his treacle run

He stamped and raved and then declared he wouldn't pay a meg
And carter vowed until he did he wouldn't stir a leg.
A neighbour chap saw state a things and pitied their distress
And telled 'em not to be so sower of such a sweet a mess

"And thar'd be sower," t'old Grocer said, "if job was thine old lad
And somebody wanted thee to pay for what thar'd never had."
"Fault isn't mine," said driver, "I've done my business right I hope,
I've brought thy treacle, there it is, and tha ma sam it up."

The neighbour left 'em to themselves, he'd no more to say
But went to guard what was left and drive young kids away
Na this din't suit young lads a bit, some meant to get a lick
But some of oldest got a taste a neighbour's walking stick

At last one lad says, "Ah know a plan if we all agree to do it
Let's shove one reight down into mess and let 'im roll reight through it."
"Agreed, agreed," they all replied, "And here comes little Jack"
He's forced to pass reight close this side, we'll do it in a crack."

Up comes young Jack just like a sucking duck
He never thought a sweeter would ever be his luck.
An' down they shoved him reight into mess
An' out he comes an awful sight as you may easily guess.

They marched him off in famous glee, all stickyfied and clammy
And them they sent him home to get licked by his Mammy
Then grocer and driver comes all in a dreadful flutter
To save some but they'd come too late, it had all run down gutter.

It taught a lesson to 'em both, befor' that jod war ended
Instead of falling out they should have tried to mend it
For what some saves about their loss, some sharper's forced to pop
And out of their misfortune they continue to get a sop.

(By courtesy of Mr. & Mrs. Hobson)

'Old Tup'

Christmas time brought with it the traditional playing of 'Old Tup' as familiar as Carol singing was or is today. 'Old Tup' was played by children to earn some extra pennies.

Ethel Pass "They used to come at Christmas time with their faces blackened and knock at your door and say, "Do you want 'Old Tup'?"

They were about six lads - they were always lads - and they'd have a brush handle with a cow's head on (not a real one) and with horns on. There was a song but I can't remember it all. 'The butcher that killed is Tupsy'....

One of the lads used to stick his knife (not real) into this 'Old Tup' and it used to fall and the children fell down still singing. I used to be a bit frightened of it when I was a kid. We used to clap and me dad used to say,"That's reet good 'oud lad!" and they'd get a penny. They'd made a hole in a cigar box for the money to be put in and then they'd go next door.

We loved it even though we were frightened. All Gleadless and Hollinsend kids used to do 'Old Tup'. It was a tradition

Stan Robertson "At Christmas time I used to go round all pubs doing 'Old Tup'. We used to have like a cow's head on and horns and butcher used to knock him down and cut him up. Somebody was dressed up as butcher."

Rose Martin "At Christmas time they used to come around with the 'Old Tup'. Four or five children aged between 12 and 14 years old used to bring a sheep's head (I think they used to get it from the butchers) and they used to have it on a brush which they held between their legs.

They used to knock at your door and say, "Do you want 'Old Tup'?" Nobody ever refused because they used to say it was bad luck it you didn't have 'Old Tup'.

Then they would come inside and sing:-

'The Old Tup'

(1st verse spoken) Here comes me and 'ar 'owd lass
We've cum because we're short of brass
Up with cup and let's all sup
And then we'll try to act 'owd tup

(Sung) As I was going to Darby
Upon a market day
I met the finest tupsy
That ever was fed on hay
Failey, Failey follow me all the way

The horns that grew on this tupsy
They grew so mighty high
That every time it shook its head
They rattled against the sky
Failey, Failey follow me all the way

The ears that grew on this tupsy
They were so long and fine
They'd mek a leather ap'pron
To last a long, long time
Failey, Failey follow me all the way

The eyes that grew in this tupsy
They were so big and round
They kicked 'em about for footballs
For they were just the size
Failey, Failey follow me all the way

And now my song is ended
And I'll be on my way
So please will you give me a trifle
Towards a bale of hay
Failey, Failey follow me all the way.

Then after they had sung the 'Old Tup' song they would say:-

We wish you a Merry Christmas
And a Happy New Year
A pocket full of money
And a cellar full of beer
A horse and a gig and a good fat pig
To last you all next year

A hole in my stocking
A hole in my shoe
Please will you give us a copper or two
If you haven't a penny a ha'penny will do
If you haven't a ha'penny
God Bless you.

I am most grateful to Rose Martin for having such a marvellous memory and reciting 'Old Tup' for me.

'Old Tup' is no longer played in Gleadless now. When it lost its identity as a village traditions like the 'old Tup' and the reciting of monologues seemed to become extinct too.

Stood the Test  for 70 Years. 

TOM RICHARDSON

: *BUTCHER* :

785, GLEADLESS ROAD,

GLEADLESS, :: SHEFFIELD

A 1929 Advert

10 HERBS, REMEDIES AND THE LOCAL DOCTOR

"Anything green that grew out of the mould
Was an excellent herb to our fathers of old"
— Kipling

Unless someone was either dying or had some terrible disease, "calling the doctor in," cost money, and so most folk made 'do" with their own little remedies however weird or unpleasant they may have been. Childhood illnesses were treated and cured by the children's mothers for they had some magical cures usually handed down to them from their own mothers. Almost medieval concoctions they were ; a pinch of this and a sprinkling of that. One can picture the unwilling "victim" with eyes tight shut to avoid seeing the distasteful medicine being thrust down his throat. Then immediately afterwards, in an effort to camouflage the horrible taste, jam on a spoon was pushed into the "patient's" mouth! Mind you, if you could keep the offending potion down, then a cure seemed almost certain. Today's revival in herbal remedies points to the fact.

The old Gleadless villagers "swore" that these remedies did you a "power of good." A fact verified here by *Ethel Pass*, as she recalls her own upbringing which were full of these medicinal compounds.

"My Mother's garden was full of herbs. When we were, what she would call, "out of sorts," we had wormwood, hyssop and herbie grass. These she would wash, boil and mash them all together. Then this mixture was put in a big jug on the oven top and we had to drink a wine glass full. When the wine glasses came out you knew that you were going to get some of this awful, horrible stuff! That was the only time that the wine glasses came out!

I can see these herbs now, stuck together in this jug with their stalks still on. Whether you wanted it or not you were made to have it. We drank this potion when it was "the fall o'leaf" (in the Autumn time) and the "Spring of leaf" (Spring). In Spring you were supposed to be prone to having "spots" so you had to drink this concoction at this time and when you were out of sorts."

Weekends brought another dread to the Pass household in the form of Brimstone and Treacle.

"When weekends came we were given Brimstone and Treacle. The treacle was black and the brimstone was a yellow powder which we bought from the chemist. We used to plead with my Mother and say, "Oh, can't we have Golden Syrup instead?"

She'd say, "Oh, no, that's no good!"So this awful, black treacle used to be put in a jar on top of the over and we were given a teaspoonful.

"It'll clear you out!" me Mother would say.

My....it certainly did!

When we had a sore throat, Mother used to say, "Open your mouth," and then she would hold a piece of brown paper to your throat. Brimstone (flowers of sulphur) was put on this brown paper and then blown down your throat. Well, you can imagine what it was like. We nearly choked!"

Surrounded by the open countryside, Gleadless was never short of the herbs that gew wildly in the open fields and hedgerows. Wild roses and honeysuckle grew along Jaunty Lane, while growing in a nearby garden was a Siberian crab apple tree. A penny worth of these apples, filled a "newspaper bag". Crab apple jelly made from the apples, tasted delicious.

Polly Wainwright - the herb lady

Nestling behind the "Old Harrow" was a group of little cottages. The Bownes and Mansell families lived there. So too did Polly Wainwright (nee Moseley) with her chimney sweep husband and son Alan, who knew everything there was to know about flowers and sold plants and seedlings locally. His little business was similar to a cottage nursery and his Mother, Polly, would help by taking the plants into Sheffield to sell.

"When you went into their house," remembers *Mrs Layden,* "the smell of herbs used to greet you. All sorts of herbs were hung across the beams in the ceiling. Mention any herb and Polly would have it. She would come round to your door with her herbs and at Christmas time she would bring everlasting flowers. She used to say, "Will you have an everlasting basket?"

She seemed to me to be a really old woman, so thin and wryly and she lived to an old age."

Little Book Remedies

If you wanted to know how to 'Renovate your brown boots', 'crimp your hair,' or re-lacquer your brass or just cure your cold, then you would look through your remedy book. The colour of course is of no significance. Remedy books (blue, red and brown) were always crammed full of recipes and potions and were kept by mothers as a useful source of information, not only for themselves but also to be passed onto their daughters who would of course eventually run a household of their own. Daughters helped their mothers in the kitchen from a very young age and would no doubt help their mums write down certain prescriptions for remedies in the little, well worn and dog earred, notebooks.

Mrs Layden, treasures her mother's little red book of remedies and although well thumbed, one can still read the many intriguing recipes.

"In those days we made our own medicine," remarks *Mrs Layden*, "My mother used to make a lot of jams and syrups out of the elderberries. During winter time, she made raspberry vinegar and blackberry vinegar to keep you well and free from colds.

Hyssop made you eat and herbie grass was good for you. It was a very strong smelling herb though and we used to put it in a cup or a jug, pour water onto it, stir it and then let it stand. We drank a wine glass full and afterwards it made you want to eat.

My mother's little book was full of these remedies and potions."

Space allows only a few of the recipes to be included here:-

Remedies and Recipes

Blackberry Vinegar (for colds)
1lb Blackberries } mash and stir together
1pt Vinegar }
Leave for 24 hrs or more. Strain and add 1lb of sugar to each pt. of juice, then boil up and bottle when cold.

Coughs and Colds Cure
Equal quantities of onions, sugar and turnips. Slice the vegetables, put a layer of onions, cover with sugar, add turnips and so on. Set aside for three days. Press the juice but do NOT bottle.
1 tablespoon for adult. 1 teaspoon for a child.

For Bronchitis
½oz Castor Oil
½oz Syrup of Rhubarb
Juice of 1 lemon
1 teaspoon 3 times a day.

Medicine for the Blood in Spring
3d (money in old coinage) Columbia Root
3d Sarsaparilla Root
1qt water and boil to 1 pint
1 wine glass full morning and night.

Recipe for Crimping Hair
1 white of an egg
1 teaspoonful of fine sugar
1 gill of boiled water
Bottle and use any time.

Marrow Jam
6lb Marrow
6lb Sugar
3 Lemons
1½ozs Bruised Ginger
Weigh marrow after peeling and removing seeds. Cut into 2″ squares. Put in a vessel with sugar on the top. Let it stand for 24 hrs.
Place the whole in a stewpan and add the lemon rind. Cut in thin strips. Tie lemon and bruised ginger in muslin bag so that it can be removed after boiling for 2½ hrs.

Potato Wine
Wash well. Do not peel.
½ gal. = 5 to 6lbs of small potatoes
Cut into small pieces, put them into a pan with 1 gal. of cold water, bring to the boil and boil exactly 5 mins not more or it will be cloudy. Have ready in stone jar 3lb demarara sugar, rind of 3 oranges and 2 sliced lemons. Strain through a sieve and boiling liquor from potatoes. Stir to dissolve the sugar and return to boiling pan, adding 1oz bruised ginger and boil for ½hr then strain off into stone jar and leave till next day. Then bottle but cork lightly till the working has stopped. Put a little sugar candy in each bottle to feed it. Store for 6 months if you want a good wine, the longer the better.

Pear Marmalade
8lb Pears
8lb Sugar
½lb preserved Ginger
4 Lemons
Peel the pears and cut into small pieces, add sugar and boil gently for 1hr. Boil lemons in water till tender, remove the pips, squeeze the jiuce in pears and chop the peel very finely together with the ginger. Add the pears and boil gently for another hour or until transparent.

I have to confess that I have not tried any of these recipes or remedies but I have been assured that they do work!

Doctors

Gleadless, like other similar communities, relied on various women who could be called upon to help at births and deaths. These strong ladies coped at births and would 'lay' people out when they died. Although this seems a harsh way of life for us today, at this time, before any National Health Service was created, there was little alternative. People would know a 'woman' who could be relied on to give assistance through births and deaths. The most notable one in Gleadless was Elizabeth Sharpe, the village midwife of whom we shall read later. But other ladies helped too, like *Stanley Crofts'* mother. "My mother was well known in Gleadless, Hollinsend and Intake where she used to work voluntary with the Doctor and District Nurse, to help those who were sick and to comfort those who had lost a relative.

She used to be called in the middle of the night and she would get up and go without question."

The late Reg. Cartledge recalls Gleadless' first surgery

"The first doctor that came to Gleadless had a room in me Mum's house in the old cottage, No.10 Grassthorpe Road, (now No.22) as a surgery. It was Dr Davison and he came on a sit-up and beg pushbike with his little black bag. This was in the 1920's.

He didn't stay very long and then Dr Billington, whose main surgery was at the top of Duke Street, came and took over the surgery. Eventually he took on as a partner Dr Hollingworth and he still had this room at our house but eventually they built the surgery which is now opposite Gleadless Church. Dr Holden, Green and Aker moved up here and that surgery began down Grassthorpe Road.

They formed a Nursing Association and this was before the days of National Health obviously and if I remember rightly the first nurse that came was called Whitchurch or something like that and then came Nurse Anderson, eventually Sister Anderson and she stayed with Mrs Simpson who kept the shop at the bottom of Smithfield Road.

When they built houses on Ridgeway Road, the Simpsons moved up there and Sister Anderson went to live with them. She was the midwife, everybody loved her. She was really well thought of in the village. As I say they formed this Nursing Association and everybody who agreed to join paid a small amount each week or each month. My wife used to go round in the mid 1940's with me Mum, collecting these contributions. The first Secretary of the Association was Miss Millicent Drewry who was also a teacher down at Gleadless School."

Elizabeth Sharpe

Elizabeth Sharpe was Gleadless' village midwife who, no matter what time of day or night it was, used to travel to all her 'calls' on foot whatever the distance. Both Elizabeth and her husband John attended the Gleadless Methodist Church, and lived in what is now called South Close Farmhouse on Gleadless Road.

Today, many of the older Gleadless residents who were 'brought into the world' by Mrs Sharpe, speak of her with warmth and affection. This endearment to the Sharpe family by the Gleadless people was shown in the erection of a cross in the Gleadless Methodist Church yard in 1920.

This simple memorial, erected by public subscription, is a fitting tribute to their memory.

The Sharpe Memorial Cross

The inscription reads:

Erected by
Public Subscription
To Honour the Memory of
Elizabeth Sharpe
of this Village
Also John Sharpe
Husband of the above
They have wrought good work
1920

John Sharpe

Elizabeth Sharpe

Elizabeth Sharpe Memorial, 1988 (Pauline Shearstone)

11. ROUND AND ABOUT MYRTLE SPRINGS

Myrtle Springs was a quiet backwater of old quaint cottages, secluded from Gleadless Road by the large trees and thick bushes. (Could Myrtle Springs have derived its name from the flowering evergreen shrub, the myrtle and from the predominance of springs in the area?)

Stan Taylor:

Well Meadow

"Well Meadow was at the top of the Common and my Mother when she was a young girl and lived on the Common, had to fetch all the water from these wells which were fed from Myrtle Springs. In my position as Playing Fields Officer with the Education dept., I was responsible for construction and maintenance of the playing fields of Hurlfield and Ashleigh Schools and in the course of construction several of these wells were discovered in perfect condition and the water was still pure."

Myrtle Springs

Once, the Myrtle Springs Toll Bar, stood at the top of Hurlfield Hill and by paying a toll at the Lodge, traffic was allowed to journey through from Gleadless Road into Myrtle Springs and from there to Hurlfield Road and so on to the Manor Top. It was a much shorter journey than by the regular route.

John Riley, who was a famous composer of hymns and songs, lived in Myrtle Springs in the old school house tht once belonged to Dr Flory. Mr Riley composed the hymn the "Golden Gate" which was sung all over England and sold more than one million copies. Later he published a "Sunday School Songster" in seven volumes.

Also in the area was Ashleigh House a marvellous residence where the Wattam family lived while close by was Ashleigh Nurseries, home of the Wakelin family, with its many greenhouses and large shrubbery.

New buildings have now been erected in this pretty, picturesque area and the old Toll Bar and Boarding School now only remain in people's memories.

The Myrtle Springs Toll Bar

This Toll Bar was situated at the top of Gleadless Road and the road that travellers passed through led them to Myrtle Springs and on the Hurlfield Road. In days before Ridgeway Road was built it was a very convenient route for travellers to take.

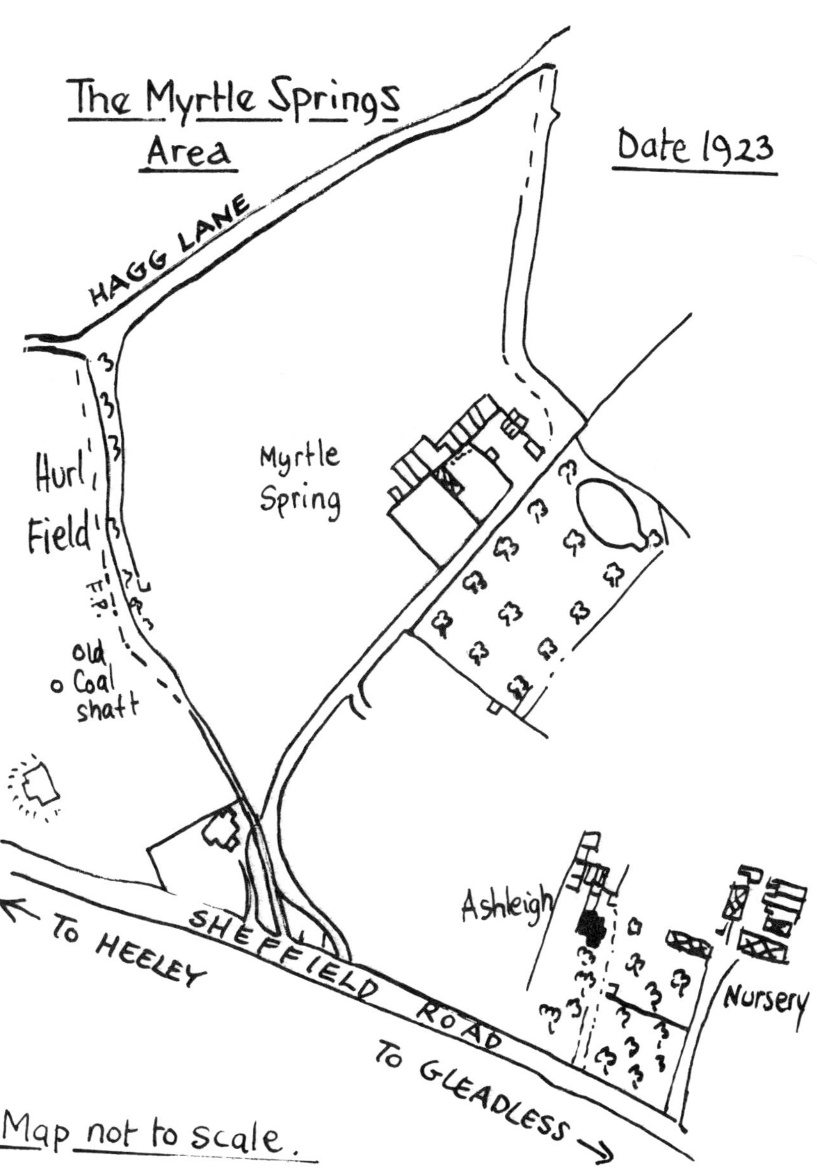
The Myrtle Springs Area
Date 1923
HAGG LANE
Hurl Field
F.P.
Old Coal shaft
Myrtle Spring
Ashleigh
Nursery
SHEFFIELD ROAD
TO HEELEY
TO GLEADLESS
Map not to scale.

Myrtle Springs Toll Bar, Gleadless

The little road was never a Turnpike road but was privately owned by the Duke of Norfolk who owned it until 1900 before he sold it to Mr Wakelin of Richmond Road. The Toll Bar was still operating in 1958 when the property then belonged to Mrs Needham of Frecheville and for a modest sum (see 'Toll Charges') one could take advantage of this short cut to the Manor Top.

Private Toll

Toll for 2 wheeled carts	*2d*
4 wheeled Carts	*3d*
Horses, Cattle, Cyclists & Foot Passengers	*1d*
Pay at the Lodge.	

Unfortunately, the Toll Bar sign was lost when the building was demolished.

The Toll Bar's demise came with the advent of the car when an extra mile or two did not matter to an engine!

In its early days, the Riley family lived at the Toll House (Myrtle Lodge) before they moved to Dr Flory's old schoolhouse in Myrtle Springs. Later a family called White lived there but most villagers remember Mrs Florence Darby as the Toll Keeper of the Lodge. She lived there with her son who had been badly injured during the War.

Annie Benton "Mrs Darby lived at the Toll Bar for many years and I remember her collecting tolls but you never paid to walk through. We used to walk through to Elm Tree that way. The Lodge was only a very small place - a bedroom and a living room and she had rats and when she was in bed she had to throw her shoe across the room to make them go! It was a very old place. The green-grocery people used the road a lot. They paid 3d for their four wheeled carts and they came through with their drays."

If Mrs Darby endured the company of rats then she was fortunate in the fact that she had an electricity and water supply. The unfortunate lady who lived there during the 1920's had to carry a bucket to fetch water from a pump along Gleadless Road and her only means of lighting was by candles and an oil lamp.

In the grounds behind the old Toll Bar was the Boarding school that once belonged to Dr Flory.

Gleadless Toll Bar on Norton Avenue (Mrs Layden)
A family called Drury/Drewery lived at this house in the 1920's. They had three daughters named Emily, Elsie and Edith. No one ever remembers any tolls being taken. It was demolished to make way for the Herdings estate.

Dr Flory's Boarding School

Described as being situated in Myrtle Springs an 'elevated, healthy and picturesque' area in 1871, this school was established in 1838 by the distinguished Dr H.C. Flory, (a descendant of a Huguenot family named Fleury) for the education of middle class children. Set in grounds of 13 acres the school afforded every facility for recreative enjoyment as well as preparing the pupils for the 'London University, Middle Class, and other competitive Examinations.' Instruction was also offered in Modern languages. (For a more detailed account of Dr Flory's school please refer to book, "Gleadless from Village to suburb".)

No. 3 Myrtle Springs (Mrs Wild)
Dr Flory's Boarding School and later the home of John Riley, famous composer. Now demolished.

Dr Flory continued with the school until his death in 1863. His son Henry succeeded him but later disposed of the school in 1870 to Caleb and Joshua Allen. However, in 1877 the land was sold and measured out for building allotments. The schoolhouse building survived for many years after but the actual date of its demolition is uncertain.

After living for a short time at Myrtle Lodge, John Riley and his family came to live at the old school house. (see John Riley section)

Annie "There were several cottages at Myrtle Springs and some stood back in a yard and one cottage was in the corner. The biggest house there was where the Riley family lived and they had a big family. Mr Riley's daughter married Frank Penistone and they lived in Bartle Road and had three children.

The Archers lived at 'The Castle' and I remember that being built."

Ashleigh House was a beautiful house set in its own grounds.

Annie "Mr & Mrs Wattam lived at Ashleigh House with their children, Ted, Tommy, Raymond, Dolly and Kathleen. Mr. Wattam had a stall in the old Market Hall where he sold cutlery.

It was a big place with a lovely lawn on the front and a Summer house and a field at the back where they kept pigs. A builder bought the land and built some houses there but Mr & Mrs Wattam were dead then."

T. WATTAM,

Cutlery Manufacturer,

37. NORFOLK MARKET HALL,

SHEFFIELD.

Cases of Stainless Cutlery - from £1 1s. upwards.
Carvers, Scissors, Razors, Pocket Knives.

Dealer in Fancy Leather Goods, Handbags, Purses, &c.

CUTLERY REPAIRED.

A 1929 Advert

Dolly Worrall (nee Wattam) "Ashleigh House was my home as a child. My Father, Thomas, was a cutlery manufacturer and sold cutlery and other goods in the Market Hall. My Mother, Emily, was a lovely, kind hearted woman and we loved living at the big house.

We had over 50 fruit trees in the orchard, a big shrubbery and kitchen garden and then there was a drive and the next drive led up to Ashleigh Nurseries where Frank Wakelin and his family lived. His cousin, Timothy Wakelin, built the house next door. The Nurseries had many greenhouses and they grew tomatoes and flowers.

The Barlow Hunt

"I remember one Boxing Day our big gate at Ashleigh was pushed back and the huntsmen came up. They said to me Father, "Any damage that's done to the fences we will be responsible for."

They drew right up the drive, right round (we'd a paddock at the back) and right over the fences. It was a lovely sight. They were all dressed in red coats. They came from Barlow and once fox came and I'd got some lovely pullets and it killed 'em. It bit their heads off but he didn't get the banties because they flew onto bedroom windowsills. Banties can fly you see."

Ashleigh House was compulsory purchased in 1960/61 and was subsequently demolished.

Bartle Road

Before moving to Ashleigh House the Wattam family lived at Rose Villa on Bartle Road. The name Bartle probably was derived from a man called Thomas Bartle who was not a Gleadless person but who developed the land and sold it in sections. There was Myrtle Springs Building Society dated around 1872 with the deeds to the houses stating that the 'occupier of the dwelling can keep a cow but not a traction engine!'

There was once an old caravan 'parked' at the bottom of Bartle Road where 'old' Roadhouse Pearson lived. He was a shoemaker and later a family called Rhodes lived there as did Cissy Croves.

Annie: "Living down Bartle Road was a lady called Nutt who had two sons and one daughter Eliza, who was a teacher at Gleadless School. Joe Nutt is the son of Percy Nutt who married a widow called Mrs Shaw who had the little farm in what is now the 'Heeley & Sheffield' pub's car park.

The Hastings, Mrs Richardson, Alices, Cockrines and Hagues also lived down Bartle Road."

Springfield House

Springfield House was a large dwelling that was situated off Gleadless Road, down in the valley, where the Gleadless Valley estate houses are today.

Dolly "A gentleman called Mr Kent lived there with his daughter before he had a bungalow built on the Common, then Mr Jackson who was a solicitor's clerk, came to live there. After Mr Jackson left, Irvine Patnick's Grandfather bought it and lived there before the Valley Estate was built."

Hurlfield House, the large building that is perched near the top of the quarry off Hurlfield Hill, was once the family home of the Parker family. The Parkers lived there for many years, handing it down to one of their sons who married and lived there with his wife.

This house fortunately still survives today.

Ivy House (Gleadless Road/Bartle Road)

Annie Benton: "My Father, John Smith, made Ivy House into a farm and he rented it from a Mr Tebbit of Meadow Street. Father had two pasture fields that stretched down to the bottom of Bartle Road but he ploughed one of them and grew vegetables. The other field he had for pasture for his cows and he had some pigs. He used to 'feed' some for Gunstones. We had to walk the pigs down to Granville Street to be killed at the slaughterhouse off Duke Street. The children used to follow us and we gathered more and more children the further we walked!

We used to have some milk come from Edale to Heeley Station and we fetched it from there. With our little pony and trap, I used to go to Sheffield and take the milk to Heeley and Sharrow. I delivered the milk every day for 24 years! sometimes my Mother, Martha went with me. We delivered milk in cans that were made out of tin and when it was wet it made them all rusty so we had to rub them with 'monkey brand' to clean them.

My father employed casual work to help us in the fields and when it was threshing day we sometimes had the Earnshaws and another time the Birds. Some people would come with dogs because when we'd threshed, there was always a lot of mice and rats about and the dogs used to catch them.

The farm at the side of the 'Heeley & Sheffield House'

Snooks kept the 'Heeley & Sheffield' when we lived nearby and at one time there used to be a farm where the pub's car park is today. My grandfather, Thomas Smith had that little farm and he had the lands that stretched down Gleadless Bank, Drive and Avenue for pasture land where he used to graze his cows in the fields.

Then he left and went to live at Dronfield and a family called Shaws took it over. When Mrs Shaw was widowed she married Percy Nutt."

John Riley, the Miner and Composer who lived at Myrtle Springs

In the 'Daily Herald' in 1913 was an article titled 'Three Talented Miners' which mentions three miners one of whom is John Riley of Myrtle Springs.

I quote, "Little by little the curtain is being lifted on the hidden genius of the mine and the workshop.... John Riley, of Myrtle Springs, Sheffield composer of the hymn, "Golden Gate", sung all over England and of which over a million copies have been sold. He has compiled and published a "Sunday School Songster" in seven volumes."

It is perhaps fair to say that few people living in Gleadless today have heard of John Riley and his music but in the first few decades of this century, Mr Riley was quite an accomplished composer and brought recognition to Gleadless through his musical accomplishments.

Apparently, one of the hymns he composed was sent to Queen Mary who wrote a letter in return thanking him for the gift. This letter was treasured for many years by the family.

Born in 1857, John Riley was a miner who worked at his composing in whatever spare moments he had. As one Gleadlessite remembers, "Mr Riley who was a very good organist, would have his windows wide open and he'd sit playing and singing away. It used to sound so beautiful."

An accomplished musician, he together with his daughter Elizabeth, who was a mezzo soprano singer, would give musical concerts in the neighbourhood. John was also a regular attender at the Intake Methodist Church.

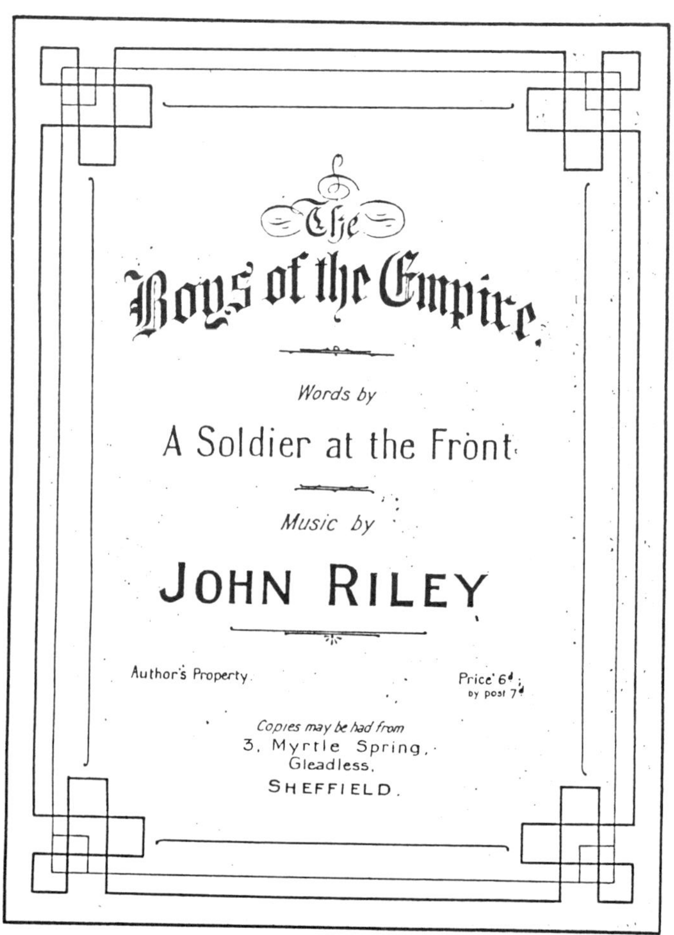

BY THE SAME COMPOSER

No 1.	*Come unto Him*	Price 1/- nett
2.	*Tell Mother I'm going to Jesus*	Price 1/- nett
3.	*Abide with me*	Price 1/- nett
4.	*Christian Mariner*	Price 1/- nett
5.	*Old England*	Price 1/- nett
6.	*The Boys of the Empire*	Price 6d, by post 7d

Copy of Original Sheet Music by John Riley

Originally, the Rileys lived at the old Toll Bar at the top of Hurlfield Hill, which was then called Myrtle Lodge, until the family began to grow and a bigger house was needed. The family then moved to No 3, Myrtle Springs which had once been the former building of Dr Flory's Boarding School. Henry Flory sold his Father's school in 1870 so the Rileys would have lived there much later.

John Riley composed many songs including a version of 'Abide with Me' but his 'best seller' was the hymn the "Golden Gate" which sold over a million copies. The chorus states:-

"Enter now the golden gate Where the happy angels wait
Where the narrow path is straight, Dear children, enter in."

When John Riley died on July 27th, 1922 he was buried in Intake Cemetry and engraved on the Memorial Stone is a fitting epitaph to such a gifted man. It states, "Entered now the Golden Gates."

John Riley & his family at Myrtle Springs (The late Mr Gabbitas)
Back Row: Albert Riley, Sarah, Anne Riley, Percy Riley, Eva Riley, Faith Riley and Elizabeth Riley. *In Front*: John Riley, Harold Riley and Faith Riley.
Taken when Percy was home on leave from the Hussars.
Missing from the above photo, is Carlo the Newfoundland dog. This family pet was so hugh it wore a dog collar 8 inches in diameter!

Family details

The oldest child, *Albert Riley* worked in the Pit but came out of it and entered the Liverpool Cathedral Choir.

Sarah Anne was the eldest daughter and *Percy Riley* after the 1st World War ended came out of the Hussars and became a tram driver. His wife was called Mabel.

Eva Riley, later became Mrs Price and had a shop at 30 West Street in Eckington.

Faith Riley (the daughter) went to live in Scunthorpe

Elizabeth Riley was born in 1891 and *Harold Riley* the youngest child was born in 1901 at the time Queen Victoria was 'lying in state'.

12. HOLLINSEND & INTAKE

Hollinsend was a close neighbour of Gleadless and because of the insularity of neighbouring communities some fifty years ago, Hollinsend and Gleadless tended (or tried to) live their lives separate from one another. Today, this is not so and the two are now so merged together that they have become more or less one big community.

Whenever, I asked anyone about Hollinsend, I came to expect the same reply, "Oh, Hollinsenders, were much tougher than the Gleadlessites!"

According to Hollinsenders, if you lived at Gleadless, you were deemed to be "posh". Although, neither community was rich by today's standards, it seems that Hollins End was in fact the poorer of the two.

Hollins End was predominately a mining community. The colliers' homes were built to house the men who worked at the neighbouring pits. In 1872, Hollins End (now spelt Hollinsend) was described as a "collection of cottages principally inhabited by colliers who work at the Birley Vale, Birley Planting, Hollins Ends and the Intake collieries....." ("Le Tall's Woodhouse" p.46.)

Life was hard for this mining village. "When the pit "hummer" sounded we knew they'd been an accident and we'd rush out to see if "our man" had been "lost". They had their escapism too in the form of drink. "After they (the colliers) had been paid on Friday night some would spend their money on beer and when they'd drunk enough at pub you could hear them arguing and fighting wi' one another."

The children were tougher too. "Gledless kids were quieter than us. Sometimes at home time (from school) we used to say, "Let's wait for Gledless kids and we'll war 'em!" (fight them)

The "Barracks" the back to back houses built by the Birley Pit to house their workers, was well known in the area.

"If you lived up at Gleadless, you were a bit better class because the "Barracks" were down there. They were like one up and one down and the women used to be fighting and the men getting drunk and all the rest of it. I got to know a little girl who lived at Hollins End. She was a nice girl and she sat next to me at school and I asked her if she'd like to come to tea at our house. She said she'd like to but first I had to walk home with her to tell 'er Mother that she was coming with me. When we got to their house I nearly died! Stone flags on the floor, jam jars to drink out of. They used to fetch beer in jam jars down there. When she got to our house she thought she'd gone to Buckingham Palace!"

Although times were difficult and starvation and poverty were always close at hand, there was a community spirit that prevailed throughout. Without this neighbourliness of helping others worse off than yourself, people would have found it more difficult to survive. Vandalism hardly existed, "muggings" were unheard of and rent money could be left for collection on the window sill and would never be stolen. "Rough and ready" they may have been but they had a certain pride where poverty was concerned. They hated admitting that they were poor and would conceal the fact as much as ppossible.

Living in Hollins End, during the early part of the 1900's was difficult, due to the hardships and poverty that the Coal Strikes of 1912, 1921 & 1926 brought.

Ethel Pass, Rose Martin and Stan Robertson were just a few of the many people I spoke to concerning Hollins End. Hard times and hard work were no strangers to these people. Their impressions of what life was like for them living in Hollins End are re-lived here and I am grateful for their most touching and vivid stories.

Stan Robertson:

Early Riser

"When I was about ten years old, two or three mornings a week, my Mother used to wake me up at 6am in the morning for me to go to Elm Tree to bring two horses back. There were all fields down Jaunty Lane and one horse would manage a load of cabbages, rhubarb, cauliflower and anything like that. They used to take the horses and stand in the Old Rag Market, in Sheffield, to sell the food. I had to bring them back from Elm Tree and I had to stand on the manger (because he was small) to fasten them up. The other men used to come at 7am. Then I used to get a little cream coloured pony, which was only small, and "yoke" him up by myself and go and help empty the "Middens".

The "Middens"

There were no water toilets in those days, only middens which had to be emptied. All ashes from coal fires used to be thrown into middens and 'my' pony used to held empty the middens in the steep yards where the men couldn't get the wheel barrow up. The pony would pull the red barrow up, with all the ashes and the toilet in, and then we'd tip it on the road. There was no tip for the middens then and it all had to be put on the fields. Ashes made the soil lighter. It had to be spread in with a shovel and ploughed in. After they'd cleaned the middens, all the roads were disinfected with a red powder which we had to fetch from the Woodhouse Depot.

One of the places I used to go to, to empty the middens, was the "Yew Tree" yard (near Frith Road). That was very steep with all the houses down the back. The "Yew Tree" was on top of the houses. Another steep place was Brierley Terrace, a row of red bricked houses. (Where the Carlton Club is today.)

About 8.30am I used to get on the pony's back and ride him as fast as I could. Put him in the stable, dash in house for a cuppa tea and a slice of toast and them I was off to school!"

The "Claming House"

"At the top of Frith Road was Bob Beverley's shop (before Phylliss Holmes had it) and it was (before my time) a butchers. In our back garden was what they called a "Claming House", the killing house. That was where they used to put the beasts so they couldn't get amything to eat before they killed them. There was a big round drum there where they used to pull them up after they'd been killed. That was before my time but the place was still there when I was a lad. There was a big boiler in there as well and we used to boil little potatoes, scrape 'em and eat 'em and give some to pigs.

The Old Lamplighter

In the street we used to have gas lamps. They weren't worked on a clock then and every night an old lamplighter used to come round lighting the lamps. He had a sort of little flame at the end of a stick and he'd pull the gas on and light the mantle. There was a gas lamp at the top of Frith Road, one up the Croft and another by Vaughan's shop opposite the "Hollin Bush"."

"The Barracks"

Their correct address was "The Square" but these three blocks of houses which formed a pattern E, were known locally as "The Barracks". All the houses faced into a yard and little imagination is required to understand how this group of houses derived their nick-name. The houses, so close in proximity, afforded very little privacy and therefore family disagreements were often shared by everyone living nearby!

"At the other side of Croft Road were "The Barracks". They were back to back houses with the backs of the houses in Croft Road coming into "The Barracks". There was number 1 Square, number 2 and number 3 Square. Some of the families I remember living there, were Martin Towers, Bottomleys, Mitchells and Crouchs. There were two Crouchs, "Tich" and Joe. Joe used to fly short, flyer pigeons and he lived in one of the little cottages nearest the Croft. Mrs Whalley lived next door to Joe."

Old Cottages on Croft Road, Hollinsend

The 'Old Row' cottages on Hollinsend Road, 1963 (Mr H. Clayton)

The "Old Row"

Mr Robertson's Father was called George Clayton Robertson. He was raised by blind Emmanual Buck who lived in Rose Cottage which was later the home of Mr Bernard Lancaster.

"My Father was known as "Judler" Buck because he was brought up by Mannie Buck who owned all the "Old Row" of cottages in Hollins End. Mannie owned the cottages where Crouchs lived. When we were kids we used to go and read "The Star" to Mannie every night because he was blind.

In these "Old Row" houses lived the Grade Family (in the 1st one) Mitchells (the 2nd) Broadheads (the 3rd) and Dodds, Shaws and Fenwicks in the others and an old lady in the end house.

Cottages near the school

There were a row of houses near the school. Up the side of the school wall was a field gate and Billy Young from Intake had that field. There were four houses there. Potters lived in the first one (furthest from the school), Haywards in the next, Murphins and then Crappers nearest to the school."

The "Yew Tree"

In 1871, The "Yew Tree" existed as a beerhouse and John Clark was the keeper. In earlier days, it seems to have been a shop as well as a beerhouse. In the 1870's it was listed as a grocery and beerhouse and in 1902 John Clark (the late Miss P. Holmes' Grandfather) owned it.

The property, which was situated beyond Frith Road and facing Croft Road, was eventually sold to Duncan Gilmore. The building was in evidence in July 1964 but its demolition was due shortly afterwards to make way for the building of houses.

"The "Yew Tree" was just one big room with a bar and one entrance. Underneath the Inn were houses and the Weldons lived there. Greggs were the first people I remember having the Inn, then Whites who used to live at the end of Sharrard Road, took it over. All the colliers used to go in "Yew Tree".

George Henry Skelton had the big field passed the "Yew Tree" and his field stretched right down to bottom of Birley Vale. He was a "big chap" with the Wesleyan Chapel and he used to let Hollinsend Football Club play football on his ground. Bob Beverley's field went right round to where the brick yard used to be and Old Tom May used to have a brick yard down there."

The "Hollin Bush" Inn

Matthew Cutts was the 'victualler' at the "Bush" in 1871 and he was still there in 1902.

"The "Bush" had two rooms and in the yard was a horse drawn caravan (but it didn't have any horses). It stood there for years and a family lived in it. One of the girls was called "Tilley". Near the "Bush" was a little house where the Skidmores lived.

Schooldays

Playing "Wag" from school

One day they were cutting corn in this field where Welwyn Road is today) and they were using the old binders, you know ... with a pole in the front and a horse on each side. It was a big, heavy "cop" and it wanted a horse on the front to help them pull it.

I was only about seven or eight and I was riding the front horse when Miss Baynes-Smith came along and saw me. She was the Infants' Headmistress and she lived at the first bungalow in Hollins End Road. She came into the field, took me off the horse's back and marched me into school.

In those days, the teacher had a big, high chair with a step on the front of it. She stood me on one of these chairs and chalked on a slate, "This is the boy that plays truant." I had to stand on this high chair at the front of the class holding this slate and I daren't put the slate down because I'd get my knuckles rattled. At school if you did anything wrong you used to get a "good hiding".

Mrs Robertson "Most girsl in those days were good needlewomen and Stan's sisters used to do all the sewing. Apparently one of the teachers used to bring her underwear for them to repair. It was passed on from one sister to the next as they came to school!"

Pea-Picking

Mr Robertson "In pea time, women from village used to pick peas in those fields down Jaunty Lane and at the back of the Church as well. When we came home from school, we used to say, "Where's the bucket Mother?"

She'd say, "Why, where ye going?"

"We're going to pick some peas off straws what women'll have left on," we told her.

They used to miss one and old Bob Beverley never bothered about us picking 'em off. We used to look through the straws then pick the peas off and put them in the bucket. When we'd got a bucket full we'd sit down in the field and "shill" (shell) them so that we could get some more.

Potato-Picking

In our childhood days, there were no tractors and when it came to potato picking time they used to plough the potatoes out using horses. It was all horse work then. The women used to go along and pick up the potatoes but they'd leave the little ones.

After the women had finished, we used to go with a bucket and collect the small ones that they'd left. We'd bring them home and my Mother would have a "Set Pot" going in kitchen. It was a big pot over fire. Then she'd put these potatoes in the "pot" to boil them and then give them to pigs.

Milk Round

We used to do anything to earn 2d or 3d. Billy Dodgson used to come round delivering milk. He lived in Woodhouse Road and not on the Common then. Fox's had the farm then.

Billy had only one leg and on a Saturday and Sunday morning, I used to go and meet him and help deliver milk. I'd only be about 10 or 12 years old. Ridgeway Road wasn't built then so while Billy delivered milk down Gladstone Road and Kirkby Road, I used to go up to Birds on Gleadless Road and take their milk. Birds used to keep all the threshing engines there, the old steam engine.

Billy had one crutch and a walking stick but he could get around so fast. He had a little pony called "Bubbles" and he was a "Bubbles"! He knew when he'd done. He could fly home like a race horse when he'd finished! When I was going home and we wanted him to stop at Frith Road for me to get off, we had a job to stop him he was going so fast!"

Domestic Life

People living in the 20's and 30's had a certain pride about accepting charity. Only desperate measures made them give in to charitable aid.
Mrs Robertson

The Pit Strike

"Stan's Mother was a very proud woman and her husband being a collier had to be on strike with all the rest of them. She had nine children born to her and she raised seven so she had a good sized family to provide for.

One day while the strike was on, she was walking down Hollinsend Road when she saw the soup kitchen (they had them every day to feed the miners' children) and all her children were waiting in the queue so she gave them all a back-hander and sent them home!

In order to feed them she used to go to a big, stone house at the corner of Hurlfield Avenue and Hurlfield Road where a family called Meadows lived. She used to go there for about 5am and do all the washing and everything and then call for some meat or something on the way home for their dinners. She'd wash and scrub so that they didn't have to ask for charity.

Plastered Pie!

If she made a meat and potato pie, she used to make it in a big enamel washing up bowl because an ordinary pie dish wasn't big enough for them. One particular day she'd made a meat and potato pie for them all and she'd just cut off a piece of the pie crust when somebody ran up the stairs and caused some of the ceiling plaster to fall off and land straight in the pie!

I said, "What on earth did you do?"

She said, "I just had to pick out every piece of the plaster because we couldn't afford not to eat it."

In the kitchen

Mr Robertson. "We only had one cold water tap and to get hot water we had to boil it. We either boiled it in the kettle or in the "set pot". We didn't have a bathroom and if we wanted a bath, we either got bathed in the kitchen or we'd go down to the Park Baths.

The "set pot" was used for cooking but it was always washed and scrubbed out choose what had been in it. The washing used to be boiled in it just the same. At the side of the sink was a boiler where Mother used to boil the washing and when we came home from school she used to say, "Come on, in this kitchen."

Then she used to get the washing out of the boiler while we had to turn the mangle with the wooden rollers and while we were turning she'd be putting clothes through the boiler.

We always had a ham hung up in the kitchen and hanging from the ceiling were big hooks where we used to put it and if we wanted a piece we'd just cut a slice off. Mother would make all her own bread in a big pancheon and bake it at the side of the fire and I remember she always called children "childer".

Coal cellars

Most of the houses had cellars underneath the house where the coal was kept. All the colliers were allowed a ton of coal a month. They didn't have to pay for that, only for the carting. They used to fetch the coal all the way from Orgreave Colliery to Gleadless.

A collier who lived near the "Nailmakers" at Norton, had his coal delivered on the Saturday morning because they couldn't carry two loads if they went all that way. A pair of horses and a man in the cart could only cart two loads of coal at a time. It was about 3/6d a ton in those days.

Workdays

My brother Harry, who was the eldest, started work when he was only twelve but I started when I was 14 years old. My pay was 2/- a day and this was for pony driving at Birley Pit. I couldn't leave the horses and I remember that one pony was called Charlie, he was a grey and the other was dark and we called him Merriman.

Pit Yard and the Pit Strike

Frith Road was always called Pit yard because years ago there was an old tip there. During the 1921 Pit Strike, we were short of coal at home so me and some other lads started digging in the old tip and we found coal.

We got underneath and we dug it out. When we arrived home with it my Father said, "Where've you got that from?"

We told him we'd got it from "bine hills" (we didn't call it tip then). Well, he went to look and when he saw where we got it from he said, "They're lucky to be alive!" It was all loose stuff and we'd been right underneath to get coal out. He said we'd been lucky we hadn't been buried because it could have caved in on us. When others saw where we'd been then there were dozens there getting it out after we found it!

My father worked at Orgreave. He used to walk there, do a shift then walk back home again.

When we were lads there were "screens" at the Manor Top (where the army camp is now) and men with their horses and carts used to fetch coal out of there. In the morning when I was fetching the horses back from Elm Tree, people with their coal carts were waiting for the gates to open. They came from town (Sheffield) to collect the coal. There used to be a pit where the Fire Station on Mansfield Road is today and the coal tubs used to come under the road from there and come up full for the carters to collect.

Paddocks Farm

Later I went to work for Albert Needham at Paddocks Farm. Walter Elliott and Herbert Clements worked there as well. I used to do the horse work at the farm. The land that belonged to the farm stretched from Myrtle Springs right down to Deep Pits to where the pond is on the Arbourthorne. It was farmed by Albert Needham but it was owned by the Duke of Norfolk before the Sheffield Corporation took it over to build the Arbourthorne Estate (late 1930's).

The Needhams then moved from Paddock Farm and went to live at Dunstone Hole Farm at Sheepbridge. They wanted me to go with them but I didn't want to leave my Mother on her own so instead they found me a job with the City Engineers which I kept until I retired.

Paddocks Farm (Noreen Walker, Canada)

Lawsons and Newfield Green Farm

There were three Lawson brothers. Walter Lawson who used to come round with the milk had the farm that was in the middle of Hurlfield Hill. There was another little farm at the bottom of the hill but there wasn't much land to it.

Another Lawson had Newfield Green Farm which was just under Buck Wood which was on the right hand side as you went to Sheffield.

Newfield Green was an old farm. It was arable and they used to keep a few beasts as well but it wasn't a very big farm. I remember, that the the foxes they caught locally, were hung on the wall!"

Rose Martin was born in 1907 and lived on Albert Road (now Alnwick Road) Hollins End. She very kindly talked at length about her childhood and early adult life which she spent in Hollins End. Like Stan Robertson, Rose always had a "job to do", even from a very early age, for life and times were hard. "Mama" Jackson was a very kind lady and one of the characters of Hollins End. Rose speaks of her with affection and we begin our conversation with Rose talking about "Mama".

""Mama" Jackson owned our houses. She lived at No12 Albert Road and they had a beer-off cum grocery shop called "Tom and Beatrice

Jackson" but we always called them "Mama" and "Papa" Jackson. I don't remember them living at the beer-off which was on the Main Road at the bottom of Albert Road. There were two cottages at the side of it and round the back there were two cottages at the back of those. There were back to back houses. On the left were two more cottages; it was like a yard.

"Mama" sold coal because her husband was a coal carter at Hollins End. She was a very kind person and very good to us. She loved animals, cats and dogs and she kept pigs.

'Ikey"

She had this special pig called "Ikey" and he even went into the house and he'd nudge "Papa" while he was eating! Even the hens went on the table while "Papa" was having his tea. They'd be picking off his fork and he would let them! Even cat used to be table pawing off his fork and he'd say, "Na then! Na, Then!"

They didn't have a table cloth on the table and the lighting was by paraffin lamps and they had candles to go to bed with.

"Ikey", the pig, grew big. Oh, ever so big and of course people were always killing pigs and so it came to "Ikey's" turn. When he was going to be killed "Mama" said, "We're going away for the day." She couldn't bear to be there when her "Ikey", who was really a pet, was going to be killed.

In those days, people had hooks in their ceilings to hang pieces of pig there. When she came back from her trip out, "Ikey" was hanging up from the hooks in the ceiling!

I don't know how she could have killed him, really. He was such a pet.

Waggonette travel

Once we went to Grindleford with "Mama" in a waggonette. Two horses pulled the waggon and some people sat inside but most of us were on the top and it was open. When we were coming up the hill from Grindleford to Fox House, everybody had to get out and walk because the horses couldn't pull us. Anyone who was lucky enough to go to the seaside travelled in a charabanc. These had no sides and they were open to the weather so if it rained you just got wet!

Childhood Days

Scarlet Fever

If you caught Scarlet Fever, you were taken away to Swallownest Fever Hospital. There were quite a few of us in the village that went and they came and collected us. It you had any brothers and sisters, they couldn't go to school while you had Scarlet Fever. I caught it off my friend because she had it and was walking about with it. She said, "Look, I can pull skin off my hand."

Well, you used to peel you see if you'd got it. When you were getting better you'd started to peel and that's when you were contagious.

At that time there were no trams or buses to Swallownest so if anybody wanted to visit you they had to walk. They could only visit on a Sunday and they weren't allowed inside so they had to stand outside at the window. I was in hospital in winter time and my Mum and Dad were frozen with the cold but they never missed coming to see me. You were usually kept in hospital about six weeks.

"Old" milk

Every night, all through the year, winter and summer, we had to walk up to Rhodes' farm (opposite the 'Old Harrow') to fetch what we called "old" milk. It wasn't old but we called it old because the cream had been taken off. I suppose you would call it non-fattening milk today. Sometimes, we had to wait while they separated the cream from the milk. The milk was cheaper than ordinary milk; it was about 2d a quart. That's why we bought it. We'd fetch it for other people in the village and when we were coming home with it we'd cheat a bit because we used to drink some (it was lovely and warm). At the bottom of Jaunty Lane was a beautiful stream and we'd stop there to put some water in the bottles to make up for what we'd drunk!

"Muck gathering"

We always had a job to do. We didn't get a Saturday penny but we had to look after somebody's children all week for just 3d.

Sometimes when me and my sister came out of school, my Dad would be waiting for us with a "cratch" which was a box on wheels with two handles.

He would say to us, "Here, two slices of bread and lard."

We used to live on bread and lard but it was home rendered lard or leaf fat, not shop lard. Then he would send us off to go all round the streets, gathering horse muck with a shovel. We daren't come back home until the "Cratch" (box) was full. We'd walk as far as Normanton Springs, collecting muck so that my Dad could put it on his garden. He was a marvellous gardener.

Haytime

Hay-making time was a lovely time. "Papa" Jackson had several fields down where Pit Lane (Frith Road) was. There were houses all down there and he and his son-in-law had gardens, there. "Papa" had hay fields as well and when it was harvest time, he always wanted plenty of helpers. Tea was mashed in big jugs and ham and salmon (mostly salmon!) sandwiches were made. We used to take tea and sandwiches to the men in the fields and then stop there. Oh, it was lovely and the weather always seemed to be fine then!

Hay-making seemed to last about a week. The hay was always cut by hand with a scythe and when it was cut we'd make "Billycocks" (a form of stacking the hay) and we used to love that! Then a horse and cart would come and a haystack would be made in the corner of the field of Jaunty Lane. Some time later, the threshing machine would come into the field to separate the corn from the chaff. The corn was bagged and when they'd stacked it all, my Mother used to say, "Ask "Papa" Jackson if you can go and glean."

So we went round and collected what they'd left and we'd put the corn into our aprons or pinafores. That was called gleaning and the corn went to feed the fowls that my Mother kept.

"Papa" had another corn field where Ridgehill Avenue is today. There were four cottages that went right up to the school and there was just a little passage between them so that you could get into the field.

Pea-Picking

During the Summer holidays, we'd go pea-picking. My Mother went as well. This was at Brewster Bradley's farm on White Lane. He'd come and say to this one particular person in the village, "Bring your regulars."

Mind you there'd be a few more than the regulars who used to go and he'd say, "I don't want you. 'I don't want you." So they had to go.

Some of the women got up to all sorts of tricks. If nobody was looking they'd fill their blouses with peas! Then they'd leave some in their buckets and put their aprons on top. If you ate a pea, you had to make a hole in the ground with your heel and put the shell in and cover it up with soil. If Mr Bradley found a pod he'd be angry.

We'd go pea-picking every day in the holidays and I got a 1/- a week for doing it. For a sack of peas which was about one cwt they got a 1/-. You had to pull up the peas by their roots. You couldn't just pull the peas off. Mr Bradley would then take the peas to sell at Sheffield Market.

He always went to Christ Church, him and his wife and at Harvest time there were always sheaves of corn in the Church. There used to be an arch that stretched from one side to the other, across the Church, filled with rambling roses and in the windows were lots of flowers and fruit.

Workdays

In those days a lot of girls went into "Service". My sister did. She was "In Service" at a doctor's house at Firth Park but "Service" work never appealed to me.

When I was 13 years old I left school on the Friday and started work on the Monday. In Hollins End there were only two people I knew who weren't colliers. One was a Mr Davies and he worked at Kirkbys the cabinet case makers. He got me a job there. My first week's wage was 8/- (40p).

Kirkbys were on Arundel Street and we had to take a wooden barrow through the streets to Richardsons, right up Scotland Street, I felt so ashamed of pushing this barrow that I tried to go through the back streets. Although I was only thirteen I thought it was so degrading having to push a barrow like that through the streets. Anyway, I had to do that job for so long before they put me in a shop. (They used to call it a shop.) First, I was a coverer and I'd cover cases to hold the cutlery. The smell of glue was horrible. Then I learned lining so then I could cover and line. We were on what we called "Piece Work".

At the end of every week when I got paid, I had to turn every penny over to my Mother 'til after I was 21. No matter how I tried to pay my board, I couldn't.

Shops in Hollinsend

From Frith Road to the bottom of Hollinsend Road, there were twelve shops. The only fish and chip shop we had was in the 'Hollin Bush' yard. It was a little wooden hut and Mrs Damms owned it.

There was Bob Beverley's shop, then Alick Butlers and then Levi Whittakers. His was a lock-up shop and we'd sit on his steps.

Next was Skeltons. That was a beer-off and the shop which "Mama" once owned. Further down there was Lorrimans, then across the road from that there was another shop but I can't remember who owned that and just below was Mrs Whittaker's (Levi's wife) shop. That was a sweet shop. Below was a clothes shop that belonged to Mrs Flowers. If you wanted to buy a vest or anything, she'd take a key and open the shop for you so you could get what you wanted. Some people had things "on the slate" but we never did.

Next was Fred Willeys, the butchers. On the other side was Harry Holmes' shop and just below that was a sweet shop. I don't know why the shops closed. They just did, it wasn't the supermarkets that put them out of business and the beer-off was demolished."

Today, none of the shops remain in Hollinsend. Sadly, when Mr Willey died in July 1988 his business closed and finished a family tradition of butchering in Hollinsend.

The "Yew Tree"

"At the bottom of Croft Road on the Main Road was the "Yew Tree'. They sold Alum beer there and it was dark in colour. My dad liked a drink of beer and we'd fetch it in a jug. We'd say that if we put jug down it would walk to pub. It used to go that often!

If you took a jug they would fill it with beer at the pub. They didn't serve under sixteens with a jug so you had to take a bottle. When I went as a girl with a bottle, they'd fill it then put a label over the top and seal it. I think it was the law so you couldn't drink it. Older ones would take a pint pot for half-a-pint because they knew they would get a long pull which would give them more than half-a-pint!

Everyday life in Hollins End

Mum

We had a wonderful, hard working Mother. There were five of us to look after so she had to go out 'papering and washing. She'd scrub the washing at the butchers to earn 2/6d and then she'd take washing in. We were fed up with seeing washing.

Then if anybody was ill or having a baby or needed to be 'laid out" they used to come to my Mother for help.

"Moonlighting"

Some people couldn't pay their rent and when they were going to be thrown out they'd do a "Moonlight Flit". When they did a "Moolight" they'd move during the night so people wouldn't know where they'd gone. They used to be a lot of "Moonlight flitting" done then.

Pigeons

Nearly everybody in the village had pigeons so there were a lot of pigeon flying. Some men would take their pigeons to Chesterfield (they had to walk there) just to let them race back home. When they saw the pigeons coming back, they would be whistling for them to come so that they could clock them in. The pigeons that flew home the quickest won.

Then at the weekend they were always rows and fights in the village when they'd been to pubs and came home drunk.

Pit accidents and burials

The Birley hummer used to go when they'd been an accident but it also went when they were going on shifts. I remember a man, who lived across the road from us, getting killed in the pit. Then another two got killed. They were no funeral homes then and when anybody died they used to be left in the house until they were buried.

It were only the wealthy people that had conveyances for funerals. The coaches were pulled by horses. The coffin used to be in front. You had to climb up the steps of the coach and then you'd sit facing each other. These coaches held about eight people.

They used to come right from Gleadless Town End because Ridgeway Road wasn't built then. Two lots of bearers were used. One lot carried the trestle and the other the coffin. They had to keep resting to change over. The procession came through the village and when they reached Alnwick Road, Mrs Corker, who wore a black dress with a white apron, was looking out for them coming. They couldn't take a short cut by coming along Stanhope Road, instead they had to keep to the Main Road and go right round. When they reached Stanhope Road, Mrs Corker used to go in and toll the bell at Intake Cemetery. The bell was tolled three times and this was done for everybody.

Jimmy Hoyland was the undertaker and him and another man used to bring the coffins by carrying them on their shoulders. They used to walk aross the fields which is Sharrard Road now but then they were just fields. From Christ Church we used to call it Church Fields.

Hard Times

I remember a man called "Rat" Pearson and in his house, hanging on the walls were hams and sides of bacon. They was all grease on the wallpaper! They'd only one room downstairs and two up and they'd quite a family of lads. If they gave you anything you thought it was marvellous.

Most people in Hollins End were poor. One family in the Barracks were so poor that their children used to run about naked - even in the cold weather and they never "ailed" anything!

I wouldn't go back and live in those times, except I suppose for some things but the happiness I've got now makes up for all the unhappy times that I had then."

Ethel Pass Was a Gill before her marriage. She is related to Sam and Walter Gill who are also contributors to this book.

Ethel was born in 1910 and lived in Stanhope Road, in Hollins End and (as the reader will soon discover) possesses a dry wit. Unfortunately, lack of space only permits a few of the stories she told me to be related here. To be in conversation with Mrs Pass is quite an enjoyable experience for she is excellent at telling a story. Whereas today we tend to rely less on the spoken word for our "entertainment", people in the past told stories as a form of amusing others, as Ethel illustrates so well here. (See also the 'Mining' chapter.)

Family background

"My grandfather was called Joseph Lomas and he was the village blacksmith. He had his own little, hand smithy near the top of Gleadless Hill and used to shoe horses because nobody had a car in Gleadless then, not even the doctor. It was all horses and carts.

He was also a local Methodist preacher. Now my grandmother Lomas was the village tailoress. (The old tailors used to sit crossed legged on a table to work.)

My Aunt Francis was in 'Out Service" at Charnock Hall which has now been demolished. She was only ten years old when she started to work there. She did "slushing". That's what they used to call it for scrubbing floors. Oh, she did work long hours. Mind you this was a very long time ago.

My father, David Gill, was born in 1879 and was down the Pit when he was eleven (1890). My Mum was always very busy, working. She worked at Walter Foxes on the Common and she was Nannie to Mr & Mrs Foxes kids. There were four of 'em and to help out she'd sometimes take the milk float round and deliver the milk.

The Old Cottages in Croft Road, Hollinsend 1963 (Mr H. Clayton)
Joe Crouch was the last resident in Croft Cottage. He died in 1961 at the age of 79.

Grandfather Gill

My grandfather Gill kept pigs and his house belonged to a chap called "Piggy" Ward who used to come and collect the rent. Once when he came my grandfather said, "Can I build another pig-sty,Mr Ward?"

"I don't see why not, Samuel," said "Piggy".

So me grandfather got to work and started to build this 'ere pig-sty and then Piggy came round again to collect his rent, Sam said, "I'm going to put my pig in it now."

But "Piggy" said, "Well, I don't think you can, Samuel. I've decided that you've got to take it down."

Well, my grandfather was so angry that he picked up hatchet and ran Piggy right up Gleadless Hill, right along top and down fields, shouting, "If I catch thee, I'll kill thee!"

He kept his pig-sty!

When he used to kill a pig, grandfather Gill never went to work. He sold pork and then didn't work after, so me Gran was worse off!

A chap called Jack White used to come and kill the pigs and he used to bring a trestle and things with him. When my father used to have a pig killed my Mother used to bring a jug and catch the blood in it to make black pudding. We kids used to go and watch and we'd wait so that we could have the pig's bladder and we'd blow it up for a football. That's the only football we had.

Jack Brock

One Hollins End character who lived on Hollins End Road was a chap called Jack Brock. There was a court case that came up and Jack was a witness and when the judge said, "And what do you know about this case, young man?"

He replied, "Me Lord, I know it all."

So the judge said, "Dismiss the other witnesses, this man knows it all."

So when we were kids and we thought we knew all about something and couldn't be told, we'd say to me dad, "I know, Dad."

And he'd say, "Shut up, Jack Brock!"

"Sugar" Taylor

"Sugar" (I don't know why they called him that, perhaps he liked sugar!) Taylor lived in the Barracks and he was the local grave digger and he'd mend clocks as well.

Well, one night me father was going up road for a pint when he saw a leet (light) in church yard (at Christ Church) so he went through gates to find out what this light was. And there was "Sugar" digging a grave!

So me dad says, "Oh, it's thee is it "Sugar"!"

And "Sugar" says, "Aye, why David?"
Me dad says, "Tha late aren't that wi' this?"
So "Sugar" replies, "Whey, I've got a rush on!"
But there he were, digging away in pitch dark except for his stone lamp!

Rough times

There were some right characters who lived in the Barracks. They used to bring kids outside and bath them in cold water. They were as tough as nails! Half of 'em never went to school because they had no shoes. We'd buy our shoes from "Greenleys" at the bottom of Duke Street and our best ones were bought from the "Public Benefit" at the Moorhead. The Barracks used to belong to the Birley Pit and a lot of them wouldn't pay their rent so they used to stop it out of their wages. The Barracks were back-to-back houses.

In Hollins End was a big house where the Lancasters lived and they were middle class people. Down at the bottom of Frith Foad was The Orchard and where Gleadless Middle School is today were fields and a couple of horses grazed there. We used to play in those fields but they were always very wet and marshy. Near Jaunty Lane was a house called Ash Grove House and a family (I think) called Flewitts lived there.

The School

At school there used to be a wall down the middle of the playground. The boys were rough and they were on the right hand side and the girls and infants were together on the left. (Notice on the school wall today, the words inscribed 'Boys' and 'Girls'.)

At home time, Hollins End kids used to wait for Gledless kids to 'war' 'em. I never used to be in at it because I used to go home but my brother used to say, "Robbo's after me, will you come and fight for me?"

It was worse in winter because they'd be snowballing then and they'd run Gleadless kids home! It was open warfare. Although they were really rough kids, there was never any fighting with knives or anything like that, it was just fists. They thought it was wonderful for they knew the Gledless kids were quieter.

Some of the Gleadless kids' fathers were miners like the Hollinsenders but they lived in two entirely different atmospheres. They were better class. A lot of us who lived in Hollins End didn't like living there. I always wanted to go back and live in Gleadless but me father would't go. He used to say, "There's enough Gills in Gledless without me."

Women

The women led a rough, hard life. My husband's Aunty who lived at Handsworth had 22 children and 17 lived! They lived in a two bedroomed house with an attic so lor' knows where they all slept!

Mind you, in those days all the girls used to go into "Service". Not many had trades but I did. I was a tailoress at "Stewarts and Stewarts" in town. One woman I knew used to wear gloves, three men's waistcoats and an old mac. and sometimes a black shawl to keep herself warm!

Oh, Hollins End was a rougher part than Gleadless but I enjoyed my childhood all the same."

Mr & Mrs Hobson

"One character I do remember living in Hollins End, was a chap called "Rat" Pearson (his real name was Ralph). He had ducks and little pigs that used to follow him about like they were dogs. "Rat" had an allotment and he made a plough so that two of his dogs could pull it to turn his soil over. A duck and a pig used to follow him across to "Hollin Bush".

Adam Oldfield kept the "Hollin Bush" then and the old rag man used to go in there for a drink. He had a row of balloons on two sticks fastened onto his rag cart and once he had to run out of pub because the balloons were going pop! pop! pop! Some rogues were popping them with air guns!"

Fred Willey - the Family Butcher

When Fred Willey died on the 9th July 1988 a long tradition of Willeys "The Family Butcher" finished in Hollinsend. Fred, who was said to be around 80 years old when he died, worked constantly in the little corner shop until his death like his Father before him (who was also called Fred.) Fred (senior) had two sons called Fred and Cecil who both entered the butchering business. Cecil continues to work today but not in Hollinsend, for with the passing of Fred, Hollinsend lost its last remaining "old" corner shop whose once regular customers in the 20's and 30's usually had numerous mouths to feed.

40, HOLLINSEND ROAD, SHEFFIELD.

Advert from G.I. Chapel's Centenary Celebrations Souvenir Booklet. (1929)
(Loaned M & Stan Taylor)

Mr Hobson. "In the old days they used to drive cattle along the road from Bakewell to the slaughterhouses and I remember Mr Willey, the butcher, used to deliver the meat in a pony and trap. Where the "Royal Oak" pub is today, there used to be two cottages and an old shed at the side. They used that old shed as a slaughterhouse and beasts were killed there. Willeys and Walshams at Intake used to share it. School kids used to go down there when they were killing beasts and they used to shout, "Come on lads!" and they'd throw rope out and kids used to be pulling at rope until they got this beast in a particular position and then they used to poll-axe it. Then they'd shout, "Let go! Let go!"

Intake

Intake is a very close neighbour of Gleadless and Hollins End. In 1872 it was described by Le Tall as a village of considerable size with its principal inhabitants being colliers. "There are eighty cottages here at least. Only some three or four appear of any age, and these perhaps not more than sixty years old; as the late George Hunter's house, Woodthorpe Arms, the Ball inn &c. John Bower Brown owns the greater part of the property here. The Newbolds, colliery proprietors, lived here about thirty years ago, and owned a great protion of Intake."

By 1902 White's Directory informs us that near Intake are several collieries. Intake is in Gleadless ecclesiastical district and that the Primitive Methodist Chapel built in 1874 cost about £1,000 and was enlarged in 1886.

Just glancing through the 1902 Directory, it is interesting to see who was living in Intake at this time. The following are just a few of the inhabitants.

Charles Blakey, Board schoolmaster
Stephen Bacon, Colliery manager, Woodthorpe Colliery
William Buxton, Eagle house, Thomas Cartledge, farmer, Fox Farm
Rev. John Thomas Collier (Primitive Methodist)
George Corker, school attendance officer
James Corker, Sexton Intake Cemetery (the Cemetery covering 4 acres, was opened in 1879)
William Dodson, butcher
Joseph Fidler, builder & contractor
Thomas Robert Gainsford Esq. J.P., managing director, Sheffield Coal Co. Ltd., h Woodthorpe Hall
John Keeton, joiner & builder
Joseph R. Payley, vict. Woodthorpe Arms
Pinder Bros. & Boul, builders & contractors
Mrs Lucy Ann Ramsden, Ball Inn
Electric Cars to Sheffield every 12 minutes

Tram Terminus Intake — 1914 (Mr H. Clayton)
Woodhouse Road is on the right.

For people living in the Gleadless area, the nearest tramway was at Intake. The opening dates for the Intake route were as follows:

10th Jan 1900 Wicker to Manór Lane via Blonk Street
17th Apr 1902 Manor Lane to Woodhouse Road
2nd Feb 1903 Diversion via Commercial St. & Sheaf St.
8th Feb 1935 Woodhouse Road to Hollinsend Road
29 Dec 1935 Hollinsend Road to Birley Vale *

(* *The Tramway Era in Sheffield*', Sheffield Transport Dept., 1960)

The closing date of the Intake route was on 7th April 1956 (although workmen's cars continued to operate to Intake via Prince of Wales Road.)

Intake memories

Born in Buxton's Yard in Intake, Mrs Thorpe remembers very well her early life in Intake. She was only ten when she left the area but made frequent visits to her Aunts who lived in Gleadless. After her marriage she returned once more to the area and today Mrs Thorpe relects on how life has changed in Intake over the passing of the years.

"I'm afraid I've nothing of interest to tell you," began Mrs Thorpe when our conversation started. However, I'm sure the reader will agree with me that her reminiscences of life in Intake (which was typical of most villages of this type at the early part of this century) are most interesting and add a valuable contribution to oral history.

Domestic life in Intake

"Black Clocks"

At the Manor Top (Elm Tree) were coking ovens and the heat from these ovens attracted to the neighbourhood, "black clocks". In the evening these black beetles came out from below the stone, flag floors as Mrs Thorpe's mother soon discovered to her horror one night!

"They were back-to-back houses in Intake and people had peg rugs on the floor. Well, one night when me Mum first moved into this (her) house she came down in her bare feet with a candle in her hand (nothing else was used for lighting then) and she felt this cracking and crunching underneath her feet. She wondered what it was so she put the candle down on the floor to have a look and she saw all these "black clocks" scurrying about - well, she nearly fainted!

My dad came rushing down to see what was the matter and he got some stuff called "Keetings (Keetons) Powder" and they spread it all over the floor and it gradually killed them. My mum said there must have been hundreds but everybody else had the same trouble.

Mice

We had trouble with mice as well. Mice were in the pantry and you had to keep everything in a "crock" with a lid on. Your bread, your flour and everything had to be covered. In fact we had a flour bin. It was a big metal bin, with half a lid and my mother used to buy a sack of flour at once and then put it in and keep the lid down so that the mice wouldn't get at it. Every night we used to set a mouse trap and put a piece of cheese in it to catch them. In fact, you'd hear these traps clicking anytime during the day because, you see, the pantry was dark when the door was shut.

I used to hate mice! You'd be having your tea and you'd hear a trap go off in the pantry and me mum used to go in, "nobble" it one and then throw it on fire! Oh, she used to put me off my tea and I couldn't eat it then! And we had a cat at that! She used to sit, curled up on the newspapers in the bottom of the nice, warm cupboard near the fire. She was a marmalade cat and when she had kittens (she was always having kittens!) the neighbours used to have them to catch their mice. Some kittens though weren't so lucky

Cleaning windows

The houses had floorboards upstairs. The stairs went round and then there was a landing and off that was a small bedroom which had a fireplace. Then you went up another flight of stairs to reach the attic which was about the same size as the room below. The houses were three storeys high.

My mother used to say it was awful cleaning the windows because she had to lean outside and sit on the window sill. Then she'd pull the window down so it rested on her knees. That's the only way they could clean them. Once she got the window on her knee and she couldn't get it up again. It'd stuck! So she had to sit there and wait for a neighbour to come round and release her and it was a fair height - three storeys!

The house we lived in used to go down a yard, like a slope. They called it Buxton's Yard. Buxton's Cottages were two houses with Eagle House in between. You couldn't go anywhere near that house. If you lost your ball in there you couldn't go and fetch it. I think a doctor lived there but I'm not sure. I was only 10 years old then. We left Intake when I was that age. It was about 1924. I was born in Buxton's Yard and much later when we came back to live in Intake, I saw them being demolished and I was upset to think they were knocking them down and I hadn't taken a photograph of where I used to live all those years ago.

My dad had a job as a gardener at a big house called Eastcliffe on East Bank Road so we all moved out of Intake but we came back often to visit all my Aunts who lived in Gleadless.

Family

My Auntie Nellie (Stubbs) had a milk round. Her husband had been in the Pit but he had to come out becuse of ill health so my Aunt bought this milk round and and all their sons helped out. They had a dairy with old fashioned stone flags on the roof. It had been an old barn or something like that. It was near the "Heeley & Sheffield" house on Gleadless Road. Then it was demolished.

Aunt Hannah's first husband was killed in the pit and later she married Tom Urton who was also a miner and lived up Smithfield Road.

In Service

Most girls in the village left and went into "Service" in Sheffield. My mum was "In Service" to the Thornton family who owned Thorntons Chocolate Cabins. She practically brought their family up. Some girls "In Service" were away sometimes for a month before they came home again.

In the Summer holidays, Thorntons used to take a country cottage in Hathersage and my mother used to go with their children. There were about three or four of them and she used to look after the kids while they were at the shop. They'd leave me mum on her own looking after them until the weekend and then they might come up if they were lucky because they were trying to get the shops going, you see.

Mr Thornton used to be a traveller with "Don Sweet Co." and perhaps he thought he could do better on his own. At weekends him and me mother experimented on gas stove making different sorts of toffee. Thornton's original toffee - my mum and Mr Thornton did that together and when he opened his first shop, which were at the corner of Norfolk Street, he let her serve the first customer.

She always remembered it. She used to say to us, "Do you know what it was? It was a chap from "Walker & Hall's", the cutlery place, who came in for 1d of acid drops!"

He didn't want toffee but acid drops. Mr Thornton was really "narked"!

"Laying-out"

Nurse Walls was the district nurse for Intake people. She lived down Main Road and was the midwife. My mother (after she was married) used to do the "laying-out" for people. I think she must have gone with Mrs Sharpe a few times and helped her.

A lot of colliers got killed down the pit and I remember a man getting killed who lived near us. They brought him home in all his muck and put him on the hearth rug. Me mother washed him and changed him but they had to leave him on the hearth rug because there was nowhere else to put him and the house was full of kids at that!

Families

They had large families in those days. In my friend's family were ten children and they lived in a one up and one down house. I don't know where they all slept. Perhaps on floor or anywhere they could. There was little room downstairs. I remember they had a horsehair sofa (they were bristly things to sit on), a big table and a fireplace downstairs. Some of the children were sent to their Gran's to be looked after. Usually, people with the largest families didn't send their children to Sunday school. I suppose they had enough to do to look after their family.

They used to send my friend's mother little potatoes (those they fed to the pigs) but she'd put them in a big, iron saucepan and boil them on the stove, then give them to kids to eat.They used to be lovely! We used to wrap them in newspaper, just like chips and go and sit on planks of wood in wood yard nearby, and eat them. We'd peel the skins off first. You were lucky if you got any butter to put on them though.

Food

Hedgehogs were a delicacy then. All the old men would go into the fields to try and find them. Of course they would have dogs sniffing them out but they'd find them and bring them home and put them in cellar.

Then they would feed 'em on bread and milk while they got them nice and fat and then they'd kill them. They said they were delicious. They'd keep them in the cellar because there was nowhere else you see.

They caught rabbits as well and sometimes when me dad's been mowing, rabbits have come running out.

Pigs

Hams were hung up in the house and with me dad being a pig-killer, he'd go out and kill a pig if anybody asked him, even though he worked at Pit.

He used to say,"Well, can I have a pig's leg if I cure it for you?"

And they'd most likely say, yes so he would cure it and then buy the leg off 'em and bring it home.

Big "pot hooks" used to hang from ceiling with hams with muslin wrapped round 'em hanging on them. (The muslin was put round to keep the flies off.)

A "flitch" of bacon used to hang from the hooks and you'd get it down and cut some off and cook it for Sunday dinner and then hang the "flitch" back up. It used to be hung up so that the air could get to it. When it had been salted it looked green sometimes with the curing. They'd cure it with salt and something else.

My mother was a cook so we always had good food. We used to have gruel that was made out of rough oats and she'd make it in a big, iron saucepan and put it on the stove. Dad would be stirring it all night to stop it lumping. Then some ginger was added to it. Oh, it was lovely to go to bed on! In winter it was supposed to do you good and keep you warm and it'd keep the cold out.

Washing

You used to hang your washing in the yard from a clothes pole and people were friendly and say, "Are you using washing line today?"

If you weren't they'd put their washing on your line. My mother had a zinc tub with a "peggy leg" in the middle of it and she'd twist it round. It was like an agitator in washing machines today.

She'd wash in pancheon as well as bake bread in it. It was made of cream porcelain inside so it could be washed out and used for baking as well.

Baking

My mother would make a stone of bread at a time in her big pancheon. Oh, and when it was baking it would smell gorgeous! It was delicious bread and if you had a slice of bread with real butter, it was like nothing on earth!

Lard in those days was better. It was lovely and "leaf" lard which was the actual fat with the skin round, gave you smooth hands. There was no better handcream then. You just rubbed the lard into your hands.

Bath night

Like I said, the houses only had a living room, a bedroom and an attic and when you wanted a bath you had to get bathed downstairs in living room. Bath night was usually Friday night, just once a week.

The living room had a stone sink in corner and a copper next to it. (That was a big, round metal object with a little thing underneath for a fire.) The copper was hotted up on bath night and out came the oval, zinc bath. All the family had the same water. You were lucky if you got in first!

We were always quite warm though because we got bathed in front of the fire, with bath on a rag rug. Round the fire was a fireguard with all your clean clothes on - warming.

Peg-rugs

Women always did sewing and knitted a lot and made stockings. My mother thought it was Heaven when she had some inlaid lino over the flag floor. She was a wizard at making peg rugs. She had little tins with different colours in. She'd make the rug on her knee and the rugs were so big sometimes. When I helped her shake them in the yard, she used to pull me all over shaking these big rugs!

Mattresses

When me mother was a young girl she used to live in a country cottage and she'd sleep on a straw mattress. They were always a lot of fleas about in those days and when they'd get up in the morning they'd been bitten with the fleas!

These mattresses had straw stuffing and I suppose the fleas were in there to start with and once you'd got fleas in your house they'd jump like mad! My mother couldn't stand it any longer so she got a "flock"mattress. These flocks were better but when you were constantly turning round on them in the night the flock used to form into little lumps and after a while it was like pebbles - even if you shook them. To get rid of the lumps you had to undo the casing, put them all on the floor and pick them out like that! Then you had to put them all back in again. I can remember her having two baths, one with the pebbles in and the other without.

We have a brass bedstead with brass knobs that you had to clean and they weren't lacquered in those days! Oh, you used to bang your head on the things and today most people think they're wonderful! Mind you, they were great at Christmas time for hanging your stocking on!

Christmas

At Christmas we used to get a new penny, spice (sweet) walking sticks, chocolate mice and mice made out of icing sugar with a little bit of wool for their tails.

If you got a box of chocolates you were wealthy. I think I must have been about twelve before I got my box of chocs.

My mum used to buy us what they called celluloid dolls (which used to dent) but these dolls were lovely and they were jointed. We spent time making frocks and clothes for them to wear.

And finally....

I suppose what you could say about people in those days, is that you could leave your door undone all night and nobody would bother you. People would walk into one another's and say, "Have you a cuppa sugar?" and things like that and they used to give it to one another if they'd got it. They were always generous with one another which was such a good thing."

Mrs Thorpe's vivid account of her early life in Intake paints a very true picture of the lives and living conditions experienced by most people in the 20's and 30's. I feel sure that people who lived through these times in Intake (and Hollins End and Gleadless for that matter) will nod their heads in agreement to Mrs Thorpe's fascinating recollections. My thanks once more for her very moving and entertaining memories.

13. A TIME TO REMEMBER AND A TIME FOR CHANGES

A Time to Remember

To bring the story of Gleadless to a close it is perhaps fitting to hear the recollections of one lady I spoke to. During our conversation I had to remind myself that the way of life she was talking about, was only fifty or sixty years ago and yet it seemed to me to be the reminiscences of a much earlier age. Times indeed were hard but as my friend constantly reassured me, they were indeed happy with everyone helping one another.

"I first remember Gleadless when as a child I walked with my Father from Sheffield through Arbourthorne. It was all fields then and there was a farm at the top where Wards lived. My Father said, "We'll go and have a look at this cottage." So we came and had a look at where we were going to live in Gleadless. We lived in that cottage before we moved to a bungalow type house at the back of Honeymoon Row. Oh, it was cold in there for they were all stone floors and at night I've stayed awake for hours listening to corncrakes in the field.

Then we moved from there to a cottage across the road and there were pigs there. They used to kill them on the spot and afterwards they'd give us the pig's bladder to kick about and the pig's feet to eat.

If you could get any bacon with relish on, it was marvellous but we had a lot of toast and tea and newspaper on the table when we'd no cloth. Once the cat got into the oven and me Mother lit the fire! Well, she smelt some burning and rushed to get it out! It was alright but it used to sit in there to keep warm.

We'd have meat at the weekends and sometimes me Mother would get a sheep's head (she called it a sheep's 'jimmy') and she'd clean it and put all the herbs in it and carrots, turnips and celery. My Father always had the brains from the sheep's head.

My Mother used to work in all sorts of weather in the fields, chopping turnip heads off. Mum was only 50 when she died of consumption.

Wedding Day

I always remember when we got married. We were there at Christ Church at 9 o'clock one Saturday morning and there was nobody there except my husband's brother and his sister who stood for us. There was nobody in church! A cottage came empty and we asked for it and we got it so we got married.

Well, it was tumbling down with rain and we had to walk all the way back to our little cottage and standing under Websters' shelter (at the Butcher's shop) were Mrs Richardson and Mrs Hall and they said, "Oh, what a morning!" And I said, "It is."

Well, me Mother said she would go up to our cottage and make a fire, which she did and make our Wedding Breakfast. Well, do you know what it was? A boiled egg! That was our Wedding Breakfast! (I've been having boiled eggs ever since!) Them were the days and yet I was happy!

When we'd had our breakfast my husband said, "Hey, kid do you know, we haven't got a clock." And I says, No, we haven't but I've no money." So he took money out of his pocket and said, "I've got 1/6d (7½p), I think we'll get an alarm for that don't you." So we went to town to buy a clock.

The Irish Channel — cottage

We spent many happy years in that cottage in the 'Irish Channel'. When you went in at the door you saw in one corner the stairs door. The kitchen was about 3ft square with a stone slab and just a sink with one cold water tap but no hot water. There were no pit baths so you had to boil water in buckets and saucepans and we had an old boiler with a fire underneath it. At the side of the fireplace was a boiler with a tap. The room had a very small window.

The Irish Channel, Old Gleadless
The 'Irish Channel' is on the left. Wood Lane Cottages are in the centre of the picture. The old Gleadless Post Office is on the right near the lamp post.

Upstairs there was a landing and just this one bedroom — we called it a bedroom but it was really a landing. Both my children were born in there.

We were poor. I've gone to school and sat on the 'causeway edge' many a time because my shoes have been crippling me. My feet have hurt me that much, but I had to wear them boots because there was nothing else.

We moved into that cottage in 1926 and the rent was 7/- a week. I remember as plain as anything going into it. We had no light and had to use candles upstairs and a paraffin lamp downstairs but we lived in there eleven years and it was ever so comfortable. I loved it. They were broken down cottages. I think at one time they may have been stables.

Our door key was like a big, stable door key and once the lock was frozen so much we couldn't get in. When it was cold we used to put the warm oven plate in bed to warm it and even hot house bricks wrapped up in a piece of cloth.

If you looked up the chimney you could see daylight and once our next door neighbours decided to sweep their chimney. So Mister went and got a holly bush from woods and he said to kids, "When I say pull, pull!" Then he went on top of roof while they were down below. Well, they'd pulled alright and all soot fell down! All you could see were whites of their eyes! He'd pushed holly bush down that much!

Every time that anybody used to open the front door, the soot used to fall down anyway. The fireplace in the bedroom was really only about three or four bricks surrounding a grate.

Mr Wainwright was the village chimney sweep and he was married to Polly who used to sell herbs and plants. They lived in a little place near Richardson's before they moved to a cottage behind the 'Old Harrow'.

We had a flagged stone floor and I used to donkey stone them around the edging. We got 'Pot mole' from the rag man. It was a brown colour and we scrubbed the floor. We made peg rugs from old coats and when we were well off, we had coconut matting.

The place was alive with cockroaches and black clocks! We tried all sorts to try and get rid of them. When you opened your cupboard door they were there. You even got them in your sugar basin!

My mother had crickets where they lived. You walked down Gleadless Hill and you'd company all the way down with the whistling of the crickets!

It was lovely countryside though and you knew everybody. You could be out at night and hear footsteps but you wouldn't be frightened. You could even leave your door unlocked and nobody would bother you. I often think back to what Gleadless used to be like. I can see it all as it was. They were really, very happy days."

A Time for Changes

'City Road Schemes to Start'

That headline made the front page of 'The Star' newspaper in 1959 and showed the cottages on Ridgeway Road (on the side of Grassthorpe Road) that were intended for demolition.

One of the road schemes called for the elimination of the "bottleneck" in Ridgeway Road between Kirkby Avenue and Hollinsend Road in an effort to reduce accident risks on Sheffield's "outer ring road," "where traffic has increased fourfold since 1946."

Church Row Cottages (Ronald Ward)
Once Gladstone Road, now Ridgeway Road, this photo shows Church Row cottages on the left and Skelton's corner shop. Suggestions are that Mr Bellamy is the coal man and Teddie Hoyland is leading the horse in the picture.

"The Ridgeway Road scheme involves the demolition of the cottages on the left had side facing away from the city and also the removal of the raised portion of the footpath at that point.

The road will be both straightened and widened here too, a dual carriageway is envisaged eventually." ('The Star', 2.1.59.)

Ridgeway Road with Kirkby Road (D. Higgins)
On the left, before the road widening (1950's).

The demolition of Church Row cottages, Ridgeway Road (D. Higgins)

This road development was not the first sign that changes were on the way for the village of Gleadless. Earlier in 1952, newspaper reports predicted that Sheffield's housing programme would include land at Gleadless. In 1952, Sheffield Corporation had made an application for confirmation of compulsory purchase orders involving 433 acres in Green Belt land at Fox Hill, Stannington, Gleadless, Totley and Bradway.

Efforts had been made to avoid using agricultural land and housing estates had been 'combed' for sites and room for 258 houses had been found. While a Derbyshire County Council spokesman suggested that, "if the Ministry accepted the cumpulsory purchase orders the Green Belt reservation on the south side of the city would virtually disappear."

When it was suggested that the taking of 500 acres of agricultural land was doing the country ill-service, the Sheffield Alderman, stated that, "it was a matter of priorities. The first priority in this case was the city."

Suggestions were made for the housing of more Sheffield people in surrounding villages and "because of the need for speedy action" another spokesman was convinced that the Green Belt sites were "the only practical solution."

As we all know now the housing and road schemes that have been brought into Gleadless have completely altered the village's character. Cynics will say, "That's progress!" But did Charnock Hall, Base Green Farm, one of the Herdings farms, and Ashleigh House, really have to be demolished even though their land had been taken?

What do the future years hold for Gleadless? Unveiled in 1985 was the "supertram". These sleek new electric trains will run (so we are told) every 4½ minutes on a 16 mile route from Mosborough through Gleadless and the Manor across the city centre and up to Hillsborough.

Supertrams will hunt in pairs with the two-section vehicles being 89ft. long and eight ft. wide and powered by overhead electric wires. There has been fierce opposition to this 'mode' of transport but will the 1990's be the age of the 'Supertram'. Will we see this train slithering down Ridgeway Road and along White Lane and onto Mosborough?

One wonders what the past Gleadless residents would have made of it all. For they enjoyed wonderful walks on Sunday nights along White Lane to Ridgeway and rambles down Carter Hall Lane, with hardly a car in sight!

"I can see the old places now as they used to be, the farms, the houses and everything and I re-live it in my memory," one elderly lady remarked. Old Gleadless has not vanished, for it lives on in the minds of people, some of whom have shared their memories with us in this book. For these people, Gleadless will always be their, "little country village."

BIBLIOGRAPHY

J. Roberts *'Woodhouse'* (1966)
Pauline Shearstone *'Gleadless from Village to Suburb'* (1985)
'The Star' newspapers — 1952/54/55/59
'The Sheffield Telegraph' 1951
Thomas Baines *'Yorkshire Past & Present'* Vol 1, pub William Mackenzie
Willis Fox *'Ridgeway Village and its Industries'* (1950)
William Cobbett *'Cottage Economy'* (1822)
Margaret Slack *'Yorkshire Fare'* pub. Dalesman
(Wentworth MSS 18th cent MD 6333. Original in Sheffield City Archives.)
Mrs Beeton *'Household Guide'* (1901)
White's Directories
'A History of Gleadless School' pamphlet
Sheffield Daily Telegraph 1915 (Sheffield Local Studies Library)
'Peter Harvey's Sheffield'. Sheaf Publishing
'Gleadless United Reformed Church'. Booklet, privately published
Daily Herald 1913
Le Tall *'Le Tall's Woodhouse'.* Holly Resources Centre
'The Tramway Era in Sheffield'. Sheffield Transport Dept, 1960
Census Returns Derbyshire Library Service
'Gleadless Methodist Church Centenary'. Booklet, 1965 pub.
The *'Bright Papers', 'Rentals of Totley and tithes of Bradfield'* (1625-30). Sheffield City Libraries, Archives
Maps of Newton and Shawe Estate. Sheffield City Libraries, Archives.
William Fairbank's Map of Carter Hall Estate, 1801
'The Victorian Kitchen' Museum of Lincolnshire Life
1851 Ecclesiastical Census

-Hurlfield Hill Farm- Old Gleadless-